Praise for *A CURIOUS MIND*

"*A Curious Mind* is not a classic autobiography but a rumination on how one trait, curiosity, reinforced by a readiness to pay attention and then to act, has forged such a remarkable career. . . . It's like spending a couple of hours in the bar of a Hollywood hotel with an amusing raconteur."

—*The Wall Street Journal*

"Curiosity leads to insights and fuels the creative process—and nobody knows more about curiosity than Brian Grazer. In his delightful book, *A Curious Mind*, we get to see that curiously creative process in action."

—Dick Costolo, former CEO of Twitter

"If you feel stuck in your business or career, or if your company is failing to stay ahead of its competition, perhaps Grazer's method of 'curiosity conversations' might provide the spark you need to ignite your best ideas."

—*Forbes*

"As Brian's friend and partner, while reading *A Curious Mind* I was returned to many key turning points in our movies and TV shows that were inspired by experiences he gained on his unique quest for understanding. I also learned a hell of a lot that I didn't actually know, even after thirty years. How is that possible? Well, Brian is a hell of a storyteller."

—Ron Howard, chairman of Imagine Entertainment
and Academy Award–winning director

"To read a book written by one of the most creative and high-quality human beings talking about his love affair with curiosity and how it can help you to have a more rewarding life is a real privilege."

—Robert K. Kraft, owner of the Kraft Group and the New England Patriots

"To have a great life, you need to be curious. Curiosity is what makes us human and moves our world forward. Brian Grazer tells this story in an exceptional way and demonstrates how everyone can tap into curiosity to live a bigger life."   —Eric Schmidt, former CEO of Google

"A powerful tribute to the ways innovation and disruptive thinking stem from a common trait: curiosity. Because the little girl who asks, 'Why is the sky blue?' becomes the woman who can change the world."

—Sheryl Sandberg, former COO of Facebook and founder of LeanIn.org

"A very stimulating blend of behind-the-scenes Hollywood machinations and business and personal self-help. Verdict: This unusual and quick read is ideal for public libraries and as nonrequired reading in business schools."   —*Library Journal*

"An appealing argument for maintaining open-minded receptivity, with special appeal for film buffs."   —*Kirkus Reviews*

"Lively . . . As Grazer further explores how curiosity has shaped his life, he sprinkles in numerous anecdotes about the hundreds of people whom he's sought out for one-on-one sessions he terms 'curiosity conversations.'"   —*Publishers Weekly*

"[*A Curious Mind*] is straightforward and full of great advice for anyone trying to rise and shine. You don't have to try to become a movie producer. In its own way, the book could be a guide for anyone with ambition, nerve, and common sense. But first comes curiosity."   —*HuffPost*

"Grazer himself comes across as a humble seeker, who never let his huge Hollywood success crush his inner child—the child who wants to know everything."   —*2paragraphs*

"Stories like de Negri's take Grazer's book beyond Hollywood dish into the mysteries of existence. What makes you curious, it turns out, can also make you stronger."   —*7x7*

"Grazer knows that curiosity doesn't merely kill the cat, it morphs it into a roaring lion worthy of a Hollywood logo—in this case, a cool cat with a wild, spiky mane after a career of petting his projects against the grain." —*WTOP*

"It'll encourage you and your partner to engage in novel conversations." —*Bustle*

"Grazer's book is conversational, funny, and inspiring. A business book like this one can be an excellent resource when it provides a different perspective of thinking and taking action." —*Palm Beach Post*

Praise for *FACE TO FACE*

"Mr. Grazer—as you might imagine for someone who helped create *A Beautiful Mind, American Gangster,* and *Friday Night Lights*—is a skilled storyteller.... In a world where people appear to carry out love affairs and pursue business relationships solely by text, making the effort to meet someone in person, undistracted, is a strategy worth considering." —*The Wall Street Journal*

"Brian Grazer's book reminds us of the fundamental ingredient to success: human connection. This is essential reading for the digital age." —Bob Iger, chairman and CEO of The Walt Disney Company

"I remember countless times when Brian made the impossible, possible, through a single face-to-face conversation. In his new book, he has done a deep dive into the subject of influential face-to-face communication and why it gets things done in business and in life." —Ron Howard, chairman of Imagine Entertainment and Academy Award–winning director

"In this digital age, connecting is what humanity is all about. Brian Grazer's captivating and very personal stories are a call to action for us all to see one another. *Face to Face*'s message is essential for our time." —Anne Wojcicki, cofounder and CEO of 23andMe

"In our increasingly digital world, Brian Grazer takes us on his personal journey of human connection. He proves that the simple step of making eye contact transformed his life and can change yours too. This is a must read for our time."

—Neil Blumenthal, cofounder and co-CEO of Warby Parker

"I loved this book. Grazer's stories convey both the power of personal connection and the importance of meaningful, face-to-face interactions to create a sense of belonging."

—Brian Chesky, cofounder, CEO, and head of community at Airbnb

"No matter where you are in life or career, *Face to Face* will help unlock your full potential. This is a compelling must read for all!"

—Whitney Wolfe Herd, founder and CEO of Bumble

"Being connected is not the same thing as connecting. Only when we meet people, face to face, can we form the kinds of meaningful connections that truly matter in our lives. And Brian Grazer is the master. Told through the stories of his own journey, *Face to Face* is a great reminder and a valuable guide for how we too can connect with people in deeper, more meaningful ways."

—Simon Sinek, optimist and *New York Times* bestselling author of *Start With Why* and *Leaders Eat Last*

"At a time when human connection is increasingly interrupted by our growing addiction to screens, this captivating book reveals how we can all transform our lives by truly connecting with others. Using highly personal stories, Brian Grazer shows how the simple act of looking up can change your life."

—Arianna Huffington, founder of *HuffPost* and CEO of Thrive Global

"Brian's gift is being able to get to the essence of what, and, more importantly, why a person feels the way they do. His stories and insights will open your heart and mind to the urgency of human connection."

—Jimmy Lovine, entrepreneur

Also Produced by Brian Grazer

FILM

A Beautiful Mind

Frost/Nixon

8 Mile

The Da Vinci Code

The Doors

Made in America

Rush

tick, tick ... BOOM!

American Gangster

Inside Man

Friday Night Lights

Dr. Seuss' How the Grinch Stole Christmas

Apollo 13

Blue Crush

Liar Liar

The Nutty Professor

Parenthood

Splash

TELEVISION

The 84th Academy Awards

Friday Night Lights

Empire

Genius

Sports Night

Arrested Development

24

Parenthood

BOOKS

A Curious Mind: The Secret to a Bigger Life

Face to Face: The Art of Human Connection

A CURIOUS MIND
EXPANDED

THE SECRET TO A BIGGER LIFE

10th anniversary edition

Brian Grazer *and* Charles Fishman

Simon & Schuster

NEW YORK   LONDON   TORONTO   SYDNEY   NEW DELHI

Simon & Schuster
1230 Avenue of the Americas
New York, NY 10020

A Curious Mind copyright © 2015 by Brian Grazer
Face to Face copyright © 2019 by Brian Grazer

All rights reserved, including the right to reproduce this book or portions thereof in any form
whatsoever. For information, address Simon & Schuster Subsidiary Rights Department,
1230 Avenue of the Americas, New York, NY 10020.

This Simon & Schuster hardcover edition November 2023

SIMON & SCHUSTER and colophon are registered trademarks of Simon & Schuster, Inc.

For information about special discounts for bulk purchases, please contact Simon & Schuster
Special Sales at 1-866-506-1949 or business@simonandschuster.com.

The Simon & Schuster Speakers Bureau can bring authors to your live event. For more
information or to book an event, contact the Simon & Schuster Speakers Bureau at
1-866-248-3049 or visit our website at www.simonspeakers.com.

Manufactured in the United States of America

1 3 5 7 9 10 8 6 4 2

Library of Congress Cataloging-in-Publication Data is available.

ISBN 978-1-6680-2550-5
ISBN 978-1-6680-2799-8 (ebook)

From A Curious Mind

*For my grandma Sonia Schwartz. Starting when I was a boy,
she treated every question I asked as valuable. She taught me to think
of myself as curious, a gift that has served me every day of my life.*

From Face to Face

*For my wife, Veronica, my soul mate in every way.
You see all of me.*

Contents

Introduction to the New Edition

Curiosity to the Rescue

> I think, at a child's birth, if a mother could ask a fairy god-mother to endow that child with the most useful gift, that gift would be curiosity.
>
> —*Eleanor Roosevelt*[1]

It was June 27, 2022, and I was at the United States Military Academy at West Point to deliver my son Patrick to his plebe year as a cadet.

That day was also the change-of-command ceremony for the head of West Point—the outgoing superintendent was being redeployed to be the head of U.S. Army forces across Europe and Africa—and I was in the audience to see the new head of West Point take command.

The ceremony was conducted by the Army Chief of Staff, General James McConville, and all of a sudden, in the middle of this very formal, buttoned-down event, McConville said, "We have with us in the audience today an Oscar-winning movie producer—Brian Grazer." And he pointed in my direction. I couldn't have been more stunned. I smiled and nodded as people turned to look at me.

Then McConville said, "We'd really like him to make the Army version of *Apollo 13*."

I get ideas for movies all the time, from all kinds of people. But not usually delivered in public by the highest-ranking officer in the U.S. Army, in front of a hundred other senior officials of all kinds.

But McConville wasn't really suggesting a movie idea.

He was laying down a challenge.

After the ceremony, General McConville and another general found me in the audience, and he told me he was quite serious about trying to intrigue me with the possibility of getting the Army into the movies.

He certainly piqued my curiosity.

That's how I came to find myself—just ten weeks later—strapped into an M1 Abrams tank, maneuvering in the middle of the desert.

That morning, I'd woken up at home in Santa Monica.

I'd gone with a handful of colleagues to an airport in Burbank, where we boarded a pair of Black Hawk helicopters and flew to Fort Irwin, the U.S. Army's largest training center, which comprises about one thousand square miles of Mojave Desert, twice the land area of Los Angeles.

We'd watched soldiers training. We'd been shown a range of Army weapons and had the chance to fire some of them. We'd had a lunch of MREs, which are exactly as unappealing as you've heard. We'd tramped through the desert, ending up covered in dust.

And now, in the midafternoon, I was deep inside an M1, trying to absorb what it must be like to crew a battle tank for real—or even in one of Fort Irwin's live-fire exercises. It was like nothing I'd ever done before—the confines of the tank cockpit, the heat (tanks don't have air-conditioning), being immersed in the smell of metal and oil and lots of previous crew members.

During two days at Fort Irwin, we got up close with some of the equipment the Army uses every day—we hopped on and off those Black Hawks a half dozen times—and we also got to know scores of young people, how they'd come to be in the U.S. Army, what they liked about it, what they didn't like about it.

I wasn't at Fort Irwin to learn how to drive an M1, of course. I was there, with a dozen people I make movies with, including a writer we'd asked to come along, to get a flavor of the U.S. military today, especially the people.

I was following my curiosity—we were all following our curiosity. What's the modern Army like? What are the people in the Army like? Where's the story moviegoers could connect with?

We learned a lot talking to the soldiers. Two things in particular have stuck with me.

I asked what was fun about being a soldier.

"Any time a group of us has a really hard task," one soldier said, "and we're sucking at it, that forms a bond. The tasks often aren't fun, but the bonds we form doing them are. They're rewarding." More than rewarding, of course: That training creates the shared experience and the trust that will serve these soldiers if they end up on a battlefield together.

Another soldier explained why, when we have such sophisticated drones, we still need people on the ground: soldiers trained, equipped, ready to deploy anywhere in the world.

Why ever put Americans directly in harm's way?

Because, he said, it's people who understand other people.

"Human connection—human influence—that can't happen with drones," the soldier said. "You win by influencing people, not killing them."

And the way to influence people is with human connection. By showing up in person.

The soldiers we talked to were excited to give outsiders a taste of their world. And we were thrilled to spend two days out in the desert in Fort Irwin, away from screens and everything else, immersed in their world.

I'm compelled to take on the challenge of making an inspirational and highly entertaining action film about the men and women who sacrifice for our country as members of the United States Army. Given the fair share of Army films set on the battlefield, I want to ensure that this project is special and different than what we've already seen.

And the points those two soldiers made will be woven throughout it: Sometimes life sucks, but if it sucks together, that creates connections and value that can't be created any other way.

Curiosity allows us to reinvent the world, as we continue to innovate with new technologies like AI and expand our creativity. It's important to note that curiosity cannot be found in anything other than humans. AI doesn't have or initiate curiosity. It doesn't have a consciousness; it doesn't feel fear or pain; it can't process feelings of hurt or a broken heart. But more distinctly, it doesn't carry a soul. Artificial intelligence is simply a patchwork of those human ingredients to create seemingly original and authentic stories. It's our responsibility to remember the difference.

Curiosity is the tool we use to solve problems—big problems, urgent problems, and our own problems. It was the curiosity of people who run pasta companies and flour mills, mask factories and seaports and middle schools. And every one of our own families too. With AI in the mix, both human curiosity and contact will become all the more powerful in the era of tech.

Having lived through uncertainty reminds us of the uncertainty we live with every day. If you don't understand a problem, you can't fix it. And the first step to understanding is leaning into the uncertainty, leaning into the *not knowing*. Asking questions.

Curiosity opens the door to adaptability.

Curiosity also opens the door to empathy.

In the last decade, I wrote two books that tried to capture the two most important things I'd learned to that point in my life:

A Curious Mind is about the underrated power of curiosity to help you live a better life.

Face to Face is about the power of human contact face to face—the importance of being with people in person. Because being in the room changes everything.

Those two deceptively simple concepts are really a single whole idea—they are the yin and yang of human connection, and also of discovery.

Nothing has so reinforced those two ideas—for me, but also in our wider cultures—as the pandemic years have: Curiosity, because of its absolute indispensability to how the world survived COVID-19. And human connection, because of how its absence during the pandemic shriveled our sense of well-being, underscoring so vividly how central our human connections are not just to surviving emotionally but to thriving.

To live a life with both meaning and happiness, we need curiosity, and we need each other—and those two things in turn reinforce each other.

And so as we reinvent ourselves, we're putting out a fresh edition combining the two books into a single volume: *A Curious Mind Expanded.*

Curiosity isn't just a tool for figuring out the structure of a molecule or how to tell a story about the Army.

It is that, of course. A tool to learn about how the world works. But curiosity is also a way of bridging gaps. Curiosity is itself a tool of human connection. If you ask someone a sincere question and listen to the answer with an open mind (and an open heart), you're learning how that person sees the world.

Curiosity is a tool of empathy. It is as powerful for helping us relate to each other as it is at helping us design faster computer chips.

Through the politics of the last decade, through the social divisions and uncertainty, we needed fewer snap judgments and fewer assumptions and more genuine curiosity.

One of the things that's magic about curiosity is that you don't need anyone's permission to use it, you don't need a team, and you don't need any special tools you don't have with you all the time.

Curiosity is a mind-set.

It's the mind-set that sees something—in the newspaper, or on TikTok or Instagram—and doesn't say, "What an idiot!" but "Why would she think that? Hmm."

Another powerful quality of curiosity is that it's positively reinforcing. If you approach the world with questions, you get one of three experiences:

You learn something completely new.

Or you learn that something you thought you understood is different than you thought.

Or you learn that you were right.

One of those three things always happens.

That's why I love asking questions. I really love all three of those results. Whether I was ignorant or confused or right, I'm never sorry I asked the questions.

This is true, and obvious, when it comes to our intellectual pursuits. But it's just as true—it's just as powerful—in our relationships with other people.

Here's a very personal example.

My son Patrick was finishing high school, and he still had to pick and apply to colleges. One of his friends had gotten into West Point, and Patrick was impressed with the experience his friend had there. From never having shown any particular interest in the military, or in going to West Point, Patrick moved over the course of a year to deciding that West Point was his first choice for college.

Not many parents I know have kids who go to the military academies. I was baffled. I was puzzled. And yes, I was worried: Everyone who graduates from West Point spends eight years as a commissioned officer in the U.S. Army, and I don't know any parents who want their kids to go to war. Not to mention that West Point is a stunningly demanding place to go to school—it's not the stereotypical college experience.

I remember a particular conversation I had with Patrick that opened my eyes. He told me two things that will always stay with me.

First, he said, "The things I care about are embodied in the values of West Point. Service to country. Service to one another."

He wanted to go to a college that would teach him, explicitly, to put those values into practice every day.

And then Patrick said, "Dad, you like to be challenged. I know that. I've seen it growing up. But I like to be challenged too. I like to be challenged even more than you do. I like to be challenged every minute of every day."

You probably couldn't find a better one-sentence description of West Point than that: Challenged every minute of every day.

I know my son well, and I love him—and all my children—with all my heart. This was a conversation that changed how I saw Patrick. I wasn't so much surprised as I was impressed and humbled.

I'd asked the simplest of questions about this key decision he was making—a decision, frankly, I disagreed with. The result was that I discovered my son had grown up. He'd thought about this carefully, thoughtfully. He was much less naive about it than I was, in fact. He understood himself, he understood his convictions, he understood what he was looking for, and he understood what he was getting himself into.

And that's how I became the father of a West Point cadet.

We often get confused about something that has to do with curiosity—confused or maybe even a little scared.

It seems easier, or safer, to fall back on our easy assumptions, especially if those assumptions reinforce what we already think.

We think that if we ask a sincere and thoughtful question of someone we disagree with, we might be dragged into an argument or coerced into agreeing with their opposing viewpoint.

Neither is correct.

It's often just the opposite. When you use curiosity with thoughtfulness and compassion, you don't have to agree with that person. But, you end up understanding them better, and that understanding is a form of connection.

So you're holding a book that does two things:

It asks you to ask more questions—to recognize the power of your own curiosity, to help you at work, to help you at home, to help you make friends, hold people accountable, discover what you love. Curiosity doesn't require a crisis. It doesn't even require an occasion. It can add depth and empathy, insight and joy and understanding to your life, moment by moment.

And this book asks you—whenever possible—to see people in person. To meet them, to look them in the eye. And it tells what I hope are memorable stories about how that changes your conversations and your relationships—and why.

In early 2023, we got the latest results from an extraordinary study on human satisfaction and human health—the longest, most detailed longitudinal study of people in history. It's the Harvard Study of Adult Development, begun in 1938, which has tracked hundreds of people, and their spouses and children, through eight decades.

The core finding of the study, which is now irrefutable, has surprised even the scientists conducting the research: human connection, our relationships, are the most important thing to our happiness, our satisfaction with our lives, and our actual physical health. Strong relationships with family and friends are a better predictor of happiness, and also of health and longevity, than income or IQ, than genetics or your cholesterol. That's a stunning and priceless insight.

Curiosity and connection. The keys to a long and happy life, and a satisfying and interesting one as well.

Brian Grazer
May 2023

PART ONE

1

There Is No Cure for Curiosity

The cure for boredom is curiosity. There is no cure for curiosity.

—Dorothy Parker[1]

One Thursday afternoon, the summer after I graduated from the University of Southern California (USC), I was sitting in my apartment in Santa Monica with the windows open, thinking about how to get some work until I started law school at USC in the fall.

Suddenly, through the windows, I overheard two guys talking just outside. One said, "Oh my God, I had the cushiest job at Warner Bros. I got paid for eight hours of work every day, and it was usually just an hour."

This guy got my attention. I opened the window a little more so I wouldn't miss the rest of the conversation, and I quietly closed the curtain.

The guy went on to say he had been a legal clerk. "I just quit today. My boss was a man named Peter Knecht."

I was amazed. Sounded perfect to me.

I went right to the telephone, dialed 411,[2] and asked for the main number at Warner Bros. I still remember it: 954-6000.[3]

I called the number and asked for Peter Knecht. An assistant in his office answered, and I said to her, "I'm going to USC law school in the fall, and I'd like to meet with Mr. Knecht about the law clerk job that's open."

Knecht got on the line. "Can you be here tomorrow at three p.m.?" he asked.

I met with him on Friday at 3 p.m. He hired me at 3:15. And I started work at Warner Bros. the next Monday.

I didn't quite realize it at that time, but two incredible things happened that day in the summer of 1974.

First, my life had just changed forever. When I reported for work as a legal clerk that Monday, they gave me a windowless office the size of a small closet. At that moment, I had found my life's work. From that tiny office, I joined the world of show business. I never again worked at anything else.

I also realized that curiosity had saved my ass that Thursday afternoon. I've been curious as long as I can remember. As a boy, I peppered my mother and my grandmother with questions, some of which they could answer, some of which they couldn't.

By the time I was a young man, curiosity was part of the way I approached the world every day. My kind of curiosity hasn't changed much since I eavesdropped on those guys at my apartment complex. It hasn't actually changed that much since I was an antsy twelve-year-old boy.

My kind of curiosity is a little wide-eyed and sometimes a little mischievous. Many of the best things that have happened in my life are the result of curiosity. And curiosity has occasionally gotten me in trouble.

But even when curiosity has gotten me in trouble, it has been interesting trouble.

Curiosity has never let me down. I'm never sorry I asked that next question. On the contrary, curiosity has swung wide many doors of opportunity for me. I've met amazing people, made great movies, made great friends, had some completely unexpected adventures, even fallen in love—because I'm not the least bit embarrassed to ask questions.

That first job at Warner Bros. studios in 1974 was exactly like the tiny office it came with—confining and discouraging. The assignment was simple: I was required to deliver final contract and legal documents to people with whom Warner Bros. was doing business. That's it. I was given envelopes filled with documents and the addresses where they should go, and off I went.

I was called a "legal clerk," but I was really just a glorified courier. At the time, I had an old BMW 2002—one of the boxy two-door BMW sedans that looked like it was leaning forward. Mine was a faded red-wine color, and I spent my days driving around Hollywood and Beverly Hills, delivering stacks of important papers.

I quickly identified the one really interesting thing about the job: the people to whom I was bringing the papers. These were the elite, the powerful, the glamorous of 1970s Hollywood—the writers, directors, producers, stars. There was only one problem: people like that always have assistants or secretaries, doormen or housekeepers.

If I was going to do this job, I didn't want to miss out on the only good part. I didn't want to meet housekeepers; I wanted to meet the important people. I was curious about them.

So I hit on a simple gambit. When I showed up, I would tell the intermediary—the secretary, the doorman—that I had to hand the documents directly to the person for the delivery to be "valid."

I went to ICM—the great talent agency—to deliver contracts to seventies superagent Sue Mengers,[4] who represented Barbra Streisand and Ryan O'Neal, Candice Bergen and Cher, Burt Reynolds and Ali MacGraw. How did I meet Mengers? I told the ICM receptionist, "The only way Miss Mengers can receive this is if I hand it to her personally." She sent me in without another question.

If the person to whom the documents were addressed wasn't there, I'd simply leave and come back. The guy who had unwittingly tipped me to the job was right. I had all day, but not much work to worry about.

This is how I met Lew Wasserman, the tough-guy head of MCA Studios, and his partner, Jules Stein.

It's how I met William Peter Blatty, who wrote *The Exorcist*, and also Billy Friedkin, the Oscar winner who directed it.

I handed contracts to Warren Beatty at the Beverly Wilshire Hotel.

I was just twenty-three years old, but I was curious. And I quickly learned that not only could I meet these people, I could also sit and talk to them.

I would hand over the documents with graciousness and deference, and since it was the seventies, they'd always say, "Come in! Have a drink! Have a cup of coffee!"

I would use these moments to get a sense of them, sometimes to get a bit of career advice. I never asked for a job. I never asked for anything, in fact.

Pretty quickly, I realized the movie business was a lot more interesting than law school. So I put it off—I never went; I would have made a terrible lawyer—and I kept that clerk job for a year, through the following summer.

You know what's curious? Throughout that entire time, no one ever called my bluff. No one said, "Hey, kid, just leave the contract on the table and get out of here. You don't need to see Warren Beatty."

I met every single person to whom I delivered papers.

Just as curiosity had gotten me the job, it also transformed the job itself into something wonderful.

The men and women whose contracts I delivered changed my life. They showed me a whole style of storytelling I wasn't familiar with, and I began to think that maybe I was a storyteller at heart. They set the stage for me to produce movies like *Splash* and *Apollo 13*, *American Gangster*, *Friday Night Lights*, and *A Beautiful Mind*.

Something else happened during that year of being a legal clerk that was just as important. It was the year I started to actively appreciate the real power of curiosity.

If you grew up in the fifties and sixties, being curious wasn't exactly considered a virtue. In the well-ordered, obedient classrooms of the Eisenhower era, it was more like an irritant. I knew I was curious, of course, but it was a little like wearing glasses. It was something people noticed, but it didn't help me get picked for sports teams, and it didn't help with girls.

That first year at Warner Bros., I realized that curiosity was more than just a quality of my personality. It was my secret weapon. Good for getting picked for the team—it would turn out to be good for becoming captain of the team—and even good for getting the girls.

Curiosity seems so simple. Innocent, even.

Labrador retrievers are charmingly curious. Porpoises are playfully, mischievously curious. A two-year-old going through the kitchen cabinets is exuberantly curious—and delighted at the noisy entertainment value of her curiosity. Every person who types a query into Google's search engine and presses Enter is curious about *something*—and that happens 378 million times an hour, every hour of every day.[5]

But curiosity has a potent behind-the-scenes power that we mostly overlook.

Curiosity is the spark that starts a flirtation—in a bar, at a party, across the lecture hall in Economics 101. And curiosity ultimately nourishes that romance, and all our best human relationships—marriages, friendships, the bond between parents and children. The curiosity to ask a simple question—"How was your day?" or "How are you feeling?"—to listen to the answer, and to ask the next question.

Curiosity can seem simultaneously urgent and trivial. Who shot J.R.? How will *Breaking Bad* end? What are the winning numbers on the ticket for the largest Powerball jackpot in history? These questions have a kind of impatient compulsion—right up until the moment we get the answer. Once the curiosity is satisfied, the question itself deflates. *Dallas* is the perfect example: Who *did* shoot J.R.? If you were alive in the 1980s, you know the question, but you may not recall the answer.[6]

There are plenty of cases where the urgency turns out to be justified, of course, and where satisfying the initial curiosity only unleashes more. The effort to decode the human genome turned into a dramatic high-stakes race between two teams of scientists. And once the genome was available, the results opened a thousand fresh pathways for scientific and medical curiosity.

The quality of many ordinary experiences often pivots on curiosity. If you're shopping for a new TV, the kind you ultimately take home and how well you like it is very much dependent on a salesperson who is curious: curious enough about the TVs to know them well, curious enough about your own needs and watching habits to figure out which TV you need.

That's a perfect example, in fact, of curiosity being camouflaged.

In an encounter like that, we'd categorize the salesperson as either "good" or "bad." A bad salesperson might aggressively try to sell us something we didn't want or understand, or would simply show us the TVs for sale, indifferently parroting the list of features on the card mounted beneath each. But the key ingredient in either case is curiosity—about the customer and about the products.

Curiosity is hiding like that almost everywhere you look, its presence or its absence proving to be the magic ingredient in a whole range of surprising places. The key to unlocking the genetic mysteries of humanity: curiosity. The key to providing decent customer service: curiosity.

If you're at a boring business dinner, curiosity can save you.

If you're bored with your career, curiosity can rescue you.

If you're feeling uncreative or unmotivated, curiosity can be the cure.

It can help you use anger or frustration constructively.

It can give you courage.

Curiosity can add zest to your life, and it can take you way beyond zest—it can enrich your whole sense of security, confidence, and well-being.

But it doesn't do any of that alone, of course.

While Labrador retrievers are really curious, no black Lab ever decoded the genome or got a job at Best Buy, for that matter. They lose interest pretty quickly.

For it to be effective, curiosity has to be harnessed to at least two other key traits. The first is the ability to pay attention to the answers to your questions—you have to actually absorb whatever it is you're being curious about. We all know people who ask really good questions, who seem engaged and energized when they're talking and asking those questions, but who zone out the moment it's time for you to answer.

The second trait is the willingness to act. Curiosity was undoubtedly the inspiration for thinking we could fly to the moon, but it didn't marshal the hundreds of thousands of people, the billions of dollars, and the determination to overcome failures and disasters along the way to making it a reality. Curiosity can inspire the original vision—of a moon mission, or of a movie, for that matter. It can replenish that inspiration when morale flags—"Look, that's where we're going!" But at some point, on the way to the moon or the multiplex, the work gets hard, the obstacles become a thicket, the frustration piles up, and then you need determination.

I hope to accomplish three things in this book: I want to wake you up to the value and power of curiosity; I want to show you all the ways I use it, in the hopes that that will inspire you to test it out in your daily life; and I want to start a conversation in the wider world about why such an important quality is so little valued, taught, and cultivated today.

For a trait with so much potential power, curiosity itself seems uncomplicated. Psychologists define curiosity as "wanting to know." That's it. And that definition squares with our own commonsense feeling. "Wanting to know," of course, means seeking out the information. Curiosity starts as an impulse, an urge, but it pops out into the world as something more active, more searching: a question.

This inquisitiveness seems as intrinsic to us as hunger or thirst. A child asks a series of seemingly innocent questions: Why is the sky blue? How high up does the blue go? Where does the blue go at night? Instead of answers (most adults can't explain why the sky is blue, including me), the child might receive a dismissive, slightly patronizing reply like, "Why, aren't *you* the curious little girl . . ."[7]

To some, questions like these feel challenging, even more so if you don't know the answers. Rather than answering them, the adult simply asserts his own authority to brush them aside. Curiosity can make us adults feel a little inadequate or impatient—that's the experience of the parent who doesn't know why the sky is blue, the experience of the teacher trying to get through the day's lesson without being derailed.

The girl is left not just without answers but also with the strong impression that asking questions—innocuous or intriguing questions—can often be regarded as impertinent.

That's hardly surprising.

No one today ever says anything bad about curiosity directly. But if you pay attention, curiosity isn't really celebrated and cultivated; it isn't protected and encouraged. It's not just that curiosity is inconvenient. Curiosity can be dangerous. Curiosity isn't just impertinent; it's insurgent. It's revolutionary.

The child who feels free to ask why the sky is blue grows into the adult who asks more disruptive questions: Why am I the serf and you the king? Does the sun really revolve around Earth? Why are people with dark skin slaves and people with light skin their masters?

How threatening is curiosity?

All you have to do is look to the Bible to see. The first story in the Bible after the telling of creation, the first story that involves people, is about curiosity. The story of Adam, Eve, the serpent, and the tree does not end well for the curious.

Adam is told explicitly by God, "You are free to eat from any tree in the garden; but you must not eat from the tree of the knowledge of good and evil, for when you eat from it you will certainly die."[8]

It is the serpent who suggests challenging God's restriction. He starts with a question himself, to Eve: Is there a tree whose fruit God has put off-limits? Yes, Eve says, the tree right at the center of the garden—we can't eat its fruit, we can't even touch it, or else we'll die.

Eve knows the rules so well she embellishes them a bit: Don't even *touch* the tree.

The serpent replies with what is surely the most heedless bravado in history, unafraid of the knowledge of good and evil, or of God. He says to Eve, "You will not certainly die. . . . For God knows that when you eat from it your eyes will be opened, and you will be like God, knowing good and evil."[9]

The serpent is appealing directly to Eve's curiosity. You don't even know what you don't know, the serpent says. With a bite of the forbidden fruit, you will see the world in a completely different way.

Eve visits the tree and discovers that "the fruit of the tree was good for food and pleasing to the eye, and also desirable for gaining wisdom."[10]

She plucks a piece of fruit, takes a bite, and passes it to Adam, who also takes a bite. And "the eyes of both of them were opened."[11]

Knowledge was never so easily gotten, nor in the end so hard won. To say that God was angry is an understatement. The punishment for knowing good and evil is misery for Eve and Adam, and for all the rest of us, forever: the pain of childbirth for Eve, the unceasing toil of raising their own food for Adam. And, of course, banishment from the garden.

The parable could not be blunter: curiosity causes suffering. Indeed, the story's moral is aimed directly at the audience: whatever your current misery, reader, it was caused by Adam, Eve, the serpent, and their rebellious curiosity.

So there you have it. The first story, in the foundation work of Western civilization—the very first story!—is about curiosity, and its message is: Don't ask questions. Don't seek out knowledge on your own—leave it to the people in charge. Knowledge just leads to wretchedness.

Barbara Benedict is a professor at Trinity College in Hartford, Connecticut, and a scholar of the eighteenth century who spent years studying the attitude about curiosity during that period, as scientific inquiry sought to overtake religion as the way we understand the world.

The Adam and Eve story, she says, is a warning. "'You are a serf because God said you should be a serf. I'm a king because God said I should be a king. Don't ask any questions about that.' Stories like Adam and Eve," Benedict says, "reflect the need of cultures and civilizations to maintain the status quo. 'Things are the way they are because that's the right way.' That attitude is popular among rulers and those who control information." And it has been from the Garden of Eden to the Biden administration.

Curiosity still gets no respect. We live in an era in which, if you're willing to squint, all of human knowledge is accessible on a smartphone, but the bias against curiosity still infuses our culture.

The classroom should be a vineyard of questions, a place to cultivate them, to learn both how to ask them and how to chase down the answers. Some classrooms are. But in fact, curiosity is often treated with the same regard in school as it was in the Garden of Eden. Especially with the recent proliferation of standardized testing, questions can derail the lockstep framework of the day's lesson plan; sometimes teachers don't know the answers themselves. It's exactly the opposite of what you would hope, but authentic curiosity in a typical seventh-grade classroom isn't cultivated—because it's inconvenient and disruptive to the orderly running of the class.

The situation is little better in the offices and workplaces where most adults spend their lives. Sure, software coders or pharmaceutical researchers or university professors are encouraged to be curious because it's a big part of their jobs. But what if the typical hospital nurse or bank teller gets curious and starts questioning how things are done? Outside of some truly exceptional places like Google and IBM and Corning, curiosity is unwelcome, if not insubordinate. Good behavior—whether you're fourteen years old or forty-five— doesn't include curiosity.

Even the word "curious" itself remains strangely anti-curious. We all pretend that a curious person is a delight, of course. But when we describe an object with the adjective "curious," we mean that it's an oddity, something a little weird, something other than normal. And when someone responds to a question with the tilt of her head and the statement, "That's a curious question," she is of course saying it's not the right question to be asking.

Here's the remarkable thing. Curiosity isn't just a great tool for improving your own life and happiness, your ability to win a great job or a great spouse. It is the key to the things we say we value most in the modern world: independence, self-determination, self-government, self-improvement. Curiosity is the path to freedom itself.

The ability to ask any question embodies two things: the freedom to go chase the answer, and the ability to challenge authority, to ask, "How come you're in charge?"

Curiosity is itself a form of power, and also a form of courage.

I was a pudgy boy, and I didn't grow out of it as a teenager. When I graduated from college, I had love handles. I got teased at the beach. I looked soft with my shirt on or off.

I decided I didn't want to look the way I looked. When I was twenty-two years old, I changed my diet and developed an exercise routine—a discipline, really. I jumped rope every day: two hundred jumps a minute, thirty minutes a day, seven days a week. Six thousand jumps a day for twelve years. Gradually my body changed; the love handles faded away.

I didn't drive myself to be buff. And I don't look like a movie star. But I also don't really look like what you might imagine a movie producer looks like. I have my own slightly offbeat style. I wear sneakers to work, I gel my hair so it stands straight up, I have a big smile.

And today, I'm still exercising four or five times a week, usually first thing in the morning, often getting up before six to make sure I have time. (I don't jump rope anymore, because I eventually ruptured both my Achilles tendons.) I'm seventy-two years old, and in the last five decades, I've never slipped back into being soft.

I took a resolution and turned it into a habit, into part of how I live each day.

I did the same thing with curiosity.

Very gradually, starting with that first law clerk's job at Warner Bros., I consciously made curiosity a part of my routine.

I already explained that first step, insisting on meeting everyone whose legal contracts I delivered. I took two things from my success with that. First, people—even famous and powerful people—are happy to talk, especially about themselves and their work; and second, it helps to have even a small pretext to talk to them.

That's what my "I have to hand these papers over in person" line was—a pretext. It worked for me, it worked for the assistants, it even worked for the people I was visiting. "Oh, he needs to see me in person—sure."

A few months after I started at Warner Bros., a senior vice president of the studio was fired. I remember watching them peel his name off the office door.

His office was spacious, it had windows, it had two secretaries, and most important, it was right next to the executive suite—what I called the "royal" offices—where the president of Warner Bros. worked, as did the chairman and the vice chairman.

I asked my boss, Peter Knecht, if I could use that vice president's office while it was empty.

"Sure," Knecht said. "I'll arrange it."

The new office changed everything. Just like when you wear the right clothes for the occasion—when you wear a suit, you feel more confident and grown-up—going to work in that real office changed my perspective. All of a sudden I felt like I had my own piece of real estate, my own franchise.

This was a great time to be in show business in Hollywood, the late sixties and seventies, and the "royal suite" was occupied by three of the most important and creative people of the era—Frank Wells, the president of Warner Bros., who went on to head Disney; Ted Ashley, who wasn't ever a household name but who, as chairman of Warner Bros., really brought energy and success back to the studio; and John Calley, the vice chairman of Warner Bros., who was a legendary producer, something of a Hollywood intellectual, a creative force, and unquestionably an eccentric character.

I was just a law clerk, but I had an office, my own secretaries, and I even had one of those old-fashioned speaker-box intercoms on my desk. Just outside my door worked three of the most powerful men in Hollywood. I had created a situation where I was in exactly the right place at exactly the right time.

I was baffled by the entertainment business, and it seemed as if even many of the people in the entertainment business were baffled by it. It was hard to understand how movies and TV shows got made. It was definitely not a linear process. People seemed to be navigating in a fog, without instruments.

But I was fascinated and captivated by it. I became like an anthropologist entering a new world, with a new language, new rituals, new priorities. It was a completely immersive environment, and it ignited my curiosity. I was determined to study it, to understand it, to master it.

It was John Calley who really showed me what being in the entertainment business was all about, and he also showed me what it could be like. Calley was a huge figure and an important creative force in the movies in the 1960s and 1970s. Under his aegis, Warner Bros. flourished, producing movies like *The Exorcist*, *A Clockwork Orange*, *Deliverance*, *Dog Day Afternoon*, *All the President's Men*, *The Towering Inferno*, *Dirty Harry*, and *Blazing Saddles*.[12]

When I was working just down the hall from him, Calley was forty-four or forty-five years old, at the height of his power, and already a legend—intelligent, eccentric, Machiavellian. Warner Bros. in those days was making a movie a month,[13] and Calley was always thinking a hundred moves ahead. A handful of people loved him, a slightly larger group admired him, and a lot of people feared him.

I think what he found appealing about me was my innocence, my utter naïveté. I wasn't working any angles. I was so new I didn't even know where the angles were.

Calley would say, "Grazer, come sit in my office." He'd put me on the couch, and I'd watch him work.

The whole thing was a revelation. My own father was a lawyer, a sole practitioner, and he struggled to be successful. I was headed to law school—a life of manila file folders, stacks of briefs, thick casebooks, working away at a Naugahyde-topped desk.

Calley worked out of a huge office that was beautiful and elegant. It was set up like a living room. He had no desk. He had a couple of sofas, and he worked all day sitting on one of them.

He didn't do any writing or typing; he didn't carry piles of work home from the office each day. He talked. He sat in this elegant living room, on a couch, and talked all day.[14] In fact, the contracts I delivered were just the final act, formalizing all the talk. Sitting there on Calley's sofa, it was clear that the business part of show business was all about conversation.

And watching Calley work, I realized something: Creative thoughts didn't have to follow a straight narrative line. You could pursue your interests, your passions; you could chase any quirky idea that came from some odd corner of your experience or your brain. Here was a world where good ideas had real value—and no one cared whether the idea was connected to yesterday's idea or whether it was related to the previous ten minutes of conversation. If it was an interesting idea, no one cared where it came from at all.

It was an epiphany. That's how my brain worked—lots of ideas, just not organized like the periodic table.

For years, I struggled in school. I wasn't that good at sitting quietly, tucked into a little desk, following a bell schedule and filling out worksheets. That binary way of learning—either you know the answer or you don't—didn't fit my brain and didn't appeal to me. I've always felt like ideas come from all corners of my brain, and I felt that way even as a kid.

I did well in college, but only because by then I had figured out some tricks to succeeding in that environment. But the huge classes and impersonal homework assignments didn't excite me. I didn't learn that much. I was headed to law school because I had gotten in, and because I wasn't quite sure what else to do. I did at least have some idea of what it meant to be a lawyer—although, frankly, it seemed a lot like a life sentence to yet more homework assignments, assuming I passed the bar exam.

Calley, on the other hand, was one of the hippest guys in the world. He knew movie stars; he socialized with movie stars. He was highly literate—he read all the time. He sat on his couch, with ideas and decisions winging through his office all day long without rules or rigidity.

Watching him was intoxicating. I thought, I want to live in this man's world. Who needs a life of brown accordion files? I want to work on a sofa, follow my curiosity, and make movies.[15]

Sitting there in his office, I could clearly understand that the movie business was built on ideas—a steady stream of captivating ideas, new ideas every day. And it was suddenly clear to me that curiosity was the way to uncover ideas; it was the way to spark them.

I knew I was curious—the way you might know you are funny or shy. Curiosity was a quality of my personality. But until that year, I didn't connect curiosity to success in the world. In school, for instance, I had never associated being curious with getting good grades.

But at Warner Bros., I discovered the value of curiosity—and I began what I consider my curiosity journey, following it in a systematic way.

Calley and I never talked about curiosity. But being given the big office and watching Calley in action gave me another idea, a more evolved version of my meetings with the people to whom I was delivering contracts. I realized I didn't have to meet only the people Warner Bros. happened to be doing business with that day. I could see anyone in the business I wanted to see. I could see the people who sparked my curiosity simply by calling their offices and asking for an appointment.

I developed a brief introduction for the secretaries and assistants who answered the phone: "Hi, my name is Brian Grazer. I work for Warner Bros. Business Affairs. This is not associated with studio business, and I do not want a job, but I would like to meet Mr. So-and-So for five minutes to talk to him . . ." And I always offered a specific reason I wanted to talk to everyone.

My message was clear: I worked at a real place, I only wanted five minutes on the schedule, I did *not* want a job. And I was polite.

Just like insisting on handing over the legal documents in person, the speech worked like a charm.

I talked to producer David Picker, who was at Columbia Pictures.

Then I thought maybe I could see producer Frank Yablans, and I did.

Once I'd met Yablans, I thought, *Maybe I can meet Lew Wasserman, the head of MCA.* And I did.

I worked myself up the ladder. Talking to one person in the movie business suggested a half dozen more people I could talk to.

Each success gave me the confidence to try for the next person. It turned out I really could talk to almost anyone in the business.

That was the start of something that changed—and continues to change—my life and my career, and which ultimately inspired this book.

I started having what I called curiosity conversations. At first, they were just inside the business. For a long time, I had a rule for myself: I had to meet one new person in the entertainment business every day.[16] But pretty quickly I realized that I could actually reach out and talk to anyone, in any business that I was curious about. It's not just showbiz people who are willing to talk about themselves and their work—everyone is.

For four decades, I've been tracking down people about whom I was curious and asking if I could sit down with them for an hour. I've had as few as a dozen curiosity conversations in a year, but sometimes I've done them as often as once a week. My goal was always at least one every two weeks. Once I started doing the curiosity conversations as a practice, my only rule for myself was that the people had to be from outside the world of movies and TV.

The idea wasn't to spend more time with the kinds of people I worked with every day. I had quickly discovered that the entertainment business is incredibly insular—we tend to talk only to ourselves. It's easy to think that movies and TV are a miniature version of the world. That's not just wrong, it's a perspective that leads to mediocre movies, and also to being boring.

I was so serious about the curiosity conversations that I often spent a year or more trying to arrange a meeting with particular people. I would spend hours calling, writing letters, cajoling, befriending assistants. As I got more successful and busier, I assigned one of my staff to arrange the conversations—the *New Yorker* did a little piece on the job, which came to be known as "cultural attaché." For a while, I had someone whose only job was to arrange the conversations.[17]

The point was to follow my curiosity, and I ranged as widely as I could. I sat down with two CIA directors. With both Carl Sagan and Isaac Asimov. I met with the man who invented the most powerful weapon in history and the richest man in the world. I met with people I was scared of; I met people I really didn't want to meet.

I never meet anyone with a movie in mind (although in recent years, it's clear that some people met with me because they thought that maybe I would do a movie about them or their work). The goal for me is to learn something.

The results have always been surprising, and the connections I've made from the curiosity conversations have cascaded through my life—and the movies we make—in the most unexpected ways. My conversation with the astronaut Jim Lovell certainly started me on the path to telling the story of Apollo 13. But how do we convey, in a movie, the psychology of being trapped on a crippled spaceship? It was Veronica de Negri, a Chilean activist who was tortured for months by her own government, who taught me what it's like to be forced to rely completely on oneself to survive. Veronica de Negri helped us to get *Apollo 13* right as surely as Jim Lovell did.

Over time, I discovered that I'm curious in a particular sort of way. My strongest sense of curiosity is what I call emotional curiosity: I want to understand what makes people tick; I want to see if I can connect a person's attitude and personality with their work, with their challenges and accomplishments.

I met with Jonas Salk, the scientist and physician who cured polio, a man who was a childhood hero of mine. It took me more than a year to get an audience with him. I wasn't interested in the scientific method Salk used to figure out how to develop the polio vaccine. I wanted to know what it was like to help millions of people avoid a crippling disease that shadowed the childhoods of everyone when I was growing up. And he worked in a different era. He was renowned, admired, successful—but he received no financial windfall. He cured what was then the worst disease afflicting the world, and he never made a dime from that. Can you imagine that happening today? I wanted to understand the mind-set that turns a cure like that loose in the world.

I met with Edward Teller, who created the hydrogen bomb. He was an old man when I met him, working on the antimissile "Star Wars" program for President Reagan. He was another person I had to lobby for a year in order to get an hour with him. I wanted to understand the intellect of a man who creates something like the hydrogen bomb and what his sense of morality is like.

I met with Carlos Slim, the Mexican businessperson who was then the richest man in the world.[18] How does the richest person in the world live every day? I wanted to know what it takes to be that kind of businessman, to be so driven and determined that you win bigger than anyone else.

The truth is that when I was meeting someone like Salk or Teller or Slim, what I hoped for was an insight, a revelation. I wanted to grasp who they were. Of course, you don't usually get that with strangers in an hour.

Salk was gracious and friendly. Teller was crabby. And Carlos Slim was unlike what I expected, not brisk or businesslike or ruthless in any way. He was very warm. Very Latino. At lunch, he ordered a lot of courses, he drank wine; it seemed like he had nowhere else he wanted to be—our lunch lasted three hours.

I've done hundreds and hundreds of curiosity meetings. It's the thing I look forward to and often the thing I end up enjoying the most. For me, when I'm learning from someone who is right in front of me, it's better than sex. It's better than success.

I had my first real curiosity conversation outside the entertainment business when I was twenty-three years old. I had been fired from the law clerk's job at Warner Bros. (after fifteen months, they thought I was having too much fun and delivering too few documents), and I was working for the producer Edgar Scherick (*The Taking of Pelham One Two Three*, *The Stepford Wives*), trying to become a producer myself.

I went to see F. Lee Bailey. Bailey was the most famous criminal trial attorney in the country at that point, having been the lawyer for Sam Sheppard and Patty Hearst.

I had an idea for a TV series, what I was calling *F. Lee Bailey's Casebook of American Crimes*—kind of a judicial version of *Walt Disney Presents*, using an expert to narrate the stories of these great cases.

I really wanted to talk to Bailey. He was winning a lot of important cases. How did he pick them? Does he have a moral compass? How does he communicate in the courtroom—with facts? With legal points? With the morality of the case?

I wanted to understand the distinction between a lawyer's belief system and what he or she was good at. What was Bailey's purpose in life, and how did that mesh with his talents?

When I tracked him down, he was preparing for trial in a case in Las Cruces, New Mexico. For some reason, he agreed to see me, so I flew out there.

It was kind of crazy. He was staying in this tiny town, at this Western-themed road motel, a little run-down, with a kidney-shaped swimming pool. I had no idea what was going to happen. I knocked, he opened the door—he was alone, no assistants—and he told me to come in while he practiced his arguments.

It was ungodly hot. I hung out on the couch in his room. He seemed to be creating his case right in front of me. After a little while, he sent me to the liquor store across the street to buy him a bottle of Johnnie Walker Black.

He had a drink. He was pacing back and forth in the room, getting more confident, ramping up his argument, sounding really smart. He had tons of information. I didn't really understand it, but he was testing it out on me.

Right there in the motel room, I could see that the guy was a force. Spellbinding.

I flew home thinking he would be great at hosting this TV show. In those days, before reality TV and Nancy Grace and Greta Van Susteren, we were thinking of it as a miniseries. We did a deal with Bailey, we hired a writer, but in the end it never got made.

Still, sitting there on the couch in that sticky motel room, in that small town in New Mexico, listening to Bailey build his case, I realized that there's a huge distance between the noble reasons he probably went to law school—which were still there, deeply embedded in him—and what things were like at that moment.

It was a whole new way to look at lawyers and their work.

I never made a movie about F. Lee Bailey, of course, although his life was certainly rich enough for one. I didn't even make a movie about lawyers until twenty years later, when I did *Liar Liar*, with Jim Carrey, about what happens to a lawyer who is forced to tell nothing but the truth for twenty-four hours straight.

For me, the curiosity conversations are just the most obvious, the most visible example of my own curiosity. They are a kind of discipline, like the exercise routine, because you don't get to talk to busy, interesting people unless you put steady effort into persuading them to see you.

But the curiosity conversations are different from the workouts in this way: I hate exercising; I just like the results. I love the curiosity conversations while they are happening. The results—a month or a decade later—are something I count on, but they are a bonus.

In fact, of course, all I do is talk—I talk for a living. Actually, I try to listen for a living. Being a movie and TV producer means I live a version of the life John Calley showed me almost fifty years ago. I have meetings and phone calls and conversations all day long. For me, every one of those is, in fact, a curiosity conversation. I don't just use curiosity to get to meet famous people, or to find good scripts. I use curiosity to make sure movies get made—on budget, on time, and with the most powerful storytelling possible. I've discovered that even when you're in charge, you are often much more effective asking questions than giving orders.

My first real, full-fledged producing job was at Paramount Studios. I had an office on the backlot in what was called the Director's Building. I was twenty-eight years old, and I had produced a couple of successful TV movies (including the first episodes of a twenty-hour miniseries on the Ten Commandments), and Paramount gave me a deal to find and produce films.

My office was in a corner on the third floor, with views of the walkways crisscrossing the lot. I would open the window (yes, in the 1970s and 1980s, office windows still opened) and I'd watch the powerful, famous, and glamorous walking by.

I was curious about who was on the lot and who was working with whom. This was during the time when I made myself meet someone new in show business every single day. I liked to shout down from my window at the people walking by—Howard Koch, who cowrote *Casablanca*; Michael Eisner, who would become CEO of Disney; and Barry Diller, who was CEO of Paramount and Michael Eisner's boss.

One day Brandon Tartikoff was walking by. He was the president of NBC television, in the process of reviving the network with shows like *Hill Street Blues* and *Cheers* and *Miami Vice*. At thirty-two, he was already one of the most powerful people in show business.

"Hey, Brandon!" I yelled. "Up here!"

He looked up at me and smiled. "Wow," he said, "you must be in charge of the world from up there."

A few minutes later, my phone rang. It was my boss, Gary Nardino, the head of TV at Paramount. "Brian, what the fuck do you think you're doing, screaming out your window at the president of NBC?"

"I'm just connecting," I said. "We're just having fun."

"I don't think we're having that much fun," Nardino said. "Cut it out."

Okay, not everyone was equally charmed by my style in those days. I was a little scared of Nardino, but not scared enough to stop shouting out the window.

One day I saw Ron Howard walking by. Ron was already famous and successful from his years acting on *The Andy Griffith Show* and *Happy Days*, but he was trying to make the leap to directing. As he was walking by, I thought, *I'm going to meet Ron Howard tomorrow.*

I didn't shout out the window at him. I waited until he got back to his office and called him up. "Ron, it's Brian Grazer," I said. "I see you on the lot. I'm a producer here too. I think we have similar goals. Let's meet and talk about it."

Ron was kind of shy, and he seemed surprised by my phone call. I don't think he really wanted to meet me. I said, "It'll be fun; it'll be relaxed; let's just do it."

A few days later, he did come by to talk. He was trying to become a mainstream movie director, and I was trying to become a mainstream movie producer. We were two guys trying to do something we'd never done before.

The moment he walked into my office, he had this aura about him—a glow. After talking to him, I could tell my choices in life weren't as thoughtful as his. He gave this sense of having a strong moral conscience. I know that sounds silly after just a single meeting, but it was my immediate impression. And it's true. It's the way Ron is today—and it's the way he was forty-four years ago.

When he walked in, I asked him, "What do you want to be?"

Ron not only wanted to direct, but he wanted to direct an R-rated movie. He wanted to change the way people saw him. I had no idea if he could direct. But I immediately decided I was going to bet on him and try to persuade him to work with me. I started pitching my movie ideas—*Splash* and *Night Shift*. He definitely didn't want to do a movie about a man falling in love with a mermaid. But he liked the irreverence of *Night Shift*, an R-rated comedy about two guys who run a call-girl ring out of the New York City morgue. Not the movie you'd ever predict from the star of *Happy Days*.

In fact, we made two movies together—*Night Shift* and then, despite Ron's initial reluctance, *Splash*, which became a huge hit. After working so well together on those two movies, we formed our company, Imagine Entertainment, and we've been artistic and business partners for almost forty years. Not only could Ron direct, but he's become a master filmmaker. The movies we've done together include *Parenthood*, *Backdraft*, *The Da Vinci Code*, *Frost/Nixon*, *Apollo 13*, and the Oscar-winning *A Beautiful Mind*.

My relationship with Ron has been the most important in my life, outside of my family. He's my closest work colleague and my best friend. I decided to meet Ron after seeing him from my window, and it was my emotional curiosity—my puzzling over what makes Ron Howard *Ron Howard*—that connected me to him. Again, at one of the most important moments of my life, following my curiosity opened the door.

Ron and I are different in many ways—especially our temperaments. But we share a sense of standards, including how to tell a story, and most important, we agree on what makes a great story. In fact, if there's anyone I know who is as genuinely curious as I am, it's Ron Howard. When we're in meetings together, he asks as many questions as I do, and his questions are different, and they elicit different information.

My curiosity conversations are something I've done with consistency and purpose all these years. You'll see many examples of them throughout this book. These conversations are events or occasions when curiosity itself is the motivation.

But in my everyday work and life, curiosity itself is not an "occasion." It's the opposite. Curiosity is something I use all the time. I'm always asking questions. For me, it's an instinct. It's also, very distinctly, a technique.

I'm a boss—Ron Howard and I run Imagine together—but I'm not much of an order giver. My management style is to ask questions. If someone's doing something I don't understand or don't like, if someone who works for me is doing something unexpected, I start out asking questions. Being curious.

I'm constantly meeting new people—sometimes at events, sometimes on Zoom, but often the new people are sitting on the couch in my office during the workday. I'm not particularly outgoing, but I have to *act* outgoing all the time. So how do I handle all these new people—sometimes a dozen in a single day—often sitting eagerly right in front of me, expecting me to run the conversation? I ask questions, of course. I let them do the talking. Being interested in someone isn't that hard if you know even a little about them—and as I've discovered, people love talking about their work, what they know about, their journey.

The entertainment business requires a huge amount of confidence. You have to believe in your own ideas for movies and TV shows, and you quickly discover that the safest answer for any studio or investor or executive to give is no. I'm often amazed that we get any movies made at all. But you can't succeed in Hollywood if you're discouraged by being told no, because regardless of the actual quality of your ideas, or even the quality of your track record, you'll get told no all the time. You have to have the confidence to push forward. That's true in all corners of the world—you have to have confidence if you work at a Silicon Valley tech company or treat patients at an inner-city hospital. My confidence comes from curiosity. Yes, asking questions builds confidence in your own ideas.

Curiosity does something else for me: it helps me cut through the routine anxiety of work and life.

I worry, for instance, about becoming complacent—I worry that out here in Hollywood, I'll end up in a bubble isolated from what's going on in the rest of the world, from how it's changing and evolving. I use curiosity to pop the bubble, to keep complacency at bay.

I also worry about much more ordinary things: I worry about giving speeches; I worry about the safety of my kids; I even worry about the police—police officers make me nervous. I use curiosity when I'm worried about something. If you understand what kind of speech someone wants you to give, if you understand how cops think, you'll either see your fear dissipate, or you'll be able to handle it.

I use curiosity as a management tool.

I use it to help me be outgoing.

I use curiosity to power my self-confidence.

I use it to avoid getting into a rut, and I use it to manage my own worries.

In the coming chapters, I'm going to analyze and tell stories about these different types of curiosity, because I think they can be useful to almost anyone.

And that is the most important way I use curiosity: I use it to tell stories. That, really, is my profession. My job as a producer is to look for good stories to tell, and I need people to write those stories, to act in them, to direct them. I'm looking for the money to get those stories made, and for ideas about how to sell the finished stories to the public. But, for me, the key to all these elements is the story itself.

Here's one of the secrets of life in Hollywood—a secret you learn in ninth-grade English class but that many people forget. There are only a few kinds of stories in the world: romance, quest, tragedy, comedy. We've been telling stories for four thousand years. Every story has been told.

And yet here I sit in the middle of a business devoted to either finding new stories or taking old stories and telling them in fresh ways, with fresh characters.

Good storytelling requires creativity and originality; it requires a real spark of inspiration. Where does the spark come from? I think curiosity is the flint from which flies the spark of inspiration.

In fact, storytelling and curiosity are natural allies. Curiosity is what drives human beings out into the world every day, to ask questions about what's going on around them, about people and why they behave the way they do. Storytelling is the act of bringing home the discoveries learned from curiosity. The story is a report from the front lines of curiosity.

Storytelling gives us the ability to tell everyone else what we've learned—or to tell everyone the story of our adventure, or about the adventures of the people we've met. Likewise, nothing sparks curiosity like good storytelling. Curiosity drives the desire to keep reading the book you can't put down; it's the desire to know how much of a movie you've just seen is true.

Curiosity and storytelling are intertwined. They give each other power.

What makes a story fresh is the point of view of the person telling it.

I produced a movie called *Splash*, about what happens when a man falls in love with a mermaid.

I produced a movie called *Apollo 13*, the true story of what happens when three U.S. astronauts get trapped in their crippled spaceship.

I produced a movie called *8 Mile*, about trying to be a white rap musician in the black rap world of Detroit.

I produced a movie called *American Gangster*, about a heroin smuggler in Vietnam-era New York.

American Gangster isn't about a gangster—it's about capability; it's about talent and determination.

8 Mile isn't about rap music; it isn't even about race—it's about surmounting humiliation, about respect, about being an outsider.

Apollo 13 isn't about aeronautics—it's about resourcefulness, about putting aside panic in the name of survival.

And *Splash*, of course, isn't about mermaids—only a thousand people in Hollywood told me we couldn't make a movie about mermaids. *Splash* is about love, about finding the right love for yourself, as opposed to the love others would choose for you.

I don't want to make movies about alluring mermaids or courageous astronauts, about brazen drug smugglers or struggling musicians. At least, I don't want to make predictable movies about *only* those things.

I don't want to tell stories where the "excitement" comes from explosions or special effects or sex scenes.

I want to tell the very best stories I can, stories that are memorable, that resonate, that make the audience think, that sometimes make people see their own lives differently. And to find those stories, to get to inspiration, to find that spark of creativity, what I do is ask questions.

What kind of story is it? Is it a comedy? A myth? An adventure?

What's the right tone for this story?

Why are the characters in this story in trouble?

What connects the characters in this story to each other?

What makes this story emotionally satisfying?

Who is telling this story, and what is that person's point of view? What is his challenge? What is her dream?

And most important, what is this story about? The plot is what happens in the story, but that plot is not what the story is *about*.

I don't think I'd be very good at my job if I weren't curious. And I think I'd be making movies that were pedestrian.

I keep asking questions until something interesting happens. My talent is to know enough to ask the questions, and to know when something interesting happens.

What I think is so exciting about curiosity is that it doesn't matter who you are; it doesn't matter what your job is, or what your passion is. Curiosity works the same way for all of us—if we use it well.

You don't have to be Thomas Edison. You don't have to be Steve Jobs. You don't have to be Steven Spielberg. But you can be "creative" and "innovative" and "compelling" and "original"—because you can be curious.

Curiosity doesn't only help you solve problems—no matter what those problems are. There's a bonus: Curiosity is free. You don't need a training course. You don't need special equipment or expensive clothing; you don't need a smartphone or a high-speed Internet connection; you don't need the full set of the *Encyclopædia Britannica* (which I was always a little sad I didn't have).

You're born curious, and no matter how much battering your curiosity has taken, it's standing by, ready to be awakened.

2

The Police Chief, the Movie Mogul, and the Father of the H-Bomb: Thinking Like Other People

Curiosity ... is insubordination in its purest form.

—*Vladimir Nabokov*[1]

The police officers asked me to lower my pants. That's when I wondered what I had gotten myself into.

It was April 30, 1992, and I was standing inside Parker Center, the distinctive downtown LA building that was then headquarters for the Los Angeles Police Department. I had been working for months to get to this spot—to meet Daryl Gates, the legendary chief of the LAPD, a man renowned for inventing the modern police SWAT unit and for showing big-city police departments across the country how to function more like paramilitary units.

In Los Angeles in the 1980s and early 1990s, no one wielded power like Chief Gates. I was fascinated by that power and by the personality that was able to accumulate it and use it. This type of influence is completely alien to me. I don't see the world as a hierarchy—as a chain of command. I don't want control over hundreds of people; I don't see life, or work, as an opportunity to build up power and exercise it. I don't particularly like giving orders or seeing whether people have enough respect for me, or fear of me, to obey those orders. But the world is filled with people maneuvering for power—in fact, the typical workplace is filled with people like that, and we probably need them.

As much as I'm fascinated by that kind of power, I'm also wary of it. I do want to understand that kind of personality, as a storyteller and also as a citizen. Chief Gates made a great curiosity conversation—the perfect example of a certain kind of autocratic mind-set, right in my own city.

I tried for many months to get on Gates's calendar—working my way through an assistant, a secretary, one cop, another cop. Finally, in early 1992, his office gave me an appointment to have lunch with Chief Gates—four months into the future.

And then, on April 29, 1992, the day before my lunch, the four LA police officers who had been caught on videotape beating Rodney King were acquitted of the charges against them, and rioting started across Los Angeles.

I got up that Thursday morning—April 30—and the rioting had gone on all night, with buildings being burned and neighborhoods being looted. Suddenly, it was the most chaotic moment in Los Angeles in almost thirty years, since the Watts riots in 1965. The Los Angeles Police Department was at the center of the chaos—it was the reason for it and also responsible for stopping it. Chief Gates completely embodied the militaristic approach that led to the Rodney King beating in the first place.

I thought for sure Gates would have enough to handle that morning and that our lunch would certainly be canceled. But no—lunch was a go.

When I got to Parker Center, it was locked down. There were concrete barriers out front, and a line of police officers, and a series of checkpoints to get into the building. They asked, "Who are you going to see?" And I answered, "Chief Daryl Gates."

I produced my ID. In the lobby there was another line of cops. A couple of them patted me down. They asked me to lower my pants. Being searched to my underwear by two uniformed LAPD officers did nothing to reduce my wariness of the police, but I wanted to see Daryl Gates; I'd been trying to see him for more than a year. With my pants pulled back up, I was escorted onto the elevator by a pair of officers who rode up to the sixth floor with me.

Parker Center vibrated with energy. Although the building was populated by the people we rely on to be cool in a crisis, it felt like everyone was a little freaked out.

I arrived at Chief Gates's suite—an outer room and his office. Everyone around me was in uniform, including the chief. He was sitting at an ordinary, utilitarian conference table in his office, surrounded by what looked like wooden schoolroom chairs with arms. He was seated on one side, and I took a seat at the end.

Chief Gates seemed totally relaxed. Downstairs, the city was burning, exploding. That very afternoon, the mayor would impose a state of emergency and a curfew and call out the National Guard; the next night, President George H. W. Bush would give a televised, prime-time speech to the nation about the LA riots.[2]

But Daryl Gates was calm.

He greeted me. "What would you like for lunch?" he asked.

I was so nervous I didn't quite know what to say. "What are you having, sir?" I asked.

"I'm having a tuna sandwich," Gates said.

"I'll have what you're having." A few minutes later, an aide delivered two tuna sandwiches with potato chips on the side.

We chatted while eating our tuna and chips. Or Chief Gates was eating, at least. I couldn't take more than a few polite bites of my sandwich.

As we sat there, Gates's chief lieutenant suddenly burst into the office, totally adrenalized, shouting, "Boss! Boss! You're on TV again right now; the city council says you're out—they say they are firing you!"

Gates turned to me. He didn't flinch. Nothing in his biochemistry changed at all. He appeared totally calm.

He said, to me and to his lieutenant, "No chance. I'll be here as long as I want to be. They'll never get me out."

He said it in a totally matter-of-fact way, just as he might ask, "How's that tuna sandwich?"

His ego, his arrogance, was just completely imperturbable. He had been in intense situations all his life. He wasn't acting—for him, it was the sum total of seconds, minutes, hours, days, months of working under incredible pressure, and mastering it.

He had accumulated all this authority and the ability and the willingness to use it. He was totally acclimated to it. He had become unflappable, impervious to the possibility that anything outside his own will could change his life.

In fact, the city council had announced his replacement just two weeks before the Rodney King riots broke out. Gates had been vague about when he would leave—and got more stubborn after the riots. His cool cockiness with me notwithstanding, six weeks after our lunch he formally announced his resignation, and he was gone as chief two weeks after that.[3]

My visit with Daryl Gates was strange, memorable, unsettling. In other words, it was perfect.

Some people might have been curious why Gates became a police officer, and how he climbed the ladder to become chief of an eight-thousand-officer force.[4] Some people might have been curious how a man like Gates spent his workday—what did he pay attention to, in terms of what was going on in the city? Some people might have wondered what being immersed in nothing but the crimes of Los Angeles does to one's view of such a beautiful city, and to the view of its people.

My mission was different. I wanted a sense of the personality of someone who wears the chief's uniform with absolute confidence, who commands a miniature paramilitary state.

What does an encounter like that do for me?

First, it gets me completely out of the world I live in. For a few hours, I lived in Daryl Gates's universe—a world that could not be more different from my own. From the moment he opened his eyes in the morning to the moment he closed his eyes at night, every single day, it's likely that Chief Gates dealt with things that I had probably never even considered.

The big stuff is different—his goals, his priorities, his values.

The minutiae are different—how he dresses, how he carries himself, how he talks to the people around him.

Daryl Gates and I lived in the same city, we were both in positions of influence, we were both successful, but our worlds were so different they hardly overlapped. We literally looked at the very same city from completely different perspectives, every day.

That's what Daryl Gates did for me: he completely disrupted my point of view.

We are all trapped in our own way of thinking, trapped in our own way of relating to people. We get so used to seeing the world our way that we come to think that the world *is* the way we see it.

For someone who makes his living finding and telling stories on movie and TV screens, that parochialism can be dangerous. It's also boring.

One of the most important ways I use curiosity every day is to see the world through other people's eyes, to see the world in ways I might otherwise miss. It's totally refreshing to be reminded, over and over, how different the world looks to other people. If we're going to tell stories that are compelling and also varied, we need to be able to capture those points of view.

Consider for a moment just a few of the twenty-one movies that Ron Howard and I have made together, that I've produced and Ron has directed.

There's *Night Shift*, with Michael Keaton running a call-girl ring out of the New York City morgue, and *Parenthood*, about Steve Martin's effort to juggle work and being a good father.

There's *Backdraft*, about the courage firefighters require and the split-second judgment they need on the job, and *A Beautiful Mind*, the story of John Nash, who was both a Nobel Prize–winning mathematician and a schizophrenic.

There's *Frost/Nixon*, the drama behind David Frost's television interviews with ex-president Richard Nixon, and *Thirteen Lives*, the harrowing, real-life story of the rescue of twelve young soccer players and their coach who were trapped in a cave in Thailand.

Those six movies capture the perspective of a raffish morgue attendant, a funny but self-critical father, a team of fearless firefighters, a brilliant but mentally ill mathematician, a canny TV journalist interviewing a disgraced former president, and an urgent all-hands international rescue effort.

That's a wonderfully varied range of characters, a wild array of points of view, stories that include comedy and quest and tragedy, settings that range from Princeton University during the Cold War to the inside of a burning skyscraper in the eighties, from the cold room at the New York City morgue to caves in remote northern Thailand. They don't seem to have anything in common—and yet they not only came from the same company, Imagine, but all of them were shepherded by Ron and me.

That's the kind of work I want to do, and have always wanted to do, in Hollywood. I don't want to produce the same movie over and over again with slightly different characters—even unconsciously.[5]

So how does this relate to my conversation with LAPD chief Daryl Gates?

Curiosity. I don't know how other people in the story business keep themselves from going stale, but my secret is curiosity—and specifically the curiosity conversations.

The variety in my work (and my life) comes from curiosity. It is the tool I use to search out different kinds of characters and stories than I would be able to make up on my own. Some people can dream up a person like Daryl Gates. I have to meet someone like that in person. To see how the world looks from his perspective, I have to sit in the same room with him. I have to ask him questions for myself and not only hear how he answers, but see how the expression on his face changes as he answers.

The curiosity conversations have a critical rule, an almost completely counterintuitive one: I never have a curiosity conversation in order to find a movie to make. I have the conversations because I'm interested in a topic or a person. The conversations have allowed me to build up a reservoir of experiences and points of view.

Often, in fact, what happens is not that a conversation will inspire a movie or an idea—just the opposite. Someone will develop an idea for a movie or TV show—someone at Imagine will have an inspiration, a writer or a director will come to us with a story, I'll have an idea—and a curiosity conversation I've had years earlier will bring all the possibilities of that idea to life for me.

The richness and variety of decades of movies and TV shows have depended on the curiosity conversations, but these meetings don't create the movies and TV shows in the first place. Curiosity spurs me to chase my passions. It also keeps me plugged into what's going on in science, in music, in popular culture. It's not just what's happening that's important; it's the attitude, the mood that surrounds what's happening.

In 2002, when I produced the movie *8 Mile*, about hip-hop music in Detroit, I was fifty-one years old. The movie had its spark when I saw Eminem perform one night on the Video Music Awards (the VMAs). I'd been paying attention to hip-hop musicians for two decades—I'd wanted to do a movie about the hip-hop world since the 1980s, when I met Chuck D from Public Enemy, Slick Rick, the Beastie Boys, and Russell Simmons, who founded the hip-hop label Def Jam. The idea for *8 Mile* crystallized when music producer

Jimmy Iovine brought Eminem to the office, and the three of us sat down to talk about what a hip-hop movie might look like. Eminem actually spent the first forty minutes not talking. Finally I said to him, "C'mon! Talk! Animate!" And he gave me one final glare, and then he told his life story, the harrowing tale of his upbringing in Detroit. That became the spine of the movie.

About the furthest thing you can get from the tumultuous, energetic, angry, antiestablishment perspective of rap music is the buttoned-down, perfectly compartmentalized, analytical world of covert intelligence. Just as *8 Mile* was being filmed, we were also launching the TV series *24*, with Kiefer Sutherland playing counterterrorism agent Jack Bauer, whose job is to foil terrorist attacks against the United States. The first season of *24* was already in production when the real terrorist attacks of September 11, 2001, hit the United States. (The premiere of the first episode was delayed a month out of sensitivity in the aftermath of the attacks.) I loved the idea of *24*, and I connected with the sense of immediacy and urgency we tried to create in the show by unfurling it each week in real time, with an hour of the show being an hour in Jack Bauer's life.

I was ready for a show like *24*—I've been absolutely captured by the world of intelligence and covert operations for decades. I've had curiosity conversations with two CIA directors (William Colby and Bill Casey), with agents from the Israeli intelligence agency Mossad and the British intelligence agencies MI5 and MI6, and with a guy named Michael Scheuer, a former CIA operative who in 1996 helped set up and ran Alec Station, the secret CIA unit charged with tracking down Osama bin Laden before the 9/11 attacks.[6]

I'm amazed at the amount of information that people in intelligence—people at the top like Colby and Casey, and also people on the front lines like Scheuer—can accumulate and keep in their brains. They know a huge amount about how the world *really* works, and theirs is a hidden world. They know about events and relationships that are secret from the rest of us, and they make decisions based on those secrets, often life-and-death decisions.

So I had years of being curious about the intelligence community, and trying to understand the motivations of those involved, and their psychology, when the TV show *24* came along. I knew a lot about that world, and I knew it could be the setting for a compelling story.

That's the long-term benefit of the conversations: the things I'm curious about create a network of information and contacts and relationships for me (not unlike the networks of information intelligence officers map out). Then when the right story comes along, it resonates with me immediately. Curiosity meant I was open to Jack Bauer in *24*, and also to the antithesis of Jack Bauer, Eminem's character in *8 Mile*, the young rapper Jimmy "B-Rabbit" Smith.

And after that conversation I had with Daryl Gates on April 30, 1992, as our city started to riot and burn, I recognized that personality again immediately when I got the chance to produce *J. Edgar*, the movie directed by Clint Eastwood about the career of FBI director J. Edgar Hoover. Leonardo DiCaprio played Hoover. Had I not spent time trying to understand Gates twenty years earlier, I'm not sure I would have fully grasped the reality of Hoover's controlling paranoia, which Eastwood and DiCaprio infused so well into the mood, the acting, even the lighting of *J. Edgar*.

It was, in fact, one of my earliest conversations that taught me in unforgettable terms that I needed to bring ideas to the table in order to make movies—a conversation from back at Warner Bros., when I was trying to meet at least one new person each day inside show business.

I had been at Warner Bros. about a year as a legal clerk when I managed to talk my way into that meeting with Lew Wasserman. In terms of meetings, that was a stunning accomplishment—as big a deal for me at twenty-three as Jonas Salk and Edward Teller would be decades later, maybe bigger. Wasserman was the head of MCA, and he was critical in creating the modern movie business, including

the idea of what we now think of as the event movie, the blockbuster. When I went to talk to him in 1975, he had been at MCA for thirty-nine years—since 1936. While he ran MCA, Wasserman had under contract movie greats like Bette Davis, Jimmy Stewart, Judy Garland, Henry Fonda, Fred Astaire, Ginger Rogers, Gregory Peck, Gene Kelly, Alfred Hitchcock, and Jack Benny.[7] MCA's Universal Pictures had produced *Jaws* and would go on to produce *E.T. the Extra-Terrestrial, Back to the Future*, and *Jurassic Park*.

On the day I went to see him, Lew Wasserman was undoubtedly the most powerful person in the movie business. I was undoubtedly the least powerful person. It had taken me months of patient cultivation to get onto Wasserman's calendar, even for just ten minutes. I talked to his assistant, Melody, on a regular basis. At one point I said to her, "How about if I just come by and meet you?" And I did—just to put my face and personality with my voice.

When I finally got to see Wasserman, I wasn't nervous or particularly intimidated. I was excited. For me, it was an opportunity to get some wisdom from a man who, in fact, started out in the movie business one notch lower than me—as an usher in a movie theater. He had practically *invented* the movie business. Surely I could learn something from him.

That day, Wasserman listened without much patience to me talk about my determination to become a movie producer. He cut me short.

"Look, buddy," Wasserman said, "you somehow found your way into this office. You're basically full of it. I can see that. If there are a dozen ways to become a producer—having money, knowing people who have money, having connections, having friends in the business, representing movie stars or writers—if there are a dozen ways to become a producer, you don't have any of them.

"You can't buy anything—you can't buy a script treatment. You can't buy a book. You don't know anybody. You certainly don't represent anybody. You have no leverage. You really have nothing.

"But the only way you can be anything in this business is if you own the material. You have to *own* it."

Then Wasserman reached over and grabbed a legal pad and a pencil from his desk. He slapped the pencil on the pad and handed them to me.

"Here's a yellow legal pad," he said. "Here's a number-two pencil. Put the pencil to the pad. Go write something. You have to bring the idea. Because you've got nothing else."

I was stunned but also amazed. Wasserman was the first person to cut through the swirl of the movie business for me and say, *Here's what you, Brian Grazer, can do to become a movie producer, to rise above legal clerk.*

Write.

Otherwise, you're all talk.

I was with Wasserman no more than ten minutes, but it felt like an hour. That time with him changed my whole perspective on the movie business—it disrupted my very youthful point of view.

What Wasserman was telling me was that since ideas were the currency in Hollywood, I had to get myself some ideas. And he was saying that since I didn't have any influence or money, I had to rely on my own curiosity and imagination as the source of those ideas. My curiosity was worth more than money—because I didn't have any money.

I didn't walk off with Wasserman's yellow legal pad and pencil. I'm pretty sure I got nervous and set them back down in his office. But I did just what he suggested: I got busy using my curiosity to create ideas.

What does it mean to be a great supermodel like Kate Moss, and how is that different from what it takes to be a great attorney like Gloria Allred?

If we're going to make movies that feel authentic, we have to be

able to understand many corners of the world—places that operate much differently than Hollywood. As I've tried to show, I consciously use curiosity to disrupt my own point of view. I seek out people from other industries and other communities—physics, medicine, modeling, business, literature, law—and then I try to learn something about the skill and the personality it takes to perform in those worlds.

But if disrupting the point of view of someone like me—a moviemaker, a storyteller—is useful, consider how powerful it is for people doing other kinds of work.

You certainly want your doctor to be able to look at the world through your eyes—you want her to understand your symptoms so she can give you what you need to feel better. You also want a doctor to be curious about new approaches to disease, and to care and healing. You want someone who is willing to listen to colleagues and researchers with views that may disrupt her comfortable, routine ways of taking care of patients. Medicine is full of disruptions that changed the typical ways doctors practiced it, starting with handwashing and sanitation and coming all the way forward to laparoscopic and robotic surgery, saving or dramatically improving the lives of millions of people. Medicine is one of those arenas that steadily, sometimes radically, advances precisely because of curiosity, but you need a doctor willing to step outside her comfortable point of view in order to benefit from those improvements yourself.

Being able to imagine the perspective of others is also a critical strategic tool for managing reality in a whole range of professions. We want our police detectives to be able to imagine what criminals will do next, we want our military commanders to be able to think five moves ahead of opposing armies, we want our basketball coaches to discern the game plans of their rivals and counter them. You can't negotiate an international trade agreement without being able to understand what other nations need.

In fact, the very best doctors, detectives, generals, coaches, and diplomats all share the skill of being able to think about the world from the perspective of their rivals. You can't simply design your own strategy, then execute it and wait to see what happens so you can respond. You have to anticipate what's going to happen—by first disrupting your own point of view.

The same skill, in a completely different context, is what creates products that delight us. The specific genius of Steve Jobs lay in designing a computer operating system, and a music player, and a phone that anticipate how we'll want to compute, and listen to music, and communicate—and providing what we want before we know it. The same is true of an easy-to-use dishwasher or TV remote control.

You can always tell when you settle into the driver's seat of a car you haven't driven before whether the people who designed the dashboard and controls were the least bit curious about how their customers use their cars. The indispensable cup holder wasn't created by the engineers of great Euro cars—BMW, Mercedes, Audi. The first car cup holders debuted when Dodge launched its Caravan in 1983.[8]

With the iPhone, the cup holder, the easy-to-use dishwasher, the engineer has done something simple but often overlooked: he or she has asked questions. Who is going to use this product? What's going to be happening while they are using it? How is that person different from me?

Successful businesspeople imagine themselves in their customers' shoes. Like coaches or generals, they also imagine what their rivals are up to, so they can be ready for the competition.

Some of this disruptive curiosity relies on instinct. Steve Jobs was famously disdainful of focus groups and consumer testing, preferring to refine products based on his own judgment.

Some of this disruptive curiosity relies on routine. During all the decades he ran Walmart—the largest company in the world—founder Sam Walton convened his top five hundred managers in a meeting every Saturday morning. The "Saturday Morning Meeting," as it was called, had just two purposes: to review in detail the week's sales, aisle by aisle through the store; and to ask the question "What is the competition doing that we should be paying attention to—or imitating?" At every Saturday-morning meeting, Walton asked his employees to stand up and talk about their visits during the work-week to competitors' stores—to Kmart, Zayre, Walgreens, Rite Aid, and Sears.

Walton had strict rules for this part of the meeting: participants were only allowed to talk about what competitors were doing right. They were only allowed to discuss things they'd seen that were smart and well executed. Walton was basically curious about why customers would want to shop anywhere besides Walmart. He didn't care what his competitors were doing *wrong*—that couldn't hurt him. But he didn't want them to get more than a week's advantage on doing something innovative—and he knew he wasn't smart enough, alone, to imagine every possible way of running a store. Why try to guess your way into your competitors' heads when you could simply walk into their stores?

Some of this disruptive curiosity relies on systematic analysis that evolves into elaborate corporate research and development programs. It took the H. J. Heinz Company almost three years to create the upside-down ketchup bottle—but the project got started when Heinz researchers followed consumers home and discovered they were storing their tall, thin, glass ketchup bottles precariously, upside down on their refrigerator doors, in an effort to get out the last serv-ings of ketchup. The inverted ketchup bottle that Heinz invented as a result relies on an innovative silicone valve that seals the ketchup in, releases instantly when the bottle is squeezed, then closes imme-diately again when the squeezing stops. The man who invented that valve is a Michigan engineer named Paul Brown, who told a reporter, "I would pretend I was silicone and, if I was injected into a mold, what I would do." H. J. Heinz was so determined to understand its customers it followed them home from the grocery store. Engineer Paul Brown was so determined to solve a problem he imagined himself as liquid silicone.[9]

Procter & Gamble, the consumer products company behind Tide, Bounty, Pampers, CoverGirl, Charmin, and Crest, spends more than $1 million a day just on consumer research. P&G is so determined to understand how we clean our clothes, our kitchens, our hair, and our teeth that company researchers do twenty thousand studies a year, of five million consumers, where the goal is principally to understand our behavior and habits. That's why Tide laundry detergent now comes in little premeasured capsules—no pouring, no measuring, no muss. That's why you can buy a Tide pen that will remove stains from your pants or your skirt while you're wearing them.[10]

My approach to curiosity is a blend of the approaches we see in Steve Jobs, Sam Walton, and P&G. I am, in fact, curious by instinct—I'm curious all the time. If someone walks into my office to talk about the music for a movie or about the revisions to a TV script, and that person is wearing really cool shoes, we'll start out talking about shoes.

I know that not everyone feels like they are naturally curious—or bold enough to ask about someone's shoes. But here's the secret: that doesn't matter. You can use curiosity even if you don't think of yourself as instinctively curious.

As soon as I realized the power of curiosity to make my work life better, I consciously worked on making curiosity part of my routine. I turned it into a discipline. And then I made it a habit.

But here's an important distinction between me and even the hyperanalytical folks at P&G. I actually use the word "curiosity" to talk about what I do, to describe it, and to understand it. The rest of the world, though, almost never talks about this kind of inquiry using the word "curiosity."

Even when we're being intently curious, in an organized, purposeful fashion, we don't call it "curiosity." The coach and his assistants who spend five days watching film to prepare for a game aren't considered "curious" about their opponent, even as they immerse themselves in the thinking, personality, and strategy of that team. Sports teams simply call it "watching film." Political campaigns call their form of curiosity "opposition research." Companies that spend enormous sums of money and expend enormous effort to understand their customers' behaviors and satisfy their needs aren't "curious" about their customers. They use phrases like "consumer research" or say they've developed an "innovation process." (If they've hired expensive consultants to help them be curious, they say they've developed a "strategic innovation process road map.")

In 2011, *Harvard Business Review* published a nine-page case study of P&G's innovation and creativity efforts. The story is coauthored by P&G's chief technology officer, and it is literally as long as this chapter to this point—about five thousand words. The authors say they want to describe P&G's effort to "systematize the serendipity that so often sparks new-business creation." In Hollywood, we call that "lunch." But "systematizing serendipity"—finding ways to uncover great ideas—is exactly what any smart organization tries to do. Sam Walton was "systematizing serendipity" in the Saturday-morning meetings. I have "systematized serendipity" with my curiosity conversations.

In the *Harvard Business Review* story on P&G, the word "innovation" appears sixty-five times. The word "curiosity": not once.[11]

That's crazy. We simply don't credit curiosity. We don't even credit curiosity when we're using it, describing it, and extolling it.

The way we talk about this is revealing and important. You can't understand, appreciate, and cultivate something if you don't even acknowledge that it exists. How can we teach kids to be curious if we don't use the word "curiosity"? How can we encourage curiosity at work if we don't tell people to be curious?

It's not a trivial, semantic argument.

We live in a society that is increasingly obsessed with "innovation" and "creativity."

Three decades ago, in 1995, "innovation" was mentioned about eighty times a day in the U.S. media; "creativity" was mentioned ninety times a day.

Just five years later, the mentions of "innovation" had soared to 260 a day; "creativity" was showing up 170 times a day.

By 2010, "innovation" was showing up 660 times a day, "creativity" close behind at 550 mentions a day.

"Curiosity" gets only a quarter of those mentions in the daily media—in 2010, about 160 times a day. That is, "curiosity" gets as many mentions today as "creativity" and "innovation" did a decade before.[12]

The big U.S. universities maintain online databases of their faculty "experts" so media and businesses can consult them. MIT lists nine faculty members who consider themselves experts on creativity, and twenty-seven who are experts on innovation. MIT experts on curiosity? Zero. Stanford lists four faculty experts on creativity, and twenty-one on innovation. Stanford faculty offering to talk about curiosity? Zero.

It's essential to cultivate creativity and innovation, of course. That's what has driven our economy forward; that's what so dramatically improves the way we live—in everything from telephones to retailing, from medicine to entertainment, from travel to education.

But as indispensable as they are, "creativity" and "innovation" are hard to measure and almost impossible to teach. (Have you ever met someone who once lacked the ability to be creative or innovative, took a course, and became creative and innovative?) In fact, we often don't agree on what constitutes an idea that is "creative" or "innovative." Nothing is as common as the innovation I come up with that I think is brilliant and you think is dumb.

I think that this intense focus on being creative and innovative can be counterproductive. The typical person at work in a cubicle may not think of himself or herself as being "creative" or "innovative." Those of us who don't work in the corporate research and development department may well be clear that "innovation" isn't our job—because right over in that other building is the "department of innovation." In fact, whether we might think we are creative or not, in most workplaces, it's pretty clear that creativity isn't part of our jobs—that's why customer service reps are reading to us from scripts when we call the 800 number, not actually talking to us.

Unlike creativity and innovation, though, curiosity is by its nature more accessible, more democratic, easier to see, and also easier to do.

From my own experience pitching hundreds of movie ideas to studio executives, I know just how often people get told no to their brilliant ideas—not just most of the time, but 90 percent of the time. It takes a strong stomach to absorb all that rejection, and I don't think most people feel like they get paid to come up with ideas that get rejected. (In the movie business, unfortunately, we don't get paid at all without having our ideas rejected, because the only way to get to yes is through a lot of nos.)

Here's the secret that we don't seem to understand, the wonderful connection we're not making: Curiosity is the tool that sparks creativity. Curiosity is the technique that gets to innovation.

Questions create a mind-set of innovation and creativity. Curiosity presumes that there might be something new out there. Curiosity presumes that there might be something outside our own experience out there. Curiosity allows the possibility that the way we're doing it now isn't the only way, or even the best way.

I said in chapter 1 that curiosity is the flint that sparks great ideas for stories. But the truth is much broader: curiosity doesn't just spark stories; it sparks inspiration in whatever work you do.

You can always be curious. And curiosity can pull you along until you find a great idea.

Sam Walton didn't walk the aisles of his own store trying to be inspired to do something new. That would have been as useful as looking inside empty Walmart tractor trailers for inspiration. He needed a different perspective on the world—just like I found with Chief Gates or Lew Wasserman. Sam Walton wanted to innovate in the most ordinary of settings—a store. He started by being curious about everyone else in retailing. He just kept asking that question over and over again: What are our competitors doing?

I don't sit in my office, gazing out the windows at Beverly Hills, waiting for movie ideas to float into my field of vision. I talk to other people. I seek out their perspective and experience and stories, and by doing that I multiply my own experience a thousandfold.

What I do, in fact, is keep asking questions until something interesting happens.

That's something we can all do. We can teach people to ask good questions, we can teach people to listen to the answers, and we can teach people to use the answers to ask the next question. The first step, in fact, is to treat the questions themselves as valuable, as worth answering—starting with our own kids. If you treat the question with respect, the person asking it almost always listens to the answer with respect (even if they don't respect the actual answer).

Being curious and asking questions creates engagement. Using curiosity to disrupt your own point of view is almost always worthwhile, even when it doesn't work out the way you expect.

That's part of the fun of curiosity—you are supposed to be surprised. If you only get the answers you anticipate, you're not being very curious. When you get answers that are surprising, that's how you know that you've disrupted your point of view. But being surprised can also be uncomfortable, and I know that well.

As I said, one of the people I was determined to meet and have a curiosity conversation with when I was just starting out in the movie business was Edward Teller. Teller was a towering figure from my youth, although not necessarily in a good way. He was a brilliant theoretical physicist who worked on the Manhattan Project, developing the first atomic bomb. One of the early worries about the bomb was that the nuclear reaction an atomic bomb started might never stop—that a single bomb might consume the entire earth. It was Teller's calculations that proved an atomic bomb, while enormously destructive, would have a confined impact.

Teller went on to drive the creation of the hydrogen bomb—a thousand times more powerful than the atomic bomb. He became director of the nation's premier nuclear weapons research facility, Lawrence Livermore National Laboratory in California. He was more than just brilliant; he was a vigorous advocate of a strong defense and passionate about the importance of nuclear weapons to that defense.

By the time I was working as a movie producer, Teller was in his seventies, but he had found a fresh role advocating for and helping to design President Ronald Reagan's controversial Star Wars missile defense shield, formally called the Strategic Defense Initiative. Teller was a cantankerous, difficult personality—he was widely rumored to be the inspiration for the title character, Dr. Strangelove, in Stanley Kubrick's 1964 movie.

I wanted to meet him simply because I wanted to understand the personality of someone who could be passionate about inventing the most destructive weapon in the history of humanity.

It was, not surprisingly, almost impossible to get an appointment with Teller. His office didn't respond to telephone calls at all. I wrote letters. I wrote follow-up letters. I offered to fly to him. Finally, one day in 1987, I got a call. Dr. Teller—who was then seventy-nine and working on Star Wars—would be passing through Los Angeles. He would have a layover of a few hours and would be spending those hours in a hotel near LAX. I could see him for an hour if I wanted to come to the hotel.

Two military officers were waiting for me in the hotel lobby, in dress uniforms. They rode up with me. Teller had a suite of two adjoining rooms, and there were other military staff and aides. I didn't see him alone.

Right from the start, he seemed pretty scary to me.

He was short. And he was indifferent. He didn't seem interested in my being there at all. You know, if people are interested in you, or if they simply want to be polite, they radiate some energy. Daryl Gates certainly had some energy.

Not Teller.

That indifference, of course, makes it hard to talk to someone.

He did seem to know that I had been trying to make an appointment with him for a year. It irritated him. He started out crabby, and we didn't move much beyond that.

He was clearly very smart and professorial, but in a high-handed kind of way. I tried to ask him about his weapons work, but I didn't get very far. What he said was, "I advance technologies as far as they can be advanced. And that's my mission."

In our conversation, he exuded a barrier similar to the one he was talking about creating over the North American continent. There was an invisible glass wall between us.

He was sending a very clear message: I was not important to him. I was wasting his time.

To be honest, what you're hoping for, really, when you meet someone like Teller—who has had this incredible impact on the events that have shaped the world—is some kind of secret.

The secret to global security, or American security.

The secret to who they are.

You're hoping for some kind of insight—a gesture, an attitude.

That expectation is a little grandiose, of course. It's hard to get secrets from someone with whom you spend forty-five minutes.

But it felt like I got nothing but scorn from Teller.

I asked him about television. He said, "I don't do that."

I asked him about the movies. He said, "I don't see movies. The last movie I saw was fifty years ago. It was *Dumbo*."

The great nuclear physicist had seen one of my precious moving pictures once, half a century earlier. *Dumbo*. A cartoon about a flying elephant.

He was actually saying that he didn't think what I did had any value. He certainly didn't care about storytelling. It wasn't just that he didn't care about it—he had contempt for it. In that sense, I was kind of offended by him. Why bother to see me, just to be rude to me? But I was really only offended in a part of my mind. I was mostly fascinated by his contempt.

In the end, he certainly qualified as disruptive—he really reached me in a way I'll never forget.

Teller was clearly a passionate patriot—almost a zealot. He cared about the United States, he cared about freedom, and in his own way, he cared about humanity.

But what was so interesting, when I had time to think about it, was that he himself seemed to lack humanity, to be immune to ordinary human connection.

When I met Teller, I was already well established as a movie producer. But you leave a meeting like that humbled, to be sure. I felt kind of like I'd been kicked in the stomach.

That doesn't mean I regretted chasing Edward Teller for a year. In a way I hadn't expected, his personality kind of matched his achievements. But that's the point of curiosity—you don't always get what you think you're going to get.

And just as important, you don't necessarily know how your curiosity is going to be received. Not everyone appreciates being the target of curiosity, and that too is a way of seeing the world from someone else's point of view.

In truth, though, I got exactly what I was hoping for: I got a vivid sense of Edward Teller. I got exactly the message Dr. Teller was sending about our relative places in the world.

Curiosity is risky. But that's good. That's how you know how valuable it is.

3

The Curiosity Inside the Story

Human minds yield helplessly to the suction of story.

—*Jonathan Gottschall*[1]

When Veronica de Negri narrates the story of her life, it's hard to connect the details of what you're hearing with the quiet, composed woman who is standing alongside you.

De Negri was a bookkeeper for a paper company, living with her husband and two young sons in Valparaíso, Chile, a historic five-hundred-year-old port city that is so beautiful its nickname is "the Jewel of the Pacific."

In her spare time, de Negri worked with trade unions and women's groups in Valparaíso, and in the early 1970s, she also worked for the government of Chile's democratically elected president, Salvador Allende.

Allende was overthrown in 1973 by the man he had appointed to lead Chile's military, General Augusto Pinochet. The coup was so violent that at one point, Chilean air force planes flew bombing runs against their nation's own presidential palace in Santiago in an effort to dislodge Allende. Pinochet assumed power on September 11, 1973, and immediately started rounding up and "disappearing" Chileans he saw as opponents, or even potential opponents.

Perhaps because of her trade-union work, or her work for Allende, officers from Chilean marine intelligence finally came for de Negri in 1975, taking her from her apartment to a marine intelligence base in Valparaíso. She was twenty-nine years old, and her sons were eight and two. Her husband was also taken that day.

At the time, Pinochet's forces were arresting, imprisoning, and torturing so many Chileans—forty thousand in all—that the dictator had to set up a network of concentration camps across Chile to handle them.

De Negri was first held at the marine base in Valparaíso. After several months, she was moved to a concentration camp in Santiago. At both places, she was tortured systematically, relentlessly, almost scientifically—day after day for months.

I met Veronica de Negri in the most unlikely of settings: the beach in Malibu, California. In the late 1980s, I lived in Malibu Beach, and my neighbors included the musician Sting and his wife, Trudie Styler. One Sunday afternoon, they invited a small group to their beachfront house for dinner.

"I want you to meet somebody," Sting said to me. "Veronica de Negri. She was incarcerated and tortured in Chile by Pinochet." Sting was working with Amnesty International and had gotten to know Veronica well through the organization.

Veronica at that point had moved to Washington, DC. After being released from the concentration camp in Santiago, then rearrested several times to remind her that she was being watched, she was expelled from Chile and reunited with her sons in Washington, who were in high school and junior high. When we met that day at Sting's home, Veronica's torturer, Pinochet, was still in power in Chile.

We started talking, and then we went for a walk on the beach.

For much of the time she was imprisoned, Veronica was blindfolded. Her torturers were devastatingly clever. Most of what was inflicted on Veronica was done episodically and erratically. So even when she wasn't being actively tortured, she lived in a state of sickening fear, because she knew that at any moment, the door of her cell could fly open, and she could be hauled off for another round. It didn't matter what time it was. It didn't matter whether the last torture session had ended an hour earlier, or three days earlier. The next round could always be just a tick of the clock away.

Pinochet's men had contrived to make sure that Veronica was being tortured psychologically, even if they didn't have the staff at that moment to torture her physically.

They used the same technique to make the torture itself more unbearable. One thing Veronica was subjected to was something she called "submarines." A tank was filled with the ugliest water imaginable, mixed with urine, feces, and other garbage. Veronica was bound, and the rope holding her was threaded through a pulley at the bottom of the tank. She was held just above the surface of the tank and then yanked down to the bottom, where she had to hold her breath until she was allowed to surface amid the stench of what was in the water. The time held underwater was never the same; the time at the surface to catch her breath was never the same.

She said that the unpredictability was almost worse than whatever was done to her: How long am I going to be able to breathe? How long am I going to have to hold my breath, and can I hold my breath that long?

It's one thing to hear about human cruelty on the news, or to read about it. But to walk alongside Veronica de Negri and hear what other human beings had done to her is an experience unlike any I had ever had before.

How does a person do that to another person?

Where does the strength come from to survive?

It takes enormous courage just to be able to retell that story to a stranger—to relive what was done and also to absorb the reaction of the person hearing the story.

I was completely mesmerized by Veronica because of that courage, and also because of her self-possession and her dignity. Her refusal to be silent. She opened to me a world I would never have been aware of, and a whole set of human qualities and behaviors I would never have thought about.

Veronica de Negri gave me something critical in addition to the searing details of her story. She gave me a completely new sense of human resilience.

One of the concepts that really animates me is what I think of as "mastery." I want to know what it takes to really master something—not just to be a police officer, but to be the chief; not just to be an intelligence agent, but to be head of the CIA; not just to be a trial attorney, but to be F. Lee Bailey. That's a quiet thread through my curiosity, and it's also a theme in some form of every one of my movies. The stories touch the whole range of human experience, I hope, but the central struggle is often about achievement, or the struggle for achievement. What does success look like, what does success *feel* like, to a father or the president of the United States, a rap musician or a mathematician?

Veronica de Negri really shattered the question of "mastery" for me. Of anyone I have ever met, she faced the most fearsome and enormous personal challenge. But it was also the most basic. She wasn't trying to solve a math equation. She was trying to survive. She was trying to survive in the face of smart, evil people who wanted to destroy her.

For Veronica, there was no help. There was no rescue. She was up against the most horrifying opponent—well-armed fellow human beings. The stakes were total: her sanity and her physical survival. And the only person she could turn to was herself. She had to search inside herself for the skills she needed to withstand what was done to her. Nothing else was available—not even a view of what she was facing beyond the blindfold.

I met and talked to Veronica several times after that first meeting at Sting's house. Over time, what I came to understand was that she had found a capacity inside herself that most of us never go looking for, let alone have to depend on.

Veronica figured out that to withstand being tortured, she had to separate herself out of the reality of what was being done to her. You slow your brain down; you slow yourself down. People talk about being in "flow," when they're writing, when they're surfing or rock climbing or running, when they're lost in doing something completely absorbing.

What Veronica told me is that to survive being tortured, hour after hour, every day for eight months, she had to get into a state of flow as well, but a flow state of an alternate reality that had its own narrative. That's how she survived. She couldn't control the physical world, but she could control her psychological reaction to it.

It's a mechanism, and it's how she saved herself. In fact, it's a storytelling mechanism. You have to find a different story to tell yourself to take you out of the torture.

Veronica's story is so compelling that we tried to capture it in a movie, *Closet Land*. *Closet Land* has just two characters—a woman and her torturer. It was always going to have a small audience, because it is so intense, so unrelenting. But I wanted to do a movie that gets viewers inside the mind of someone who is being tortured. Torture takes place all over the planet, and I wanted people to be able to see it.

What I learned from Veronica, her sense of mastery, connects to the psychology of the characters in many other movies and shows. When I first read astronaut Jim Lovell's account of the explosion and crisis on the Apollo 13 capsule, I couldn't really grasp the details of the spacecraft, the orbital mechanics, the issues with fuel and carbon dioxide and skipping off the top of Earth's atmosphere. What I connected with immediately was the sense Lovell conveyed of being trapped, of being in a physical setting, also a life-and-death setting, where he and his fellow astronauts had lost control. They had to adopt a mind-set like Veronica's—they had to create an alternate narrative—to have the psychological strength to get themselves back to Earth. I think that movie, too, owes a lot to Veronica de Negri.

You might expect someone who had survived what Veronica was put through to be discouraged, to be cynical, to lack a certain basic hope.

She isn't like that at all. She's vibrant. She's a person of intellect, and obviously a person of inner strength. She isn't cheery or buoyant, but she has great energy, fierce energy.

And she has this incredible human capacity to rely on her own psychic strength to survive. That's what is so urgent to me about people's emotional makeup. What saved Veronica was her character, her personality, the story she was able to tell herself.

Curiosity connects you to reality.

I live in two overlapping worlds that are often far from reality: the world of Hollywood show business, and the world of storytelling. In Hollywood, we have a sense of being at the center of the world. Our creative work touches everyone in the United States, as well as a huge part of the rest of the world. We deal with actors and directors who are famous and, in Hollywood, powerful—powerful in that they can demand large paychecks, they can command armies of staff and technicians, they can pick their work, they can create whole new worlds from scratch, and they can specify all kinds of quirky elements about things, like the food they'll eat. Our projects involve huge sums of money—both the dollars to get a project made in the first place and the dollars they make when they succeed in theaters and on TV. The millions are often in the triple digits, and we're now firmly in the era of the billion-dollar film franchise, and the era of the billion-dollar acting career.[2]

So Hollywood absolutely has a huge sense of importance about what we do, and we have a huge sense of importance about the people who do it. It's possible to lose track of the difference between the stories we're telling, with as much vividness and texture as we can possibly create, and the real world. For while the money is real—the risks are real, and they are often large—the rest of it is, of course, showbiz, make-believe.

A comedy about the New York City morgue—*Night Shift*—doesn't involve any dead bodies.

A TV drama about producing a sports news show—*Sports Night*—involves no sporting events, no sports figures, no news.

A movie about the brutal reality of drug smuggling—*American Gangster*—involves no actual drugs or brutality.

Even in a great love story, no one typically falls in love.

Just as important, storytelling itself is not reality. That may seem obvious, but it's not at all. When you come home from work and tell your wife or husband "the story" of your day, you reshape those nine hours to highlight the drama, to make your own role the centerpiece, to leave out the boring parts (which may be eight hours of the nine). And you're telling a real story about your real day.

In the movies and on TV, we're always trying to tell stories that are true—whether it's *Frost/Nixon*, about real people and real events, or *How the Grinch Stole Christmas*, about a child's fantasy. The stories need to be "true" in emotional terms, true in thematic terms, not necessarily true in factual terms. For any movie that purports to tackle a set of real events, there's now typically a website detailing all the things we "got wrong"—you can read about the departures from reality in *Gravity* and *Captain Phillips*. We released *Apollo 13* in the summer of 1995—before Google was on the Internet—but you can read about the ways the movie differs from the factual story of the rescue at a half dozen websites.[3] You can even read about the differences between 2014's movie *Noah* with Russell Crowe and the biblical Noah—that is, the differences between the movie and the "real" story of a mythic biblical figure.[4]

The truth is, we want to tell great stories, captivating stories, and so we tweak the stories all the time—in fact, when we're making a movie or a TV show, we tweak the stories every day, while we're making them—in order to get more immediacy, or to move things along more quickly. We tweak them to make them seem more realistic, even when we're actually deviating from the "facts." We're all storytellers, and in about the third grade we start to learn the difference between a story that is true and a story that is factually correct.

It is very easy to get caught up in the urgency and the charisma of Hollywood. It's a hermetic world (it doesn't help that we're in California, far from a lot of the big decision-making in Washington, DC, and New York City). And it's very easy to get caught up in the world of episodic storytelling.

Curiosity pulls me back to reality. Asking questions of real people, with lives outside the movie business, is a bracing reminder of all the worlds that exist beyond Hollywood.

You can make as many movies as you want about war or black ops or revolution or prison. They're just movies. What was done to Veronica de Negri was not a movie; it was real—her pain and her survival.

When you watch a movie that is completely engrossing, what happens to you? I'm talking about one of those movies where you lose track of time, where everything fades away except the fate of the characters, and their world, on-screen. One of those movies where you walk out onto the sidewalk afterward, blinking, reentering reality, thinking, *Wow, it's a Sunday afternoon in spring. Whew.*

When you were binge-watching *Squid Game* or *The White Lotus*, what caused you to touch the Play button just one more time, six times in a row?

When you read a book, what keeps you in the chair, turning pages way past the moment when you should have set the book down and gone to sleep?

National Public Radio knows exactly how riveting its radio storytelling can be. NPR has figured out that people often park, turn off the engine, then sit in the car in the driveway, waiting to hear the end of a particular story that isn't quite finished. NPR calls these "driveway moments."[5] Why would anyone put the last three minutes of a story on NPR ahead of going inside to dinner and their family?

Curiosity.

Curiosity keeps you turning the pages of the book, it tugs you along to watch just one more episode, it causes you to lose track of the day and the time and the weather when you're in a theater seat. Curiosity creates NPR's "driveway moments."[6]

Curiosity is a vital piece of great storytelling—the power of a story to grab hold of your attention, to create the irresistible pull of that simple question: What's going to happen next?

Good stories have all kinds of powerful elements. They have fascinating characters caught in revealing or meaningful or dramatic dilemmas. They have talented acting, good writing, and vivid voices. They have plots that are surprising, with great pacing and settings that transport you to the story's location. They create a world into which you can slip effortlessly—and then lose yourself.

But it's all in service of one goal: making you care. You can say you care about the characters or the story, but all you really care about is what's going to happen next. What's going to happen in the end? How is the tangle of plotlines going to be untangled? How is the tangle of human relationships going to be untangled?

A story may or may not make its point memorably. It may or may not be entertaining or compelling, funny or sad, upsetting, even enraging.

But none of those qualities matter if you don't get the whole story—if you don't actually watch the movie or read the book. If you don't stick around, it doesn't matter what the point of the story is. To be effective, a story has to keep you in the chair—whether you're holding a Kindle, or sitting in your car with your hand on the radio knob, or sitting in the multiplex.

Inspiring curiosity is the first job of a good story.

How often have you started reading a newspaper or magazine story with a great headline, about a topic you care about, only to give up after a few paragraphs, thinking, *That story didn't live up to the headline?*

Curiosity is the engine that provides the momentum of good storytelling. But I think there's an even more powerful connection between them.

Storytelling and curiosity are really indispensable to each other. They certainly reinforce and refresh each other. But they might actually do more. Curiosity helps create storytelling. And there's no question storytelling inspires curiosity.

Curiosity is fun and enriching personally, in isolation. But the value and the fun of curiosity are magnified by sharing what you've learned. If you go to the zoo and see the new panda cubs, or you go to Florence and spend three days looking at Renaissance art, there's nothing like coming home and telling your family and friends "the story" of your trip. We read aloud the most amazing tidbits from the newspaper over breakfast. Half of what's on Twitter is literally people saying, "Look what I just read—can you believe this?" Someone's Twitter stream is a tour through what that person thinks is interesting enough to share—a journey through their version of clickable curiosity.

If you go all the way back in time to the earliest human tribes, some kind of storytelling was indispensable to survival. The person who discovered the nearby spring of water had to communicate that. The mother who had to snatch her wandering child from the stalking cougar had to communicate that. The person who first found wild potatoes and figured out how to eat them had to communicate that.

Curiosity is great, but if what we learn evaporates, if it goes no further than our own experience, then it doesn't really help us.

Curiosity itself is essential to survival.

But the power of human development comes from being able to share what we learn, and to accumulate it.

And that's what stories are: shared knowledge.

Curiosity motivates us to explore and discover. Storytelling allows us to share the knowledge and excitement of what we've figured out. And that storytelling in turn inspires curiosity in the people to whom we're talking.

If you learn about the nearby spring, you may immediately be curious about trying to find it yourself. If you hear about this new food, the potato, you may be curious about whether you can cook it and what it will taste like.

Even modern stories that are emotionally satisfying often leave you curious. How many people watch Ron Howard's *Apollo 13*—which has a deeply satisfying ending—then want to learn more about that mission, or the Apollo program and spaceflight in general?

There is, of course, a profession that connects curiosity and storytelling: journalism. That's what being a reporter is. But, in fact, we're all storytellers. We're all journalists and novelists of our own lives and relationships. Twitter, Instagram, and blogging are modern ways of saying "Here's what's happening in my life." What is the old-fashioned family dinner table but a kind of nightly news roundup of your family?

Much of the power of stories comes from their emotional heft. That's where the humor and the joy are, the excitement and the unforgettableness. We learn how to behave, in part, from the stories of how other people behave—whether those stories are told by sixth-grade girls over lunch, or by software engineers whose product didn't succeed with a new customer, or by Jane Austen in her novel *Sense and Sensibility*. Stories are how we learn about the world, but also how we learn about other people, about what's going on in their heads and how it differs from what's going on in our heads.

From the moment we're born, from the moment we wake up in the morning, we're saturated in stories. Even when we're asleep, our brains are telling us stories.

One of the great unresolved questions of life on Earth is: Why are humans able to make such great intellectual and social progress, compared to other animals?

Maybe it's the opposable thumb.

Maybe it's the size and structure of our brains.

Maybe it's language.

Maybe it's our ability to seize and use fire.

But maybe what makes humans unique is our ability to tell stories—and our reflex to constantly connect curiosity and storytelling in an M. C. Escher–like spiral. Our stories and our curiosity mirror each other. They are what make us successful, and also human.

"Brian, look at me when I'm speaking to you!"

It's been a while since I was in elementary school, but I can still remember when my teacher Miss Jenkins would call on me. My entire body would break out in a cold sweat. My heart would pound. And my eyes would look anywhere *except* in Miss Jenkins's direction.

Miss Jenkins probably didn't look threatening to anyone else. But she absolutely terrified me. Once, when she thought I wasn't paying attention in class, she took me outside the room and hit me across the face with a wooden paddle, leaving a throbbing, red welt across my cheek. More than Miss Jenkins's temper, though, what truly petrified me was her ability to make me feel humiliated just by asking me a question. I almost *never* knew the answer, and being forced to admit that—time after time, out loud, in front of the whole class— was mortifying. The other students snickered behind my back and whispered jokes at my expense. It hurt worse than a paddle to the face. I dreaded going to school every morning because I anticipated another question from Miss Jenkins, and more humiliation.

Needless to say, short of hiding under my desk (tempting though it was), I did everything I could to stay off Miss Jenkins's radar. When she asked a question, scanning the room for a response, I would turn my head or fake a cough. I came up with all kinds of excuses: bathroom breaks, stomachaches, even a feigned broken toe. But my avoidance technique of choice was "the Look-Away." At this age, hiding my eyes was the ultimate way to disconnect. I figured if I didn't meet Miss Jenkins's eyes, she wouldn't call on me. Disaster averted. When I saw other students using the same move, I understood that they were probably averting their eyes to avoid embarrassment too.

Of course, my attempts to evade my teacher's attention weren't always successful. On those days when she called my name, rather than glance in her direction to signal I'd heard, I'd continue to stare at the ceiling . . . or the chalkboard . . . or my feet. If I didn't look at her, I thought, maybe she would look away too. Maybe she would take pity on me and move on to someone else. Maybe I would disappear entirely and she wouldn't see me anymore. It was a far-flung hope. But it was worth a shot if it meant that I could avoid looking clueless, yet again, in front of my friends and classmates.

The truth is, school was hard for me. The reason I had trouble answering questions in class was that I had trouble doing my homework; and the reason I had trouble doing my homework was that reading was incredibly difficult for me. When I was growing up, my reading ability was severely impaired.

I couldn't read at all in my early years of elementary school. I'd look at the words on the page, but they made no sense. I couldn't sound them out; I couldn't connect the symbols printed there with the language I knew and used every day.

In retrospect, I understand that I was dealing with a reading disability. However, back in the 1950s, there were only two reasons you couldn't read in the third grade. You were stupid, or you were stubborn. But I was just baffled, and frustrated, and always worried about school.

People didn't start talking about dyslexia until ten years after I was in third grade, and they didn't start really helping typical kids with it until ten years after that. Today, I might have been classified as dyslexic.

I don't think my situation at home made things any easier. More often than not, I'd barely survive a day at school just to come home to find my parents arguing. They were constantly bickering—at times full-out yelling at each other—and a lot of their fights seemed to be about what to do with me and whether to hold me back a grade. But they rarely talked to me about it. Long story short, as a kid, I felt alone and anxious pretty much all the time.

As it was, I got Fs in elementary school, with the occasional D. My savior was my grandmother—my mom's mother, Sonia, a classic four-foot-ten Jewish grandmother. She always believed in me, and she was always telling me I was something special.

My mother was upset—her son was failing third grade! She went off and found me a reading tutor, who slowly taught me to lasso the letters and the words on the page. My grandmother, on the other hand, was totally imperturbable. It was a real counterpoint.

Grandma Sonia tried to reinforce my areas of strength, one of which was verbal communication. "Never stop asking those questions of yours," she just kept telling me. "You're curious. Your curiosity is good. Think big!" My grandmother could see beyond the report card; it felt like she could see inside my head. She knew I was as hungry to learn as every other kid. I just had a hard time satisfying that hunger.

My grandmother really helped make me something of a dreamer. She said to me, "Don't let the system define you. You're already defined—you're curious!"

What a thing to say to a boy in elementary school—"Don't let the system define you!" But thank goodness she did. My grandmother taught me a lot, but one of the most important things she imparted was that all you really need is one champion.

The more I embraced Sonia's messages internally, the more assured I became at school. I started to ask questions and contribute to discussions voluntarily. Rather than avoid my teachers, I engaged and connected with them. It wasn't long before I realized that when I looked at my teachers and classmates while they were speaking, I was better able to absorb what they were saying. The more focused I was, the more intently I listened and the easier it was to understand the material. It turns out that all that time I had been trying to disengage in elementary school, hiding my eyes so that the teacher wouldn't call on me, I was making learning even harder for myself.

Since reading itself was so hard for me, I had to be resourceful to learn what I wanted to learn, and also patient and determined. Through some combination of my grandmother's faith in my abilities, hard work, and just plain luck, my reading ability gradually improved throughout high school. If what I had was dyslexia, I seemed to grow out of it as I grew up. As an adult, I do read—I read scripts and newspapers, books and magazines, memos and emails. But every page is an effort. The work never fades. Reading for me, reading for someone who is dyslexic, I think, is a little bit like what math is for many people: you have to work so hard at getting the problem into your brain that you can lose track of the point of the problem itself. Even today, in my seventies, the physical effort of reading drains some of the pleasure I might take from whatever it is I'm reading.

What I think is amazing is that, despite my struggle with reading, two vital things survived: the joy I find in learning and my passion for stories. I was the kid who wanted nothing more than to avoid questions in the classroom, and now I relish the chance to be an eager student, to ask questions of people who are themselves discovering the answers.

I was the kid who didn't have the pleasure of losing himself in all those great growing-up classics—*James and the Giant Peach, Charlotte's Web, Dune, A Wrinkle in Time, The Catcher in the Rye*—but now I spend my life helping create exactly those kinds of completely absorbing stories, just on screen.

I love good stories; I just like them best the way they were originally discovered—told out loud. That's why the curiosity conversations have been so important to me, and also so much fun. I've described some of the dramatic ones, but most of the conversations have taken place in my office. Some of them have been like reading a story from the front page of the *Wall Street Journal*, perfectly crystallizing something in a way I'll never forget.

I've always been interested in manners and etiquette: What's the right way to behave? What's the right way to treat people? Why does it matter who opens the door and where the silverware sits on the table?

I invited Letitia Baldrige in to talk—the legendary expert on protocol of every kind who first became famous as social secretary for Jacqueline Kennedy, helping turn the Kennedy White House into a center of culture and the arts. Baldrige had left Tiffany & Co. to go to work at the White House, and she went on to write a newspaper column and many books on modern manners. She was tall—much taller than I am—and already silver-haired when she came to talk. She entered my office with elegant authority.

Letitia Baldrige gave me an understanding of the difference between "manners" and "etiquette"—something I had never quite grasped before.

Manners are really the basis for how we treat other people—manners are born out of compassion, empathy, the "golden rule." Manners are, quite simply, making people feel welcome, comfortable, and respected.

Etiquette is the set of techniques you use to have great manners.

Etiquette is the by-product. The way you invite someone to an event makes a difference. The way you greet people, the way you introduce them to people already present, the way you pull a chair out for someone.

Manners are the way you want to behave and the way you want to make people feel. Etiquette is the granularization of that desire to treat people with grace and warmth.

I love that distinction. For me, it illuminates both manners and etiquette, making them more understandable and more practical. I use a little bit of what Letitia Baldrige taught me every day. You open the car door for your partner not because she can't open the door herself, but because you love her. You arrange the silverware on the table a certain way because that gives your guests comfort and predictability so they can be more relaxed at dinner.

And as Letitia told me, the feeling you're trying to convey—the hospitality, the warmth—is much more important than following any particular rule. You can follow the rules, but if you do it with a disdainful attitude, you're being rude, despite having "perfect" etiquette.

Not every conversation was so practically useful. One of my favorites was with someone who, at first glance, would seem to be the exact opposite of etiquette expert Letitia Baldrige: Sheldon Glashow, the Harvard physicist who won the Nobel Prize in physics in 1979 when he was forty-six years old, for research he did when he was twenty-eight.

We flew Glashow out to Los Angeles from Cambridge. He came to the office one morning, and he seemed as delighted at the novelty of meeting someone with influence in the movie business as I was to meet someone of his stature from the world of science.

When he came to visit, in 2004, he was seventy-two, one of the wise men of modern particle physics. Glashow's pioneering work in physics involved figuring out that what physicists thought were the four basic forces of nature might actually be three forces—he helped "unify" the weak force and the electromagnetic force. (The other two are the strong force and gravity.)

I enjoy trying to wrap my brain around particle physics. I like it the same way some people like to understand the complexities of geology or currency trading or poker. It's an arcane world all its own, with a distinct language and cast of characters—particle physics can literally seem like a different universe. And yet, it's the universe we live in. We're all made up of quarks and hadrons and electroweak forces.

Walking into my office, Glashow couldn't have been more enthusiastic or open. I'm a layman, but he was happy to talk me through the science of where particle physics is today. He had the demeanor of your favorite, patient professor. If you didn't quite understand something, he would try explaining it in a different way.

He was a teacher as well as a scientist. The morning Glashow won the Nobel Prize, he had to cancel his 10 a.m. class—which was on particle physics—for Harvard undergraduates.

Glashow was curious about the movie business. He clearly liked movies. He'd helped Matt Damon and Ben Affleck get the math right for *Good Will Hunting* (he was thanked in the credits).

Glashow was the opposite of Edward Teller. He welcomed the chance to talk—he did give up two days to make time to visit—and he was interested in just about everything. We typically put the conversations on the day's schedule for an hour or two. Shelly Glashow and I talked for four hours, and it just flew by. The main feeling I had when I walked Dr. Glashow out of the office was, *I'd like to talk to this man again.*

A newspaper or magazine story in the hands of a talented reporter could have captured much of what I got from Letitia Baldrige and Sheldon Glashow. But I would have been working so hard at the reading I think I would have missed the fun.

I understand every time that my curiosity conversations are a remarkable privilege—most people don't have a life that allows them to call people and invite them in to talk. But I get something special out of this kind of curiosity that isn't unique to me, or to this particular setting: meeting people in person is totally different from seeing them on TV, or reading about them. That's true not just for me. The vividness of someone's personality and energy really only comes alive when you shake hands and look them in the eye. When you hear them tell a story. That has a real emotional power for me, and a real staying power. It's learning without being taught; it's learning through storytelling.

That kind of direct, in-person curiosity allows you to be surprised. Both Baldrige and Glashow were surprising—much different than I might have imagined in advance.

Baldrige was focused on manners, not etiquette. For all her experience at the highest levels of what you might call precision protocol—from Tiffany's to state dinners at the White House—she really just wanted people to treat each other well. She was the legendary arbiter of the rules, but for her, manners weren't about the rules; they were about grace and hospitality.

Glashow worked in an area of science that is so arcane it requires as many years of school *after* high school graduation as before, just to get to the point where you can start making fresh progress. And yet he was the opposite of inaccessible and insular. It was refreshing to meet a brilliant theoretical physicist who wasn't at all the cliché of the distracted scientist. He was completely engaged in the wider world.

My point is that you don't actually need to be sitting down, by appointment, with the social secretary of the White House or the Nobel Prize–winning physicist to have that kind of experience. When someone new joins your company, when you're standing along the sidelines at your son's soccer game with the other parents, when you're on an airplane seated next to a stranger, or attending a big industry conference, all those people around you have tales to tell. It's worth giving yourself the chance to be surprised.

I met Condoleezza Rice at a dinner party in Hollywood. I'd always been intrigued by her. She's a classical pianist. She was a professor of political science at Stanford University, and then the university's provost—the chief academic officer. And, of course, she was President George W. Bush's national security advisor for four years and secretary of state for four years. She has remarkable presence—given her level of responsibility, she always appears composed, even calm. She also conveys a sense of being in the know. To me, she almost seemed to have superpowers.

The dinner where I met her was in 2009, not long after she had stepped down as secretary of state. She was sitting just across from me.

Condi still had security shadowing her, but she was very easy to talk to. One thing you see up close that you never saw when she was speaking on TV is the sparkle in her eyes. As the dinner was breaking up, I said to her, "Can I call you? Maybe you'll have lunch with me?"

She smiled and said, "Sure."

Not long after, we had lunch at E. Baldi, on Canon Drive, a well-known Hollywood restaurant. She arrived in a car with her security detail, and we sat in the only booth in the small restaurant.

Condi was relaxed and gracious, but I think I was more curious about her than she was about me.

I told her about a movie we were getting ready to make. It was called *Cartel*, about a man bent on revenge against the Mexican drug cartels after they brutally murdered his wife. The movie was set in Mexico, the seat of so much cartel violence, and we were going to film it in Mexico, just a couple of months away. We originally had Sean Penn set to star; when he couldn't do it, we got Josh Brolin for the lead. I was worried about filming a movie sharply critical of the cartels in the country where they were beheading judges.

Condi listened. I told her that studio security had assessed the areas where we wanted to film in Mexico and told us it was fine. She looked at me skeptically. "I don't think it's safe to do that," she said.

Cartel was at a crossroads. We had spent money. The studio thought it was safe. But what I read in the newspapers every day suggested something different. The issue of safety nagged at me. I thought, *Would I personally travel to the set of a cartel movie in Mexico?* Answering honestly, I thought I wouldn't. And if I wouldn't go, how could I be comfortable sending anyone else? I really needed another informed point of view.

Condi followed up after our lunch. She had done some checking and she said, "No. It's not safe to do what you're planning."

That was the final straw, for me and the studio. We shut the movie down. We never took it to Mexico, and it never got made. Looking back, I was worried someone might have gotten killed. I've learned to pay attention to those instincts, to those occasional nagging doubts, and I've learned to make sure we're curious enough to find really expert opinion when there's a big risk. I think making a movie about drug cartels in the nation where they were operating could have been a disaster.

I wouldn't be very good at my job without curiosity. It's infused into every step of the process now. But think about the number of people who should also say that, in professions we don't typically think of as requiring inquisitiveness—at least as the primary skill— the way we expect it in a doctor or a detective.

A good financial planner needs to know the markets and the way to arrange money for retirement, but he also should be curious.

A good real estate agent needs to know the market, the houses available, the houses that might become available, but should also be curious about her clients.

A city planner needs to be curious, and an advertising executive, a housekeeper, a fitness trainer, a car mechanic, and a good hairstylist all need to be curious as well.

And in every case, the curiosity is all about the story. What's the story of your life, and how are you hoping that money or a new house or a new hairstyle will help you shape that story, and help you tell it?

This kind of curiosity seems so routine that we shouldn't even need to talk about it. I think it used to be. But in a world where so many of our basic interactions are structured and scripted—we're talking to "customer service" on an 800 number, we're trying to be heard over the speaker in the drive-through lane, we're checking into a hotel where the hospitality is "trained"—curiosity has been strangled.

It's considered a wild card.

But that's exactly wrong. If you think about a good hairstylist, the job itself requires skill at understanding hair, at understanding the shapes of people's heads, the quality of their hair; and it has a spritz of creativity and individualism. But it's also got an important human element. As a customer, you want a stylist who is interested in you, who asks what your hair means to you, and who pays attention to how you want to look and feel when you stand up from the chair. You also want a stylist who talks to you, who asks the kinds of questions that keep both of you engaged and entertained while your hair is being washed and cut and dried. (Or a stylist who is perceptive enough to realize you don't want to talk at all.)

The great thing is that this perfectly routine sort of curiosity works for both the stylist and the customer. The customer gets the haircut she's hoping for, she gets hair that helps her present her best self, that helps her tell her story, and she also gets a fun, relaxing experience. The stylist avoids falling into a rut. She learns something about her customer, and also about how the world works—every customer in the styling chair is a chance for a miniature curiosity conversation. She's giving the best haircuts she can give while creating happy and loyal customers and having an entertaining work life.

Going to the hair salon is not like sitting down with an architect to plan the redesign of office space at your company, or to plan the addition to your house. But curiosity and storytelling add just a little bit of fun and distinctiveness—and occasionally learning and insight—to what can otherwise become routine.

If manners are the lubricant that lets us all get along, curiosity is the shot of Tabasco that adds some spice, wakes us up, creates connection, and puts meaning into almost any encounter.

4

Curiosity as a Superhero Power

Curiosity will conquer fear even more than bravery will.

—*James Stephens*[1]

I was in the bar at the Ritz-Carlton in New York City, facing Central Park, sitting alongside a man with the best muttonchop sideburns since President Martin Van Buren. I was having drinks with Isaac Asimov, the author who helped bring science and science fiction alive for a whole generation of Americans.

It was 1986, the movie *Splash* had come out and broken through, and I was using that success to make the curiosity conversations as ambitious as possible.

Isaac Asimov was a legend, of course. At the time we met, he had written more than 300 books. By the time he died, in 1992, that number had grown to 477. Asimov's writing is so clear and accessible—rendering all kinds of complicated topics understandable—that it's easy to overlook how smart he was. Although no one ever called him "Dr. Asimov," he had a PhD in chemistry from Columbia, and before he was able to support himself by writing, he was a professor of biochemistry at Boston University's medical school.

Most people know Asimov as a storyteller and a visionary, a man who was able to look at how science and human beings interacted and imagine the future, the author of *I, Robot* and the *Foundation* trilogy. But Asimov actually wrote more nonfiction books than fiction. He wrote seven books about mathematics, he wrote sixty-eight books on astronomy, he wrote a biochemistry textbook, he wrote books titled *Photosynthesis* and *The Neutrino: Ghost Particle of the Atom*. He wrote literary guides to the Bible (two volumes), Shakespeare, and *Paradise Lost*. He had a boy's mischievous love of jokes and wrote eight books or collections of humor, including *Lecherous Limericks*, *More Lecherous Limericks*, and *Still More Lecherous Limericks*. In the last decade of his life, Asimov averaged fifteen or more books a year. He was writing books faster than most people can read them—including me.[2]

Asimov was a polymath, an autodidact, and a genius. And he was an instinctive storyteller. Who wouldn't want to sit down with him for an hour?

Isaac Asimov met me at the Ritz-Carlton with his second wife, Janet Jeppson Asimov, a psychiatrist with degrees from Stanford and NYU. I found her more intimidating than I found him—Isaac was relaxed; his wife was more on guard. She was clearly the boss, or at least his protector.

Both Isaac and Janet ordered ginger ale.

We started to chat. Apparently, it wasn't going that well, although I didn't quite realize how poorly it was going. After only ten minutes—the Asimovs hadn't even finished their ginger ales—Janet Asimov abruptly interrupted.

"You clearly don't know my husband's work well enough to have this conversation," she said, rising from the table. "This is a waste of his time. We're leaving. C'mon, Isaac."

And that was it. They got up and left me sitting alone at the table, mouth half-open in astonishment.

I had arranged a meeting with one of the most interesting, inventive, and prolific storytellers of our time, and I had managed to bore him (or, at least, bore his watchful wife) so thoroughly in just ten minutes that they couldn't bear it and had to flee the black hole of my dullness.[3]

I don't think I've ever felt so much like I had been slapped—without actually having been touched—in my life.

Here's the thing: Janet Asimov was right.

It took me a few months to get over the sting of them walking out. But she had caught me, and she had called me on it. I wasn't prepared well enough to talk to Isaac Asimov. He had agreed to take an hour to sit down with me—for him, that was a sacrifice of a whole book chapter—but I hadn't respected him in turn. I hadn't taken the time to learn enough about him, or to read, say, *I, Robot* from start to finish.

Going into that meeting, I was scared of Isaac Asimov. I was worried about exactly what ended up happening: I was afraid of not knowing enough to have a good conversation with him. But I hadn't been smart enough to harness that fear to curiosity.

I never made those mistakes again.

I've learned to rely on curiosity in two really important ways: first, I use curiosity to fight fear.

I have a whole bunch of relatively ordinary fears.

I have a fear of public speaking.

I don't really love big social settings where I might not have a good time, where I might end up kind of trapped, or where I might not be as entertaining as someone thinks I should be.

Now, take a minute to consider this list. Given my fears, I sure have picked the wrong profession. Half my life—half my work life—requires me to go somewhere, give a talk, mingle in large social settings with important people who I kind of know, but not really.

Throw in that I'm a little scared of powerful people, and a little intimidated by intellectuals—exactly the kind of people with whom I want to have curiosity conversations—and it can seem like I've created a life that's perfectly designed to make me anxious from the moment I open my eyes in the morning.

In addition to using curiosity to tackle my fears, I use curiosity to instill confidence—in my ideas, in my decisions, in my vision, in myself. Hollywood, as I've mentioned, is the land of "no." Instead of spelling out the word H-O-L-L-Y-W-O-O-D in the famous sign in the Hollywood Hills, they could have spelled out N-O-N-O-N-O-N-O!

An aspiring filmmaker was in my office recently for a meeting, and he said to me, "Oh, you're cool. No one ever says no to you."

That's silly. Everybody says no to me. Everybody *still* says no to me. It's just the opposite of what it looks like.

Sure, people *like* me. People say yes to meetings.

People say, "Please come to dinner." Sometimes they say, "Please come on this cool trip with me"—and that's flattering.

But if I want to do something creative, if I want to do something edgy—a TV series about a medieval executioner, for instance, that I helped push forward in 2014, or a movie about the impact of James Brown on the music business in the United States, which came out in the summer of 2014—people say no. These days, they just smile and put their arm around my shoulder when they do.

You have to learn to beat the no.

Everybody in Hollywood has to beat the no—and if you write code in Silicon Valley, or if you design cars in Detroit, if you manage hedge funds in Lower Manhattan, you also have to learn to beat the no.

Some people here charm their way around the no.

Some people cajole their way around it, some people reason their way around it, some people whine their way around it.

If I need support on a project, I don't want to cajole or charm or wheedle anyone into it. I want them to have the same enthusiasm and commitment I feel. I don't want to pull someone in against his or her judgment. I want them to see the idea, the movie, the characters with the kind of excitement that carries them through the tough parts of any project.

I use curiosity to beat the no, and I use curiosity to figure out how to get to yes. But not quite in the way you would imagine.

I didn't turn into a full-fledged producer with the first movie Ron Howard and I made—*Night Shift*. That movie was clever, sexy, and easy to explain. It had a quick hook. You could instantly see the comic possibilities. In fact, *Night Shift* is based on a real story I read in the back pages of the *New York Times* in the summer of 1976.[4]

It was the second movie Ron and I made together, *Splash*, that taught me what producers actually do in Hollywood. Their job is to come up with the vision of the story, and to find the financing and cast to make the movie, to protect the quality of the movie as it moves along. But first and foremost, the job of the producer is to get the movie made.

The kernel of *Splash*, what I call the "ignition point" for the story, is simple: What happens when a mermaid comes out of the ocean onto dry land?

What would her impressions be, what would her life be like? What would happen if I got to meet that mermaid? What would it take to win her love—what would she have to give up? What would a man wooing her have to give up?

I wrote the first script for *Splash* myself (I called it *Wet* to start with).

The mermaid idea came to me before the idea for *Night Shift*, while I was working as a producer of TV movies and miniseries (like *Zuma Beach* and the Ten Commandments series of TV movies). I was following the advice that Lew Wasserman gave me, to come up with ideas, something I could own, putting the pencil to the yellow legal pad. I was like any other twenty-eight-year-old man in the movie business in LA in the 1970s: I was enthralled with California women. I was always trying to understand them. It's not too far a leap from these bikini-clad women on the beach to a mermaid on the beach.

Except for this: no one wanted a movie about a mermaid.

No studio was interested, no director was interested.

Everybody said no.

Even Ron Howard didn't want to direct a movie about a mermaid. He said no more than once.

Hollywood is fundamentally a risk-averse town—we're always looking for the sure thing. That's why we have movies with four sequels, even six sequels.

No one seemed to understand a movie about a mermaid. Where was the previously successful mermaid movie, anyway?

Eventually, two things happened.

First, I listened to the no. There was information in the resistance that I had to be curious about.

I would say, "It's a movie about a mermaid coming onto land. She meets a boy. It's funny!" That didn't work.

I would say, "It's a movie about a mermaid coming onto land. She meets a boy. It's kind of a fantasy, you know?" They weren't buying it.

I needed to understand what people were saying no to. Were they saying no to a comedy? Were they saying no to a mermaid fantasy? Were they saying no to me—to Brian Grazer?

It turned out that I first wrote and pitched *Splash* too much from the perspective of the mermaid.

I thought mermaids were really intriguing, really alluring (and I'm in good company—see, for instance, Hans Christian Andersen's legendary *The Little Mermaid*). Hollywood studio executives just seemed puzzled. They were saying no to the mermaid.

So I thought, *Okay, this isn't a mermaid movie—it's a love story!* It's a romantic comedy with a mermaid as the girl. I *recontextualized* the movie. Same idea, different framework. I started pitching a movie that was a love story, between a man and a mermaid, with a little comedy thrown in.

The answer was still no, but a little less emphatic. You could see that at least executives were tickled by the idea of a love story involving a mermaid.

Anthea Sylbert, whose job was to buy movies for United Artists, was one of the people to whom I pitched *Splash* more than once.

"I throw you out the door, you come back in the window," she told me with exasperation one day. "I throw you out the window, you come back down the chimney. The answer is no! I don't want this mermaid movie!"

I made a pest of myself. But as Anthea Sylbert recently told me, "You were a pest, but not like a mosquito. More like an overactive five-year-old. Impish. I kind of wanted to tell you to go sit in a corner and be quiet."

Despite saying no, Anthea was intrigued by the mermaid. "I've always been a sucker for mythology, for fables, for a fairy-tale kind of thing," she said. In fact, it wasn't too hard to make the mermaid movie into a mermaid-man love story, and from that into a mermaid-man love-story fairy tale.

Anthea got me some money for a more polished script and helped hire novelist and screenwriter Bruce Jay Friedman to rework my original version.

And I worked a little curiosity on Anthea too. She wanted rules for the mermaid.

I had no idea what she was talking about. "Why do we need rules?" I asked.

She wanted it clear how the mermaid behaved in the ocean and how she behaved on land (what happened to the tail, for instance?). She wanted the audience to be in on the rules.

"Why?" I asked again.

She thought it would add to both the fun and the fairy-tale element.

Then, out of nowhere, a second mermaid movie popped up—this one to be written by the legendary screenwriter Robert Towne (*Chi-*

natown, Shampoo), directed by Herbert Ross (*Goodbye, Mr. Chips*; *The Turning Point*), and it was going to star Warren Beatty and Jessica Lange.

One mermaid movie was totally uninteresting to Hollywood.

Two mermaid movies was one mermaid movie too many—and Hollywood was going with the one that had the Oscar-winning writer and Oscar-nominated director. Especially over the partnership of Grazer and Howard—we had exactly one movie together to our credit.

I look laid-back, I dress laid-back, I try to act laid-back. But I'm not laid-back. I'm the guy who heard people talking about a job through an open window, and twenty-four hours later, I had that job. I can list several people I had to work on for six months to a year to arrange curiosity conversations: Lew Wasserman, Daryl Gates, Carl Sagan, Edward Teller, Jonas Salk.

So what happens first is that a dozen people tell me no one is interested in mermaids, no one is making a mermaid movie. Then people say, "Aww, I'm so sorry, we'd love to make your mermaid movie, but there's already a mermaid movie in the works—they've got Jessica Lange as the mermaid! Cool, huh? We wouldn't want to go head-to-head against *that*. Thanks for stopping by."

Sorry; I wasn't going to let Herbert Ross and Robert Towne do my mermaid movie.

Ron and I ended up striking a deal with Disney for *Splash* to be the first movie from their new division, Touchstone, which had been created specifically to give Disney the freedom to do grown-up movies. Ron not only signed up, he told Touchstone he would do the movie on a tight budget and vowed to beat Herbert Ross's mermaid to theaters.

Splash was a huge hit. It was number one at the box office its first two weeks, it was in the top ten for eleven weeks, and it was at the time the fastest moneymaking movie in Disney film history. *Splash* was also the first Disney movie that wasn't rated G. We gave Disney a big PG-rated hit—the very first time.

We didn't just beat the other mermaid movie; it never got made. And *Splash* not only made money, but it helped make the careers of Tom Hanks and Daryl Hannah. People in Hollywood went from being a little skeptical of Ron Howard as a director to elbowing each other out of the way to hire him.

And, in perhaps the sweetest moment, given how many times I heard the word "no" while trying to get it made, the script for *Splash* was nominated for an Academy Award for best original screenplay. That year, *Places in the Heart*, the movie about the Great Depression starring Sally Field, won. But Ron and I went to our first Academy Awards celebration.

The night *Splash* opened, March 9, 1984, Ron Howard and I hired a limousine and drove around with our wives, looking at the lines at LA movie theaters. That was a tradition we started with *Night Shift*, but those lines were a little disappointing. *Splash* was a different story.[5]

In Westwood, there was a theater called the Westwood Avco, right on Wilshire Boulevard. For the opening of Steven Spielberg's *E.T.*, in 1982, we had seen the lines at the Avco wrapped around the block. When we drove up the night *Splash* debuted, the lines were also around the block. Not as long as they were for *E.T.*, but still incredible. People were standing in line to see our mermaid movie. It was thrilling. We jumped out of the car, and we walked from the front of the line to the back, talking to people and hugging each other.

Then we jumped back in the car and started another tradition: we drove to In-N-Out Burger, the famous Southern California drive-through, and ate burgers with a really good bottle of Bordeaux I had been optimistic enough to tuck into the limo.

It took seven years to get *Splash* from ignition point to the Westwood Avco theater. I didn't just need an idea I felt passionately about—a good idea. I needed persistence. Determination.

Just as curiosity and storytelling reinforce each other, so do curiosity and persistence. Curiosity leads to storytelling, and storytelling inspires curiosity. The exact same dynamic works with curiosity and persistence.

Curiosity rewards persistence. If you get discouraged when you can't find the answer to a question immediately, if you give up with the first no, then your curiosity isn't serving you very well. For me, that is one of the lessons of working with Anthea Sylbert—my persistence helped me stay the course, and my curiosity helped me figure out how to change the mermaid movie just a little bit so other people understood it and appreciated it. There's nothing more fruitless and unhelpful than idle curiosity. Persistence is what carries curiosity to some worthwhile resolution.

Likewise, persistence without curiosity may mean you chase a goal that isn't worthy of the effort—or you chase a goal without adjusting as you learn new information. You end up way off course. Persistence is the drive moving you forward. Curiosity provides the navigation.

Curiosity can help spark a great idea and help you refine it.

Determination can help you push the idea forward in the face of skepticism from others.

Together, they can give you confidence that you're onto something smart. And that confidence is the foundation of your ambition.

Asking questions is the key—to helping yourself, refining your ideas, persuading others. And that's true even if you think you know what you're doing and where you're heading.

I got the chance to turn one of the great Dr. Seuss books into a movie. I won the rights to *How the Grinch Stole Christmas!* from Dr. Seuss's widow, Audrey Geisel, in a two-year process competing with other great filmmakers who wanted the chance, including John Hughes (*Ferris Bueller's Day Off*, *Home Alone*), Tom Shadyac (who directed our movie *Liar Liar*), and the Farrelly brothers (*There's Something about Mary*).

In fact, *How the Grinch Stole Christmas!* would be the first Seuss book Audrey allowed to be turned into a full-length movie. Audrey Geisel was a little like Isaac Asimov's wife, in fact: she was a fierce protector of the legacy of her husband, who died in 1991. The California license plate on her car when we were working with her was a single word: "GRINCH." (Theodor Geisel also had the "GRINCH" license plate during the later years of his life.)[6]

I persuaded Jim Carrey to play the Grinch and persuaded Ron Howard to direct. Audrey Geisel insisted on meeting and talking to both of them in advance.

When I take on a project like turning *How the Grinch Stole Christmas!* into a movie, I feel a real sense of responsibility. The book was first published in 1957, and it has been a part of the childhood of essentially every American born since then.

I was as familiar with the story, the characters, the art of *Grinch* as any other fifty-year-old adult in the United States was. It was read to me as a child, and I'd read it to my own children.

But as we embarked on writing a script, on creating Whoville and transferring the mood of the book to the screen, I kept a set of questions in mind—questions I asked myself, questions I asked Ron and Jim and the writers, Jeff Price and Peter Seaman, over and over as we were making the movie.

We had won the rights; now the most important questions were: What, exactly, is this story? What kind of story is it?

Is it a verbal comedy?

Is it a physical comedy?

Is it an action picture?

Is it a myth?

The answer to each of these questions is yes. That's what made it a challenge and a responsibility. When you were working on the physical comedy, you couldn't forget that you were also the keeper of a myth. When you were working on the action, you couldn't forget that the joy and the playfulness of the story come from

Dr. Seuss's original language as much as from anything he drew, or we designed.

Asking questions allows you to understand how other people are thinking about your idea. If Ron Howard thinks *Grinch* is an action picture and I think it's a verbal comedy, we've got a problem. The way to find out is to ask. Often the simplest questions are the best.

What kind of movie is *Grinch*?

What story are we telling?

What feeling are we trying to convey, especially when the audience is going to arrive with their own set of feelings about the story?

That, too, is at the heart of what good movie producers do. You always want to create a movie that is original, that has passion. With a story as iconic as *Grinch*, you also need to keep the audience's expectations in mind. Everyone walking into a movie theater to see *How the Grinch Stole Christmas* would already have a feeling about what they thought the story was.

And no one more vividly or more firmly than Audrey Geisel. She was our most challenging audience—our audience of one. We showed her the movie in the Hitchcock Theatre on the Universal Studios lot. There were just five people in the room. Audrey sat very near the front. I sat thirty rows back from her, near the back, because I was so nervous about her reaction. A couple of editors and sound guys sat in the rows between us.

As the credits rolled, Audrey started clapping. She was beaming. She loved it. Sitting there in the screening room, I was so happy to have made her happy that I had tears streaming down my face.

Even a classic story, one that is totally familiar, can't succeed without the kind of elemental curiosity we brought to *Grinch*, so everyone agrees on the story you're trying to tell and the way you're trying to tell it.[7]

It seems so obvious. But how often have you been involved in a project where you get halfway along and discover that the people involved had slightly different understandings of what you were up to—differences that turned out to make it impossible to work effectively together, because everyone didn't actually agree on the goal?

It happens every day—in movies, in marketing, in architecture and advertising, in journalism and politics, and in the whole rest of the world. It even happens in sports. Nothing says miscommunication like a busted pass play in an NFL game.

It's a little counterintuitive, but rather than derailing or distracting you, questions can keep you on course.

Being determined in the face of obstacles is vital.

I feel like we enter the world, newborn, and at that moment, the answer is yes. And it's yes for a little while after that. The world is openhearted to us. But at some point, the world starts saying no, and the sooner you start practicing ways of getting around no, the better. I now think of myself as impervious to rejection.

We've been talking about using curiosity when the world says no. But just as often, the no can come from inside your head, and curiosity can be the cure to that kind of no too.

As I mentioned earlier, when I have a fear of something, I try to get curious about it—I try to set the fear aside long enough to start asking questions. The questions do two things: they distract me from the queasy feeling, and I learn something about what I'm worried about. Instinctively, I think, we all know that. But sometimes you need to remind yourself that the best way to dispel the fear is to face it, to be curious.

I am a nervous public speaker. I give a good speech, but I don't enjoy getting ready to give a speech, and I don't even necessarily enjoy giving the speech—what I enjoy is having given it. The fun part is talking to people about the speech after it's done.

For me, every time I do it is a test. Here's how I keep the nervousness at bay:

First, I don't start preparing too far in advance, because for me, that just opens up the box of worry. If I start writing the speech two weeks in advance, then I just worry every day for two weeks.

So I make sure I have enough time to prepare, and I start work-ing on the talk a few days before I have to give it.

I do the same thing I did with *Grinch*. I ask questions:

What's the talk supposed to be about?

What's the best possible version of the talk?

What do the people coming to this event expect to hear?

What do they want to hear, in general?

What do they want to hear from me, specifically?

And who is the audience?

The answer to each of these questions helps me create a frame-work for what I'm supposed to talk about. And the answers immedi-ately spark ideas, anecdotes, and points I want to make—which I keep track of.

I'm always looking for stories to tell—stories that make those points. In terms of giving a speech, I'm looking for stories for two reasons. People like stories—they don't want to be lectured; they want to be entertained. And I know the stories I'm telling—so even if I stumble or lose my way, well, it's my story. I can't actually forget what I'm trying to say. I won't be thrown off stride.

In the end, I write out the whole speech a day or two in advance. And I practice several times.

Writing the speech gets it into my brain.

Practicing also gets it into my brain—and practicing shows me the rough spots, or the spots where the point and the story don't fit perfectly, or where I'm not sure I'm telling the joke exactly right. Practicing gives me a chance to edit—just like you edit a movie, a magazine story, a business presentation, or a book.

I bring the full text of the speech with me, I set it on the podium, and then I stand next to the podium and talk. I don't read the speech from the pages. I have the text in case I need it. But I usually don't.

Does curiosity require work?

Of course it does.

Even if you're "naturally curious" (whatever that phrase means to you), asking questions, absorbing the answers, figuring out in what direction the answers point you, figuring out what other questions you need to ask—that's all work.

I do think of myself as naturally curious, but I've also exercised my curiosity in all kinds of situations, all day long, for more than sixty years. Sometimes you do have to remind yourself to use your curiosity. If someone's telling you no, that can easily throw you off stride. You can get so caught up in being rejected, in not getting something you're working toward, that you forget to ask questions about what's happening. *Why am I being told no?*

If you have a fear of giving a speech, you can become so distracted or put off that you avoid it instead of plunging in. That prolongs the anxiety, and it doesn't help the speech—it hurts it. The speech doesn't write itself, and the way to manage being nervous about the speech is to work on it.

I have found that using curiosity to get around the no, whether the no is coming from someone else or from my own brain, has taught me some other valuable ways of confronting resistance, of getting things done.

A great piece of advice came to me from my longtime friend Herbert A. Allen, the investment banker and creator of the remarkable media and technology conference he hosted annually in Sun Valley, Idaho. (It's now called simply the Allen & Co. Sun Valley Conference.)

Many years ago, he told me: make the hardest call of the day first.

The hardest call of the day might be someone you fear is going to give you bad news. The hardest call might be someone to whom you have to deliver bad news. The hardest call might be someone you want to see in person who might be avoiding you.

And Allen was being metaphoric. The "hardest call" might be an email you have to send, it might be a conversation you need to have in person with someone in your own office.

Whatever it is, the reason you think of it as the "hardest call of the day" is because there's something scary about it. It's going to be uncomfortable in some way—either in the encounter itself, or in the outcome of the encounter. But Allen's point is that a task like that isn't going to be less scary at noon or at 4:30 in the afternoon. Just the opposite: the low-grade anxiety from the "hardest call" is going to cast a shadow over the whole day. It's going to distract you, maybe even make you less effective. It will certainly make you less open-hearted.

"Make the hardest call first." That's not quite about curiosity, and it's not quite about determination—it's a little bit of both. It's grit. It's character. Grab hold of the one task that really must be done—however much you're not looking forward to it—and tackle it.

That clears the air. It brightens the rest of the day. It may, in fact, reset the agenda for part of the day. It gives you confidence to tackle whatever else is coming—because you've done the hardest thing first. And while the outcome of the "hardest call" usually goes just like you imagined, sometimes there's a surprise there too.

Asking questions always seems, superficially, like an admission of ignorance. How can admitting your ignorance be the path to confidence?

That's one of the many wonderful dualities of curiosity.

Curiosity helps you dispel ignorance and confusion; curiosity evaporates fogginess and uncertainty; it clears up disagreement.

Curiosity can give you confidence. And the confidence can give you determination. And the confidence and determination can give you ambition. That's how you get beyond the no, whether it's coming from other people or from inside your own mind.

If you harness curiosity to your dreams, it can help power them along to reality.

More than a decade ago, the New York style magazine *W* did a profile of me with the headline "The Mogul: Brian Grazer, Whose

Movies Have Grossed $10.5 Billion, Is Arguably the Most Success-ful Producer in Town—and Surely the Most Recognizable. Is It the Hair?"[8]

People in Hollywood, of course, know the hair.

People in the rest of the world—people who may not even know my name but know *A Beautiful Mind* or *Arrested Development* or *The Da Vinci Code*—some of them know the hair too. "That Hollywood guy with the hair that stands straight up"—that's a common description of me.

The hair is part of my image, part of my persona.

And the hair is no accident. Of course it isn't—because I have to gel it vertical every single morning.

But my hair isn't just a fashion quirk. It's not even really a matter of personal taste.

After Ron Howard and I had done a couple of movies, I was building a reasonable reputation in Hollywood. It was nothing like the visibility of Ron, of course—he was a star and a director and the icon of an era. I was a producer, and also a newcomer, especially compared to Ron.

But I wanted to make an impression. Hollywood is a land of style, a world where how you present yourself matters. Many of the people working here are so dramatically good-looking—that is their style. But not me, and I know that.

When Ron and I were getting Imagine up and running in the early nineties, it was during a period when male Hollywood produc-ers were developing a kind of collective persona. There was a group of young, successful producers doing loud, aggressive movies. They were themselves loud and aggressive—they were "yellers," people who sometimes managed their colleagues by throwing things and screaming. And many in this same group wore beards. Bearded, ag-gressive men, producing aggressive movies.

That wasn't me. I wasn't doing loud movies, and I don't look great with facial hair. I worked for a couple of screamers in my early days in Hollywood. I don't like being screamed at, and I am not a screamer myself.

But I didn't want to simply fade into the background. I felt I needed to define myself in a way that made me memorable.

So this question of personal style—what to wear, how to look—was on my mind.

It all fell into place one afternoon in 1993, when I was swimming with my daughter, Sage, who was then about five. As I surfaced in the pool, I ran my fingers through my wet hair, standing it straight up.

"That looks cool!" Sage said.

I looked at myself in the mirror with my hair standing up, and I thought, "That's really interesting."

So I gelled it straight up. I started that very day.

The hair got noticed. It instantly produced an extreme reaction from people.

I'd say 25 percent of people thought it was cool.

Another 50 percent of people were curious about it. *Why do you do your hair like that? How do you do your hair like that?*

Some people who already knew me were in this curious category. They said, "Brian, what's up with the hair? What are you thinking? What got you to do that?"

Then there was the other 25 percent—the people who hated the hair. The hair made them angry. They looked at my hair and immediately decided I was an asshole.

I loved that. I really liked getting that extreme range of reactions from people. The hair inspired curiosity about me. Right after I started wearing my hair up, I would sometimes notice people talking about it when they thought I couldn't hear them.

"Hey, what's with Grazer? What's he doing with his hair?"

Michael Ovitz, the famous superagent and Hollywood power broker, grew up in the business right alongside me. He lobbied me. "Don't do the hair," Michael said. "Businesspeople won't take you seriously."

Some people thought I was arrogant because of the hair.

The truth is that it had occurred to me that the world of Hollywood is divided into two categories—business folk and artists. I thought this hairstyle tipped me over into the artist category, where I was more comfortable.

After having my hair straight up for a few months, I did think about stopping. So many people seemed to be talking about it.

But then I realized something: yes, the hair was inspiring curiosity about me, but what was really interesting was that people's reactions to the hair said more about what they thought of me than it revealed about me or my hair.

I came to see my hair as a test to the world. I felt like I was eliciting the truth about how people felt about me much more quickly than having to wait for it to come out. So I left it up.

In a way, the hair does something else for me. It lets people know that this guy isn't quite what he seems. He's a little unpredictable. I'm not a prepackaged, shrink-wrapped guy. I'm a little different.

Here's why my hair is important.

Hollywood and show business really are a small world, and as in any industry, there is a pretty defined system of rules and practices and traditions. To get things done, you have to follow the rules.

Mind you, all I did was gel my hair straight up, just as a gambit, and some people went completely crazy about it. Not just some people—one out of four people.

My hair doesn't have the slightest impact on any script or director or talent; it doesn't change the marketing of a movie or the opening weekend grosses. But it made a lot of people—some of them important people—really uncomfortable.

Now imagine the reaction, the resistance, when you do something different in a category where it really matters.

And that's the point. The hair started as a goof, an experiment. But it conveys something quietly revealing about me. I don't want to look like everyone else.

And I don't want to do the same kind of work everyone's doing. I don't even want to do the same kind of work I was doing ten years ago or five years ago.

I want variety. I want to tell new stories—or classic stories in new ways—both because that makes my life interesting and because it makes going to the movie theater or turning on the TV interesting.

I want the opportunity to be different.

Where do I get the confidence to be different?

A lot of it comes from curiosity. I spent years as a young man trying to understand the business I'm in. I have spent decades staying connected to how the rest of the world works.

The curiosity conversations give me a reservoir of experience and insight that goes well beyond my own firsthand experience.

But the conversations also give me a lot of firsthand experience in exposing my own lack of knowledge, my own naïveté. I actually practice being a little ignorant. I'm willing to admit what I don't know, because I know that's how I get smarter. Asking questions may seem to expose your ignorance, but what it really does is just the opposite. People who ask questions, in fact, are rarely thought of as stupid.

The epigram that opens this chapter—"Curiosity will conquer fear even more than bravery will"—comes from a book by the Irish poet James Stephens. The quote goes on a little longer and makes a central point:

> Curiosity will conquer fear even more than bravery will; indeed, it has led many people into dangers which mere physical courage would shudder away from, for hunger and love and curiosity are the great impelling forces of life.

That's what curiosity has done for me and what I think it can do for almost anyone. It can give you the courage to be adventurous and ambitious. It does that by getting you comfortable with being a little uncomfortable. The start of any journey is always a little nerve-racking.

I have learned to surf as an adult. I have learned to paint as an adult. I learned to surf much better after producing *Blue Crush*, a female-empowerment movie that we shot on the North Shore of Oahu. Some of the people working on the movie were surfing there—surfing some of the biggest waves in the world—and I became fascinated with how waves work and what it's like to ride them. I love surfing—it requires so much concentration that it wipes away completely the concerns of the moment. It's also totally thrilling.

I love painting in much the same way. I find it utterly relaxing. I'm not a great painter; I'm not even a particularly good painter in technical terms. But I figured out that a lot of what matters in painting is what you're trying to say, not whether you say it perfectly. I don't need to have great painting technique to find real originality in it and to be energized by it. I learned to paint after meeting Andy Warhol and Roy Lichtenstein.

In both cases, my curiosity conquered my fear. I was inspired to do both those things by some of the people who did them best in the world. I wasn't trying to be a world-class surfer or a world-class painter. I was just curious to taste the joy, the thrill, the satisfaction that those people got from mastering something that is both hard and rewarding.

Curiosity gives you power. It's not the kind of power that comes from yelling and being aggressive. It's a quiet kind of power. It's a cumulative power. Curiosity is power for real people; it's power for people who don't have superpowers.

So I protect that part of myself—the part that's not afraid to seem briefly ignorant. Not knowing the answer opens up the world, as long as you don't try to hide what you don't know. I try never to be self-conscious about not knowing.

As it turns out, the people who hated my hair back in the beginning were right. It is a little bit of a challenge. The hair looks like just a matter of personal style—but for me, it is a way of reminding myself every day that I am trying to be a little different, that it's okay to be a little different, that being different requires courage, just like gelling your hair straight up requires courage, but you can be different in ways that make most people smile.

I gel my hair every morning first thing when I wake up. It takes about ten seconds. I never skip the gel. And thirty years after I started doing it, it has long since become my signature—and my approach to work matches my hair. It's also still a great way of starting a conversation and standing out.

In February 2001, I got to spend four days in Cuba with a group of seven friends who are also media executives. The others were Graydon Carter, then the editor of *Vanity Fair*; Tom Freston, then CEO of MTV; Bill Roedy, then also at MTV; producer Brad Grey; Jim Wiatt, then chief of the talent agency William Morris; and Les Moonves, then the president of CBS.[9]

As part of the visit, we had a long lunch with Fidel Castro. Castro was wearing his usual green army fatigues, and he talked to us through a translator for three and a half hours—I think without even taking a breath. It was the usual Castro speech, mostly about why Cuba is amazing and the United States is doomed.

When he stopped talking, he looked at me—I wasn't necessarily the most prominent person in the group—and through the translator he asked just one question: "How do you get your hair to stand up that way?" Everybody laughed.

Even Castro loved the hair.

5

Every Conversation Is a Curiosity Conversation

Connection gives meaning to our lives. Connection is why we're here.

—*Brené Brown*[1]

In the spring of 1995, we at Imagine Entertainment got a new boss. Like anyone, I wanted to make a good impression. I just wasn't quite sure how to do that.

In fact, I haven't had a boss in the conventional sense since starting my partnership with Ron Howard, someone who could call me up and tell me what to do, someone I had to check in with every few days. Ron and I had been running Imagine together—along with a lot of other people—since 1986.

During that time, we'd had our most consistent partnership with Universal Studios—they finance and distribute many of the movies we produce. So I consider whoever is running Universal my "boss" in the sense that we need to work well with that person, and we need to develop and sustain a strong personal and professional relationship so we can agree on the kinds of movies we're making together. Tens of millions of dollars are always hanging in the balance.

By the mid-1990s, we'd done a run of movies with Universal that were both great and successful: *Parenthood* (1989), *Kindergarten Cop* (1990), *Backdraft* (1991), and *The Paper* (1994).

When Lew Wasserman was running Universal, I wanted to know Lew—beyond my youthful encounter when he gave me the pencil and the legal pad.

When the Japanese electronics company Matsushita bought Universal, I got to know Matsushita executive Tsuzo Murase.

And when Matsushita sold Universal to the Seagram Company in 1995—yes, over less than a decade, Universal Studios went from being independent to being owned by a Japanese electronics company, to being owned by a Canadian liquor company—I wanted to know Seagram's CEO, Edgar Bronfman Jr.

I didn't hear from Bronfman during the first few weeks after the deal was announced. I did hear that Bronfman had called Steven Spielberg and director and producer Ivan Reitman. So I wondered what to do.

I was a movie producer, making lots of movies with what had suddenly become Bronfman's company. I wasn't quite sure how to reach out.

Should I call his office?

Should I send an email?

Bob Iger is a close friend who once gave me a piece of advice that has stuck with me. In the right circumstances, he said, "Doing nothing can be a very powerful action unto itself."

During his years as the CEO of Disney, Iger had plenty of experience in high-risk, high-pressure situations. In the space of seventy-two hours, he could be in London on the set of the new *Star Wars* movie, then in China working at Shanghai Disney, and then back home in Los Angeles at one of his kids' basketball games. That same weekend, he would be eager to talk about the eighteen-hundred-page biography of Winston Churchill that he finished reading during all his travels. Bob's insistence on excellence and his own wide-ranging curiosity were, and continue to be, tireless.

As I was thinking about how to approach Bronfman, Bob's advice occurred to me. I tend to think that *action* is the way to get action on something. I know how to be patient, but I don't usually leave things alone. I nudge them along. At least, that's how I operated in the first years of my career. This time I decided to wait. To take no action.

"Doing nothing can be a very powerful action unto itself."

Then the White House called and solved the problem for me.

That spring we were getting ready to release *Apollo 13* for a summer premiere—it was set to open June 30, 1995, in 2,200 theaters. In May, we got a call from the White House, inviting us to show the movie to President Bill Clinton, his family, and guests three weeks before it was released, on June 8, in the White House screening room.

That's how a White House movie screening works—the movie itself is invited to the White House, and all the people responsible for making it get to come along.

So Tom Hanks was going to the *Apollo 13* screening at the White House, along with his wife, Rita Wilson, and so was the NASA astronaut that Hanks portrayed, Jim Lovell. The film's director, Ron Howard, was going, and as the producer, I was going too. Also invited: Ron Meyer, the head of Universal Studios, and Edgar Bronfman, the CEO of the company that owned Universal.

What could be more perfect?

My movie gets invited to the White House—perhaps the most prestigious single movie screen in the whole country. And my new boss at Universal gets to be a guest at the White House, not just to see my movie, but *because* of my movie.

That's about as great an introduction to the boss as you could want.

It was my first time at the White House. The night started with a cocktail reception. Bronfman was there. President Clinton and Hillary joined us (Chelsea didn't), some senators and congressmen, a cabinet secretary or two.

After the cocktails, we all stepped into the White House screening room, which is surprisingly small—just sixty seats. They served popcorn; it was very homey, not fancy at all.

President Clinton sat through the whole movie. And as it ended, at the moment when NASA Mission Control reestablished radio contact with the returning Apollo capsule, as the familiar trio of orange-and-white parachutes popped out on the TV screens in Mission Control, the screening room burst into applause.

It was, as I expected, a great setting to meet Edgar Bronfman. A lot of people were competing for his attention that night, of course, but we talked for a few minutes. Bronfman, tall and lanky, is very elegant and extremely well mannered. "I love this movie," he told me. "I'm so proud of this."

He was just a few weeks into owning Universal, but you could tell how genuinely excited he was about the movie business. He came out to Los Angeles three weeks later for the official premiere of *Apollo 13* with his wife, Clarissa. The White House screening was the start of a friendship, and a working relationship, that lasted through the five years that Edgar owned and ran Universal as part of Seagram.

It was my first time meeting President Clinton, and as so many other people have related from their experience, President Clinton seemed to make a point of connecting with me—a connection that continues to this day. President Clinton clearly appreciated the spirit of *Apollo 13*, the way the movie captures the NASA engineers and astronauts turning a potential disaster into a triumph of American ingenuity.

President Clinton later became a big fan of the TV show *24*, which premiered after his second term ended. From his perspective, he told me, *24* had a special emotional punch. He said the show captured a lot of the details of intelligence and counterterrorism work accurately—and that in the end, Jack Bauer always nails the bad guy. In real life, he told me, the president and the country's intelligence and defense staff are often tangled in bureaucracy and legal limitations and red tape, not to mention uncertainty. For President Clinton, *24* was a wish-fulfillment experience: sometimes, he said, it would have been nice to move with the boldness and independence of Jack Bauer.

In writing about curiosity so far, I've tried to tease apart the kinds of curiosity—we've tried to granularize it, to create a taxonomy of thinking about, classifying, and using it.

As a tool for discovery, as a kind of secret weapon to understand what other people don't.

As a spark for creativity and inspiration.

As a way of motivating yourself.

As a tool for independence and self-confidence.

As the key to storytelling.

As a form of courage.

But I think the most valuable use of curiosity is one we haven't explored yet. In fact, I had only recently stumbled into this quality of curiosity—or at least, stumbled into recognizing it. It's so obvious that when I say it, you may briefly roll your eyes. But it's also hidden: it's a kind of curiosity that we neglect and overlook more than the others, even though it has the most power to improve our lives, the lives of those closest to us, and the lives of those we work with every day. I'm talking about the human connection that is created by curiosity.

Human connection is the most important element of our daily lives—with our colleagues and bosses, our romantic partners, our children, our friends.

Human connection requires sincerity. It requires compassion. It requires trust.

Can you really have sincerity, or compassion, or trust, without curiosity?

I don't think so. I think when you stop to consider it—when you look at your own experiences at work and at home—what's so clear is that authentic human connection requires curiosity.

To be a good boss, you have to be curious about the people who work for you. And to be a good colleague, a good romantic partner, a good parent, you have to be curious as well.

True love requires curiosity, and sustaining that love requires sustaining your curiosity. Real intimacy requires curiosity.

I use curiosity every day to help manage people at work, not just in all the ways we've talked about, but as a tool to build trust and cooperation and engagement.

I use curiosity every day with my wife and my kids and my friends—not always as skillfully as I would like, I confess—but I use it to keep my relationships vital and fresh, to stay connected.

Human connection is the most important part of being alive. It's the key to sustained happiness and to a sense of satisfaction with how you're living.

And curiosity is the key to connecting and staying connected.

I once had a meeting on the couches in my office with one of my movie production executives.

She had come in to talk about the state of a movie we were working on, with a cast of big-name movie stars and a series of intertwining stories.

The meeting was short, really just a progress report. Many movies bump and grind along for a lot of months, and a lot of meetings, before either landing on the theater screen or running out of energy and simply never getting made.

This particular movie had been in the works for more than a year already, but not a scene had been shot.

I listened to the update for a few minutes before gently interrupting. "Why should we do this movie?" I asked. "Why *are* we doing this movie?"

My colleague stopped and looked at me. She'd been at Imagine a long time and knew me pretty well. She answered my question by simply reciting in brisk shorthand how we got into this movie—who brought it to us, why it was exciting at that moment.

I knew all that. And she knew I knew it. She was answering the question of why we *were* doing this movie, but she wasn't answering the question of why we *should* do this movie.

A few minutes later, I tried again.

"Do you love this movie?" I asked.

She smiled. She didn't shake her head, but she might as well have. Without saying a word, her smile said, *Do I love this movie? What kind of question is that? I love the idea of getting this movie made after all these meetings, all these negotiations, all these changes in cast and schedule—that's what I love.*

She slipped my question like a boxer sidestepping a punch. Love? What's love? This movie was in the ditch at that moment. We loved it once: loved the idea, loved the cast, loved the package, loved the mood we were going to create for the Friday-night movie crowds . . . a year before. Now the movie just needed to be winched out of the ditch. Who knew whether we loved it anymore? We couldn't possibly love it until we saw some of it on a screen.

I just nodded.

My colleague ticked off a couple of other things—she is well organized and typically comes to my office with a list of the things she needs to make sure we talk about. When she was done with her list, she whisked off.

I hadn't told her what to do about the stalled movie.

And she hadn't asked what to do about the stalled movie.

But she very clearly knew how I felt about it. I didn't love it anymore. I couldn't really remember loving it that much. I thought it had become a burden, taking time and energy and emotion we should have been putting into projects we really did love.

But here's a key element of my personality: I don't like to boss people around. I don't get motivated by telling people what to do; I don't take any pleasure in it.

So I manage with curiosity by asking questions.

I actually do it instinctively now. I don't need to stop and remind myself to ask questions instead of giving instructions. Work these days for many people is filled with one Zoom meeting or in-person conversation or conference call after another. In a typical day, I may have fifty conversations of some substance. But I so prefer hearing what other people have to say that I instinctively ask questions. If you're listening to my side of a phone call, you may hear little but the occasional question.

My sense is that most managers and bosses, and most workplaces, don't work that way.

Sometimes you have to give orders.

Sometimes I have to give orders.

But if you set aside the routine instructions that are part of everyone's workday—the request to get someone on the phone, to look up a fact, to schedule a meeting—I almost always start with questions.

I especially think questions are a great management tool when I think someone isn't doing what I would hope they would, or when I think something isn't going in the direction I want it to go.

People often imagine that if there's going to be conflict, they need to start with a firm hand, they need to remind people of the chain of command.

I'm never worried about who is in charge.

I'm worried about making sure we get the best possible decision, the best possible casting, script, movie trailer, financing deal, the best possible movie.

Asking questions elicits information, of course.

Asking questions creates the space for people to raise issues they are worried about that the boss, or their colleagues, may not know about.

Asking questions gives people the chance to tell a different story than the one you're expecting.

Most important, from my perspective, is that asking questions means people have to make their case for the way they want a decision to go.

The movie business is all about being able to "make your case." With *Splash*, I had to make my case hundreds of times over seven years. After forty years of successfully making movies, that hasn't changed for me. In the summer of 2014, we produced the movie *Get On Up*, the story of James Brown and his monumental impact on the music we listen to every day. Tate Taylor, who directed *The Help*, directed the film. Mick Jagger coproduced. Chad Boseman, who played Jackie Robinson in the movie *42*, starred as James Brown.

I worked for years to make a movie about James Brown and his music. His story is so elemental, so American. It wasn't just that James Brown came from poverty, that he cut through discrimination—his childhood was devastating; he was abandoned by both his mother and his father and raised in a brothel. He didn't have much basic education, and no formal musical education. And yet he created a whole new sound in music, a sound that is irresistible. He created a whole new way of performing onstage. James Brown had to be totally self-reliant, totally self-created. His impact on American music is profound. But he paid a huge price. His is a story about finding identity and self-worth. It's a story of great triumph and also sadness, for him and for those closest to him.

I'd been interested in James Brown's music and his life for twenty years. I worked with James Brown himself on doing a movie for eight years—buying the rights to his life, trying to get the story and the script right, meeting with him over and over. But when he died in 2006 before we had gotten a movie made, the rights to his story reverted to his estate. I was discouraged. We had to start all over.

I knew Mick Jagger, the lead singer of the Rolling Stones, a little bit—I'd met him several times. Mick was as passionate about the power of James Brown's music and story as I was. After Brown died, Mick called me up. "Let's make this movie together," he said. He knew I had a working script. He said he would try to renegotiate the rights.

And then we had to go make the case, again, to Universal Pictures—which had already lost money during my first round trying to get a James Brown movie made.

Mick and I went to see Donna Langley, who was then the head of production at Universal Pictures. She's English and grew up adoring the Rolling Stones. It was a fantastic meeting. Mick was so graceful, so relaxed, so eloquent. He talked to Donna about James Brown, about the script, about the kind of movie we wanted to make. All in that classic Mick Jagger accent. He made it fun. He made it appealing.

And it worked. Still, after I'd been in the movie business thirty-five years, after I'd won an Oscar, putting *Get On Up* on the screen took sixteen years—and I needed Mick Jagger's help to make it happen.

So if you're going to survive in Hollywood—and I think if you're going to survive and thrive anywhere in business—you have to learn to "make the case" for whatever you want to do. Making the case means answering the big questions: Why this project? Why now? Why with this group of talent? With this investment of money? Who is the audience (or the customer)? How will we capture that audience, that customer?

And the biggest question of all, the question I'm always pulling back to the center of the conversation, is this: What's the story? What's this movie about?

Making the case also means answering the detail questions: Why these songs in that order on the soundtrack? Why that supporting actress? Why that scene?

None of these are yes-or-no questions. They are open-ended questions—they are questions where the answer can itself be a story, sometimes short, sometimes a longer one.

I ask these questions, and I listen to the answers. Sometimes I listen with a skeptical expression on my face, I'm sure. Sometimes I listen with a distracted look in my eye.

And sometimes you need to ask questions that are even more open.

What are you focused on?

Why are you focused on that?

What are you worried about?

What's your plan?

I think asking questions creates a lot more engagement in the people with whom you work. It's subtle. Let's say you have a movie that's in trouble. You ask the executive responsible for moving that movie along what her plan is. You're doing two things just by asking the question. You're making it clear that she should have a plan, and you're making it clear that she is in charge of that plan. The question itself implies both the responsibility for the problem and the authority to come up with the solution.

If you work with talented people who want to do the work they are doing, then they'll want to step up. But it's a simple quality of human nature that people prefer to choose to do things rather than be ordered to do them. In fact, as soon as you tell me I have to do something—give a speech, attend a banquet, go to Cannes—I immediately start looking for ways to avoid doing it. If you invite me to do something, I'm much more likely to want to do it.

I work every day with actors, with beautiful, charming, charismatic people whose job is to persuade you to believe them. That's what being a great actor means—it means having the ability to cast a spell over the audience, to persuade them you are the character you're portraying. A great actor creates believability.

But if you pause for a moment and think about it, you'll realize that employing people like that is really hard. Actors are hard to manage because they are often used to getting what they want, and because their talent is persuading you to see the world the way they want you to. That's why you've hired them in the first place.

Am I the "boss" of the movie? Is the director the "boss" of the movie? In different ways, of course, the producer and the director are the "bosses" of the movie.

When you're out on location, you can be spending $300,000 a day to make a movie. That's $12,500 an hour, even while everyone is sleeping.

So if an actor gets mad, or pouty, or wants their jet refueled, they are the person shaking the cage. They are the person in charge.

You can't let people behave badly. But you also can't screw up the psyche of an actor. If someone ends up with a bad attitude, you don't get the performance you want.

When there's a problem, when there's trouble at $300,000 a day, you want to find a way to have a conversation so that you can convince your star or stars to help you. You want to draw them in, not order them around.

Back in 1991, we shot the movie *Far and Away*. We had Tom Cruise as the lead. Tom was at the top of his career. He was only twenty-nine years old, but he had already made *Top Gun* (1986), *The Color of Money* (1986), *Rain Man* (1988), and *Born on the Fourth of July* (1989).

Tom isn't difficult to work with. But *Far and Away* was a challenging movie to get made. It was an old-fashioned epic, a story of two immigrants leaving Ireland for America at the turn of the last century. We shot in Ireland and the western United States. It got expensive, but it wasn't overtly commercial. When we figured out what it was going to cost, the studio told me to find ways of cutting the budget.

I went to Tom on the set. We talked. I said, "Look, you're not the producer of this movie. But we all want to make it, we all have this vision of a movie we're doing as artists, a story we care about. It's going to be expensive, but we can't spend as much money as it looks like we're going to. We need to hold the line."

I said to Tom, "Can you be the team leader here with the cast and crew? Can you be the guy that sets an example?"

He looked at me and said, "I'm one hundred percent that guy!"

He said, "When I have to go to the bathroom, I'm going to run to the trailer and run back to the set. I'm going to set the pace for excellence, and respect, and tightening up."

And that's exactly what he did. He led. He was motivated. And he motivated other people.

I didn't walk in and tell Tom what to do. I didn't order everybody to work harder, to make do with less. I explained where we were. And I went to the key player, the person other people would respect, and I asked that person a question: "Can you be the leader here?"

Being persuasive, being successful, in a situation like that is hardly guaranteed. Some of it is in how you present yourself. I think Tom appreciated that I came to him with a problem, that I treated him as an equal, that I treated him as part of the solution. I allowed Tom to be curious about both the problem and how to fix it.

Some of that is Tom's character—he isn't just thinking of himself.

But you have a much greater chance of success at a key moment like that if you ask someone to step up in a big way, rather than order them to step up in a big way. Tom did it.

I think asking for people's help—rather than directing it—is almost always the smart way of doing things, regardless of the stakes.

For instance, I think my partnership with Ron Howard only works because we never tell each other what to do. We always ask.

If I need Ron to call Russell Crowe, I don't say, "Ron, I need you to call Russell Crowe." I say something like, "How would you feel about calling Russell Crowe?"

Or, "Do you think it's a good idea if you call Russell Crowe?"

Or, "How do you think Russell Crowe would feel if you called him?"

Unless Ron asks me a specific yes-or-no question, I never tell him what to do.

The same is true of my relationship with Tom Hanks. Tom Cruise. Denzel Washington. I don't tell, I ask.

I am, of course, communicating what I want. But I'm leaving them the choice. They know what I want, but they have free will. They can say no.

This isn't just a matter of personal style. The real benefit of asking rather than telling is that it creates the space for a conversation, for a different idea, a different strategy.

I trust Ron Howard completely—I trust his artistic instincts, I trust his business judgment, I trust his affection and respect for me and for what we've created.

So I don't want to say, "Ron, I need you to call Russell Crowe."

I want to say, "Ron, what would happen if you called Russell Crowe?" Because then Ron can wrinkle his brow and come up with a different way of approaching Russell with whatever idea we've got.

I've discovered another unexpected characteristic of using questions: they transmit values. In fact, questions can quietly transmit values more powerfully than a direct statement telling people what you want them to stand for, or exhorting them about what you want them to stand for.

Why do I ask my movie production executive if she loves that movie that isn't managing to get made? Because I want her to love the movies she's making for us. We've been doing this business for a long time, and at this point the only reason to do a project is because we love it. If I say to her, or anyone else, "Let's only do movies you really love," it's easy for that to sound like a goal, or a theory, or, worst of all, a platitude.

If I ask directly, "Do you love this movie?"—the question makes it clear what I think our priorities really are.

It worked exactly the same way with Tom Cruise and *Far and Away*. If I fly to Ireland from Los Angeles and start telling everybody that we need to save money, we need to film faster, cut effects, save costs on the catering—well then, I'm just the LA executive who flies in with the bad news and the marching orders.

If I sit down quietly with Tom and ask the question, "Can you be the team leader here?"—it's a moment packed with values. We care about this movie. We've got to find a way of protecting the integrity of the story while living within a reasonable budget. I need help. And I have so much respect for Tom that I'm asking him to help me solve this problem, to help me manage the whole movie. This is a powerful message, packed into only seven words, with a question mark at the end instead of a period.

Curiosity at work isn't a matter of style. It's much more consequential than that.

If you're the boss and you manage by asking questions, you're laying the foundation for the culture of your company or your group.

You're letting people know that the boss is willing to listen. This isn't about being "warm" or "friendly." It's about understanding how complicated the modern business world is, how indispensable diversity of perspective is, and how hard creative work is.

Here's why it's hard: because often there is no right answer.

Consider for a moment an example that seems really simple: the design of Google's search page.

How many ways are there to design a web page? How many ways are there to design a page for searching the web? An infinite number, of course.

Google's page is legendary for its spare, almost stark appearance. There's a clean page, a search box, the Google logo, two buttons: "Google Search" and "I'm Feeling Lucky." And wide-open white space. Today, the Google home page is considered a triumph of graphic design, a brilliant example of taking something as complex and chaotic as the World Wide Web and making it simple and accessible.

Two things are fascinating from the story of the design of Google's search page. First, it's an accident. Sergey Brin, one of Google's two cofounders, didn't know how to do HTML computer code when he and Larry Page first launched the search engine in 1998, so he designed the simplest possible page—because that's all he had the skills to do.

Second, people found the simple page so different from the rest of the cluttered Web that they didn't understand what to do. People routinely sat in front of the clean page waiting for the rest of it to load instead of typing in their search. Google solved that confusion by putting a tiny copyright line at the bottom of the search page (it's not there anymore), so users would know the page had finished loading.[2]

So the story of Google's brilliant home page is surprising mostly because it wasn't done by design, and its brilliance took a while to become clear. Brin didn't know how to code anything fancy, so he didn't. And what has now become an influential example of online design usability was so baffling when it was first unveiled that people couldn't figure out how to use it.

But the home page isn't really Google at all. Google is the vast array of computer code and algorithms that allow the company to search the Web and present results. There are millions of lines of code behind a Google search—and millions more behind Google mail, Google Chrome, Google Ads.

If we can envision dozens, hundreds of ways of designing a search page, imagine for a moment the ways that all that computer code could be written. It's like imagining the ways a book can be written, like imagining the ways a story could be told on screen. For Google, it is a story, just written in zeroes and ones.

That's why asking questions at work, instead of giving orders, is so valuable. Because most modern problems—lowering someone's cholesterol, getting passengers onto an airplane efficiently, or searching all of human knowledge—don't have a right answer. They have all kinds of answers, many of them wonderful.

To get at the possibilities, you have to find out what ideas and reactions are in other people's minds. You have to ask them questions.

How do you see this problem?

What are we missing?

Is there another way of tackling this?

How would we solve this if we were the customer?

That's as true in movies as in any other business. I love the movies we've made. But we didn't produce the "right" version of the iconic films *Apollo 13* or *A Beautiful Mind*. We have the version of the story that we made—the very best version, with the cast and crew and script and budget we had.

Tom Hanks is the face of *Apollo 13*, as real-life astronaut Jim Lovell.

Russell Crowe captures the spirit, the struggles, and the interior intellectual life of mathematician John Nash in *A Beautiful Mind*.

They both executed those roles brilliantly.

But clearly that isn't the only version of those movies that could have been made—what if we hadn't been able to sign Hanks or Crowe for those leading roles? We would have hired another actor. And the whole movie would have been different—even if every other actor, every other behind-the-scenes person, and every word of the script had been identical.

Anna Culp, who was for years executive vice president for movie production at Imagine, had been at the company more than two decades, having started as my assistant.

"We do approach everything as 'case-building,'" Anna said about the culture at Imagine. "Being asked questions means you always have the chance to make the movie better, and to make the case for making the movie better.

"For me, the questions mean no one is ever wrong. Most of the time, these aren't those kinds of right-or-wrong decisions.

"The movies we end up loving, you can't really imagine them having come out any other way. But with something like the James Brown movie, *Get On Up*, well, over sixteen years, at different times, there have been very different versions of that movie.

"For me, questions have become a habit I use myself. I'm always asking, 'Why am I doing this material, this movie?'

"And you know, if something doesn't work out financially—if it's not a success—you want to be able to stand back and say, 'This is still something I'm proud of.'

"The disadvantages of the questions are, in some sense, the same as the advantages. You wonder if you are delivering, and if you are delivering the right thing. Because the boss isn't telling you. I can't tell you how many times I've gone back to my office after a meeting, and I'm thinking, 'Are we doing the right movie? Are we doing the movie the right way? Am I delivering?'

"This isn't a science. It's a creative business."

As Anna makes so clear, this kind of "management curiosity" ripples into the corners of how people think about their work, and their approach to their work, every day.

Questions create both the authority in people to come up with ideas and take action, and the responsibility for moving things forward.

Questions create the space for all kinds of ideas, and the sparks to come up with those ideas.

Most important, questions send a very clear message: we're willing to listen, even to ideas or suggestions or problems we weren't expecting.

As valuable as questions are when you're the boss, I think they are just as important in every other direction in the workplace. People should ask their bosses questions. I appreciate it when people ask me the same kind of open-ended questions I so often ask.

What are you hoping for?

What are you expecting?

What's the most important part of this for you?

Those kinds of questions allow a boss to be clear about things that the boss might *think* are clear, but which often aren't clear at all.

Indeed, people at all levels should ask each other questions. That helps break down the barriers between job functions in our company, and in any workplace, and also helps puncture the idea that the job hierarchy determines who can have a good idea.

I like when people at Imagine ask me questions for many reasons, but here's the simplest and most powerful reason: if they ask the question, then they almost always listen to the answer.

People are more likely to consider a piece of advice, or a flat-out instruction, if they've asked for it in the first place.

Imagine is hardly a perfect workplace. We have our share of dull meetings and unproductive brainstorming sessions. We miscommunicate, we misinterpret, we miss out on some opportunities, and we push forward some projects we should let go.

But nobody is afraid to ask a question.

Nobody is afraid to answer a question.

Making questions a central part of managing people and projects is hard. I do it instinctively, from years of using questions to draw people out, and from a natural inclination to hear how projects are moving along rather than giving orders about them.

I think questions are an underappreciated management tool. But if it's not the way you normally interact with people, it will take a conscious effort to change. And you have to be prepared that, initially, asking questions slows things down. If you really want to know what people think, if you really want people to take more responsibility, if you really want a conversation around the problems and opportunities—rather than having people execute marching orders—that takes more time.

It's like being a reporter inside your own organization.

If asking questions isn't your typical style, this approach may puzzle people at first. So the best way to start might be to pick a particular project and manage that project with questions. If you can start using curiosity in the office, you'll find that after a while, the benefits are remarkable. People's creativity gradually blossoms. And you end up knowing a lot more—you know more about the people you work with every day and how their minds work, and you know more about what's going on with the work itself.

The most important element of this kind of culture is that you can't simply unleash a welter of questions—like a police detective or a lawyer doing a cross-examination in court. We're not asking questions for the sake of hearing ourselves ask them.

There are two key elements to a questioning culture. The first is the atmosphere around the question. You can't ask a question in a tone of voice or with a facial expression that indicates you already know the answer. You can't ask a question with that impatience that indicates you can't wait to ask the next question.

The point of the question has to be the answer.

The questions and the answers have to be driving a project or a decision forward.

And you have to listen to the answer. You have to take the answer seriously—as a boss or a colleague or a subordinate. If you don't take the answers seriously, no one will take the questions seriously. You'll just get the answers calculated to get everyone out of the conversation quickly.

The questions, in other words, have to come from genuine curiosity. If you're not curious enough to listen to the answer, all the question does is increase cynicism and decrease trust and engagement.

One of my childhood heroes was Jonas Salk, the physician and scientist who figured out how to create the first vaccine that prevented polio. Salk was a towering figure.

Today, it's hard to imagine how much fear polio instilled in American parents and children. A devastating disease, polio is a viral infection of the lining of the spinal cord, and it killed children, left them permanently crippled, or left them paralyzed so severely that they had to live their lives inside an iron breathing machine called an iron lung. Polio is incurable and untreatable. Kids with a stiff or painful neck would be raced to the doctor or the hospital, and in some cases they would be dead within a few hours.

And polio is contagious, although how exactly it spread wasn't clear during the height of the epidemics. So when epidemics swept through the United States, people would keep their kids home from any place where crowds gathered—kids didn't go to the movies, summer camp, the beach, or the swimming pool.

In 1952, the year after I was born, there was a major epidemic of polio in the United States—58,000 people got the disease; 3,145 died; 21,269 were left with some level of paralysis.[3]

Just in the entertainment world, the number of people who survived polio gives a vivid sense of how widespread and dangerous it was. Alan Alda had polio as a child, as did Mia Farrow, Mel Ferrer, Francis Ford Coppola, Donald Sutherland, Johnny Weissmuller. Arthur C. Clarke, the science fiction author, had polio, as did the great newspaper editor Ben Bradlee and the violinist Itzhak Perlman, who still requires braces and a crutch to walk.[4]

Jonas Salk was a determined and fairly independent-minded virologist who developed a "killed virus" form of the polio vaccine while working at the University of Pittsburgh. The vaccine used inactivated particles of polio virus to stimulate the immune system, so people who received two doses of the vaccine were immune to infection.[5]

When the Salk vaccine was announced in 1955, Salk became a nationwide, and then a worldwide, hero. Immunization programs were launched immediately, and by the end of the 1950s, there were only a few hundred cases of polio being reported in the whole country. Tens of thousands of people were saved from lives of challenge, or from death. Everyone was able to go back to living without the shadow of polio over their lives.[6]

Dr. Salk was born in 1914, and he was just forty when the vaccine was announced. By the time I decided to meet him, he had established a scientific research center called the Salk Institute for Biological Studies in La Jolla, California, just north of San Diego.

Salk was then in his late sixties and hard to reach, almost impossible.

I worked for more than a year just to get the attention of someone in his office. Eventually, I discovered that Dr. Salk's assistant was a woman named Joan Abrahamson, who was herself a MacArthur Award winner, a so-called genius grant winner.

I talked to her regularly. She knew how much I admired Dr. Salk, and also how interested I was in meeting him. And she knew that Dr. Salk, while he kept a low profile, was not a classic absentminded scientist. Dr. Salk had a wide range of interests and might enjoy learning something about the movie business.

It was 1984, not long after *Splash* had been released, when Joan told me that Dr. Salk would be speaking at a scientific meeting at the Beverly Wilshire Hotel, in Beverly Hills, and that if I wanted to meet them there in the morning, he could spend some time with me between sessions.

Not perfect, of course. Huge association meetings tend to be crowded, distracting, and filled with hubbub. But I certainly wasn't saying no. The morning of the meeting, I woke up feeling a little fluey. I was tired, light-headed, my throat a little tickly.

By the time I got to the Beverly Wilshire that morning, I think I looked a little sick. If it had been anything but meeting Jonas Salk, I would have wheeled around and headed back home.

I met Joan, and I met Dr. Salk. It was late morning. Dr. Salk looked at me with a little concern and he said, "What's wrong?"

I said, "Dr. Salk, I'm just not feeling that well this morning. I feel a little light-headed, a little sick."

He immediately said, "Let me go grab you a glass of orange juice." And before I could say anything, he popped off to the restaurant and came back with a big glass of orange juice.

This was long before most people had heard about the research that orange juice could really help perk you up if you were just getting sick. He said, "Drink this—it will bump up your blood sugar; you'll feel better quickly."

I drank the entire glass, and he was right—it worked.

It was kind of a surprising first encounter. Dr. Salk was so accessible, so human, so perceptive—he wasn't some genius off in his own world. He behaved, in fact, like a physician. He noticed immediately that something wasn't right, and he wanted to take care of me.

That morning, our conversation was brief—no more than thirty minutes. Dr. Salk was a slight-framed man, very friendly, very engaged, very intellectual. We talked a little about his research at the Salk Institute (he spent a lot of time trying to find a vaccine for HIV near the end of his career), and we talked about the impact of saving so many people's lives. He was completely modest about that.

Dr. Salk ended up inviting me to visit the Salk Institute, which I did, and we developed a friendship. He was intrigued with the idea of my curiosity conversations, and he proposed an expanded version. He suggested that the two of us each invite a couple of really interesting people to a daylong conversation, to be held at my Malibu house. So there would be six or eight of us, from totally different disciplines, spending the day in a relaxed atmosphere, trading our problems and our experiences and our questions. What a fabulous idea. And we did it.

Dr. Salk invited a robotics expert from Caltech and Betty Edwards, the theorist and teacher who wrote the book *Drawing on the Right Side of the Brain.* I brought director and producer Sydney Pollack (*Out of Africa*, *Tootsie*) and producer George Lucas, the creator of *Star Wars* and *Indiana Jones*, and George brought Linda Ronstadt, the singer who was his girlfriend at the time.

The whole thing was Dr. Salk's idea. He was curious—in particular, he was curious about how the "media mind" worked, how people like Lucas and Pollack thought about the world and what they created, and he was curious about storytelling. It was very relaxed, very unpretentious. We didn't solve the problems of the world, but we sure did put in one room a half dozen people who wouldn't typically encounter each other.

The time I remember most vividly with Jonas Salk, though, was the first moment we met—that honest, simple, human connection right at the beginning. Although he was just in the process of meeting me, Dr. Salk noticed I was looking down and was considerate enough to ask why—and immediately offered help. These days, it seems, it's almost a shock when people ask questions about you and then stop long enough to absorb the answer.

Curiosity is what creates empathy. To care about someone, you have to wonder about them.

Curiosity creates interest. It can also create excitement.

A good first date is filled with a tumble of questions and answers, the fizz of discovering someone new, of learning how they connect to you, and of how they are different. You can't decide whether it's more fun to ask questions of your date, or to answer your date's questions about you.

But what happens months or years later is that your boyfriend or girlfriend, your husband or wife, feels familiar. That's the beauty and safety of a solid, intimate relationship: you feel like you know the person, like you can rely on the person and their responses, that you can, perhaps, even predict them.

You love that person. You love the version of that person that you hold in your mind and your heart.

But familiarity is the enemy of curiosity.

And when our curiosity about those closest to us fades, that's the moment when our connection begins to fray. It frays silently, almost invisibly. But when we stop asking genuine questions of those around us—and most important, when we stop really listening to the answers—that's when we start to lose our connection.

What happened at the office today, dear?

Not much. How about you?

If you picture for a moment the image of a married couple in their midthirties, they've got the two kids put to sleep, it's nine o'clock at night, they're tired, they're cleaning up the kitchen or they're folding laundry or they're sitting in the family room or they're getting ready for bed. They're thinking about all the ordinary things that crowd into your brain when the day quiets down: Did I remember to RSVP for that birthday party? How am I going to deal with Sally at that project review tomorrow? I wonder why Tom has been so chilly recently? I forgot to make those plane reservations again! The conversation between the couple is desultory, or it's purely pragmatic—you do this, I'll do that.

Maybe it's just a moment of tiredness and quiet before bed. But if you string a month of evenings like that together, if you string a year of evenings like that together, that's how people drift apart.

The familiarity is comfortable, even reassuring. But the couple has stopped being curious about each other—genuinely curious. They don't ask real questions. They don't listen to the answers.

It's a little simplistic, of course, but the quickest way to restore energy and excitement to your relationships is to bring some real curiosity back to them. Ask questions about your spouse's day and pay attention to the answers. Ask questions about your kids' friends, about their classes, about what's exciting them at school and pay attention to the answers.

Ask questions like you would have on a first date—ask about their feelings, their reactions.

How do you feel about . . . ?

What did you think of . . . ?

What doesn't work are the classic questions we all ask too often: What happened at work? What happened at school?

Those questions can be waved off. "Nothing." That's the answer 95 percent of the time. As if your wife spent eight hours at the office or your kids spent eight hours at school staring silently at a blank wall—and then came home.

You need questions that can't be answered with a single muttered word.

What did Sally think of your new ideas for the product launch?

What do you enjoy about Mr. Meyer's history class?

How are you thinking about your speech at the convention next week?

Who's going to try out for the musical this year?

Maybe we should have an adventure this weekend. What would you like to do Saturday afternoon?

How many marriages that drift into disconnection and boredom could be helped by a revival of genuine curiosity on both sides? We need these daily reminders that although I live with this person, I don't actually know her *today*—unless I ask about her today.

We don't just take our relationships to those closest to us for granted. We take for granted that we know them so well we know what happened today. We know what they think.

But we don't. That's part of the fun of curiosity, and part of the value of curiosity: it creates the moment of surprise.

And before the moment of surprise comes the moment of respect. Genuine curiosity requires respect—I care about you, and I care about your experience in the world, and I want to hear about it.

This brings me back to Ron Howard. I feel like I know Ron as well as I know anyone, and I certainly rely on him in professional and personal terms. But I never presume I know what's happening with Ron, and I never presume that I know what his reaction to something is going to be. I ask.

That same kind of respect, curiosity, and surprise is just as powerful in our intimate relationships as it is at work. In that sense, every conversation can be a curiosity conversation. It's another example of curiosity being fundamentally respectful—you aren't just asking about the person you're talking to; you are genuinely interested in what she has to say, in her point of view, in her experiences.

At work, you can manage people by talking at them—but you can't manage them very well by doing that. To be a good manager, you need to understand the people you work with, and if you're doing all the talking, you can't understand them.

And if you don't understand the people you're working with, you certainly can't inspire them.

At home, you can be in the same room as your partner or your kids, but you can't be connected to them unless you ask questions about them and hear the answers. Curiosity is the door to open those relationships, and to reopen them. It can keep you from being lonely.

And by the way: I love people being curious about me. I like it when people ask me interesting questions, I like a great conversation, and I like telling stories. It's almost as much fun to be the object of curiosity as it is to be curious.

Curiosity isn't necessarily about achieving something, about driving toward some goal.

Sometimes, it's just about connecting with people. Which is to say, curiosity can be about sustaining intimacy. It's not about a goal, it's about happiness.

Your love for someone can, of course, also fire your curiosity on their behalf.

My oldest son, Riley, was born in 1986. When he was about three and a half years old, we realized there was something different about his nervous system, about his psychology, and his responses. Riley's mom, Corki—then my wife—and I spent many years trying to understand what was happening with him developmentally, and when he was about seven years old, he was diagnosed with Asperger's syndrome.

It was the early nineties, and treatment for Asperger's then was even more uncertain than it is today. Riley was a happy kid. He was socially oriented. We wanted to help him connect with the world in the most constructive way possible.

We tried different styles of education. We tried some weird

glasses that changed his vision. We tried Ritalin—though only briefly. Getting Riley the help he needs has been a constant journey, for him and for his mother and for me.

As Riley was growing up, I started thinking about mental illness and the stigma attached to it. I had survived stigma myself, of course, because of my reading disability. Riley is a gracious and delightful person, but if you don't understand how the world looks to him, you might be puzzled by him. I wanted to do a movie that really tackled the issues around mental illness, that helped destigmatize it. I was always watching for an idea.

In the spring of 1998, Graydon Carter, the editor of *Vanity Fair*, called and told me I had to read a piece in the June issue, an excerpt from a book by Sylvia Nasar called *A Beautiful Mind* that told the life story of John Nash, a Princeton-educated mathematician who won the Nobel Prize but who was also plagued with devastating schizophrenia. The magazine excerpt was riveting. Here was a story about genius and schizophrenia braided together—of achievement, mental illness, and overcoming stigma—all in the life of a real man. I was thinking about Riley even as I was reading the pages in *Vanity Fair*.

I immediately knew two things. I wanted to make a movie of *A Beautiful Mind* and the life of the Nobel laureate mathematician who was also schizophrenic. And I wanted it to be the kind of movie that would reach people and change their attitudes, even change their behavior, toward people who are different—disabled or mentally ill.

Part of the power of *A Beautiful Mind* comes from this remarkable insight: It isn't just hard for outsiders to relate to someone who is different. It's hard for the person who is mentally ill to relate to everyone else. That person struggles to understand how the world works, too, and struggles to understand people's responses to him.

There was an auction for the movie rights to *A Beautiful Mind*, and as part of the auction, I sat and talked to Sylvia Nasar, and also to John Nash himself, and his wife, Alicia. They wanted to know why I wanted to make the movie and what kind of movie I wanted to make.

I talked a little bit about my son, but mostly I talked about John Nash's story. I'd already produced two movies at that point that involved buying the rights to the stories of real people—*The Doors* and *Apollo 13*. You have to tell people the truth about the movie you want to make from their lives—and if you get the movie, you have to stick to what you promised.

I told John Nash that I wouldn't portray him as a perfect person. He's brilliant, but also arrogant, a tough guy. That's important. He has a beautiful love story with his wife. I said, "I want to do a movie that celebrates the beauty of your mind and your romance."

And that's the movie we made—that's the movie the screenwriter Akiva Goldsman was able to write, the movie Ron Howard created on-screen as director, and those are the people that Russell Crowe and Jennifer Connelly were able to bring to life so vividly.

While we were in the early stages of working on the movie, I was thinking about how to convey how the mind of a schizophrenic works—how to show that on-screen. Sylvia Nasar's book doesn't have this sense of alternate reality. But I didn't want the movie of *A Beautiful Mind* to simply portray John Nash from the point of view of the people around him. That wouldn't provide the revelation or the connection we were looking for.

The solution came one day before *A Beautiful Mind* was too far along. Riley and I were watching Stanley Kubrick's *The Shining* together. There's a vivid scene in *The Shining* where Jack Nicholson is in a bar, having conversations with people who don't exist. It hit me immediately. I thought we should find a way of showing Nash's reality—show how the schizophrenic mind works by showing what the world looks like from his point of view. And that's what we did: John Nash's reality is shown in the movie no differently than everyone else's reality.

Akiva Goldsman got that idea perfectly—and I think it's the

source of the power of the movie itself, in addition to the portrayals by Russell and Jennifer, of course.

The movie was more than a success. It did well financially. It won four Academy Awards—for Ron and me for best picture, for Ron for best director, for Akiva for best adapted screenplay, for Jennifer for best supporting actress. And John and Alicia Nash were with us at the Academy Awards that night in 2002.

But the real success is that the movie has affected so many people's lives. People came up to me on the street—people still come up to me—and said, "You've helped me understand what my child or my niece or my mother is going through." I remember being at a Ralphs supermarket in Malibu not long after the movie came out, and a woman came up to me and told me she was brought to tears by that movie.

It isn't just that I did *A Beautiful Mind* because the story touched me personally. The way we did it came directly from my own experiences. And the way we did it, to me, makes it such a powerful, and such a valuable, movie. My curiosity and determination to help Riley led me to *A Beautiful Mind*. And my experience being his father, and watching how he experiences the world, led us to a totally original treatment of mental illness. *A Beautiful Mind* is unquestionably the most gratifying movie I've ever made.

6

Good Taste and the Power of Anti-Curiosity

If we are not able to ask skeptical questions, to interrogate those who tell us that something is true, to be skeptical of those in authority, then we are up for grabs for the next charlatan—political or religious—who comes ambling along.

—*Carl Sagan*[1]

The movies we've made at Imagine have a great variety of settings, stories, and tones.

We made a movie about achieving the American dream—and the central character was a semiliterate African American man trying to climb the ladder of the heroin trade in New York City in the 1970s. That movie, *American Gangster*, is also about the values of American capitalism.

We made a movie about the power and the passion of high school football in rural Texas. It's a movie about how boys grow up, how they discover who they really are; it's about teamwork and community and identity. It's also about disappointment, because at the climax of *Friday Night Lights*, the Permian High Panthers lose their big game.

We made a movie called *8 Mile* about a hip-hop artist—a white hip-hop artist.

We made a movie about the movie *Deep Throat*, and how that pornographic film about oral sex came to define a critical moment in our culture.

We made a movie about a Nobel Prize–winning mathematician—but *A Beautiful Mind* is really about what it's like to be mentally ill, to be schizophrenic, and to try to function in the world anyway.

Two things are true about all these movies.

First, they are all about developing character, about discovering flaws and strengths and overcoming your emotional injuries to become a full person. To me, the American dream is about overcoming obstacles—the circumstances of your birth, a limited education, the way other people perceive you, something inside your own head. Overcoming obstacles is itself an art form. So if the movies I make have a single theme, it is how to leverage your limits into success.

Second, no one in Hollywood really wanted to do any of them.

I've talked about using curiosity to get around the no that is so common in Hollywood and at work in general. The first reaction to most ideas that are a little outside the mainstream is discomfort, and the first reaction to discomfort is to say no.

Why are we glorifying a heroin dealer?[2]

Shouldn't the football team win the big game?

Who wants to watch a whole movie about a struggling white hip-hop artist?

For me, curiosity helps find ideas that are edgy and different and interesting. Curiosity provides the wide range of experience and understanding of popular culture that gives me an instinct of when something new might resonate. And curiosity gives me courage, the courage to have confidence in those interesting ideas, even if they aren't popular ones.

Sometimes you don't just want to attract the crowd to something mainstream; you want to create the crowd for something unconventional.

I like projects with soul—stories and characters with heart. I like to believe in something. I like the idea of the popular iconoclast—doing work that is at the edge but not too far over the edge.

That's when I run into something very important, and very contrarian. I run into the limits of curiosity.

Sometimes you need anti-curiosity.

When I have an idea I love that is unconventional, eventually I have to say, "I'm doing it."

Don't tell me why it's a bad idea—I'm doing it. That's anti-curiosity.

Anti-curiosity isn't just the determination to grab hold of an interesting idea and push forward in the face of skepticism and rejection. Anti-curiosity is something much more specific and important.

It's the moment when you shut down your curiosity, when you resist learning more, when you may have to tell people, "No, that's okay—don't tell me all your reasons for saying no."

Here's what I mean. When you're building financial and casting support for a movie, you have already built the case for the movie for yourself, in your own mind. You have gone over and over why this story is interesting, why the script is good, why the people you want to make the movie match the story and the script.

Everyone in Hollywood knows how to "make the case." That's what we do with each other all day long. And any successful producer or director or actor is great at "making the case."

When someone tells me no, you'd think I'd be immediately curious about why they're saying no. Maybe they're hung up on something small, something I could fix easily. Maybe four people in a row will make the same criticism, will give me the same reason they are saying no—and why wouldn't I want to know that? Maybe after I hear why an idea isn't winning support, like a smart politician reading the opinion polls, I'll change my mind.

But that doesn't work. You just end up reshaping an interesting, unconventional story into a different story to match the popular conception.

So when someone tells me no, almost always, that's it. I don't want them to unfurl this long, persuasive argument about why they think my idea isn't any good, or isn't right for them, or could be much better if I reconfigured it somehow.

I decline all that input because I'm worried about being persuaded out of something I really believe in. I'm worried about being persuaded into something I don't believe in—just because someone smart and persuasive is sitting in front of me, making *their* case.

If I've formed an opinion on something fundamental like a movie we should do, if I've dedicated a lot of time to it, a lot of money, a lot of curiosity, then I don't want any more information on it. I don't want you trying to "recontextualize" an artistic decision that I've made.

Thanks anyway—I don't want your critique.

Because here's another thing I know for sure.

You don't know what a good idea is.

At least, you don't know what a good idea is any more than I know what a good idea is. No one in Hollywood really knows what a good idea is before a movie hits the screens. We only know if it's a *good* idea after it's done.

That's not about success, by the way. At Imagine, we've done some movies that were successful but weren't necessarily great movies. Much more important, we've done some great movies that weren't huge box-office hits—*Rush, Get On Up, Frost/Nixon, The Doors*.

In advance, my passion for something I think is a good idea, an interesting idea, is just as valid as someone's decision that it isn't. But the certainty that something is a worthwhile idea is fragile. It requires energy and determination and optimism to keep going. I don't want other people's negativity to get inside my head, to undermine my confidence. I don't need to hear a list of criticisms—whether it's sincere or not. When you're trying to get a movie made, when you're making your case, you've spent months or years working on something, and you need to develop a kind of invulnerability if you're both going to get it made and protect it.

When I'm checking in with people I want to join us, it works something like this.

I'll send out the script and all the information—I'm the producer, Ron Howard is the director, here's the budget, here's the cast.

After a little while, I get on the phone. They'll say, "We're going to pass."

I'll say, "You're passing? Honestly? Are you *sure* you're passing? Okay, then, thank you very much. I really appreciate you reading it."

If it's something I think is really right for the person I'm talking to—if I think they're the one who's making a mistake—I might say, "You can't say no! You gotta say yes!"

But that's it. No curiosity. The wall goes up. Anti-curiosity.

Because I don't need someone casting doubt, when they've spent an hour thinking about the project, and I've spent three years thinking about it. If they're saying no, I need all my determination and confidence to grab hold of the idea and take it to the next person with the same level of passion and enthusiasm. You can't get anything done trying to absorb and neutralize everyone else's criticisms.

There have been moments when I've been a little too quick with my anti-curiosity. Ron Howard and I took Imagine Entertainment public in 1986.[3] We thought it would be an innovative way to run a creative company. But public companies are much more complicated to run than private companies—and that turns out to be particularly true in a hit-and-miss kind of business like movie and TV production. We were undercapitalized. We were uncomfortable with all the rules about public companies—what we had to reveal, what we could talk about, what we couldn't talk about. After seven years, in 1993, Ron and I bought the company back from the shareholders. Before we went public, we certainly hadn't been nearly curious enough about what being a "public" company would require of us.

When it comes to movies, there is one really memorable case

where I shouldn't have suspended my curiosity—the quirky movie *Cry-Baby* from 1990. Curiosity got me into that movie. A script came in from director John Waters. I read it. I was attracted to it.

I had just seen *Hairspray*, which Waters had written and directed, and I loved it. I thought *Cry-Baby* could either be a flop or an unexpected hit like *Grease*. I said yes. We got an incredible cast to work with John Waters—Johnny Depp as the lead (it was his big movie break), and also Willem Dafoe, Patty Hearst, Troy Donahue, Joey Heatherton, Iggy Pop, Traci Lords.

I loved working with John Waters. I loved working with Johnny Depp. But here's what I didn't do: I didn't go back and see John Waters's other movies. A couple of people told me to—before you pay for a John Waters movie, they said, go watch a bunch of John Waters movies. He's not exactly mainstream. They said to at least watch *Pink Flamingos*, which is pretty edgy, before you green-light *Cry-Baby*.

I was having none of it. I didn't want any of that hesitation in my psyche. I'd decided I was being curious enough—curious enough to see what happened with this John Waters film.

At the box office, *Cry-Baby* was a flop.

The lesson is pretty clear: I should have watched John Waters's previous movies. I should have watched *Pink Flamingos*. I didn't live with that script at all. I got excited, and I didn't want to second-guess my instincts.

So how do you know when not to be curious?

It looks harder to figure out than it really is.

Most of the time, curiosity is energizing. It motivates you. It takes you to places you haven't been before, it introduces you to people you haven't met before, it teaches you something new about people you know already.

Sometimes curiosity carries you to places that are hugely unpleasant or painful but important. It's hard to read about child abuse, it's hard to read about war, it's hard to hear about the painful experiences of people you love. But in all those kinds of cases, you have an obligation to learn, to listen, to understand.

Sometimes you have to listen to people offering criticism of you—a smart boss might have great advice about how to be more effective at work, about how to write better, or how to be more persuasive. A colleague might be able to tell you how you sabotage yourself, or undermine your work, or damage relationships you need to be nurturing.

In those instances, there's something constructive coming from the curiosity, from listening, even though the conversation itself might be unpleasant.

You know to stop being curious when your results are just the opposite of what you need—when they sap your momentum, drain your enthusiasm, corrode your confidence. When you're getting a critique but not much in the way of useful ideas, that's the moment for a pinch of anti-curiosity.

I admit that I don't know specifically where interesting ideas come from. But I know generally: they come from mixing a lot of experiences, information, and perspectives, then noticing something unusual or revealing or new. But it's not that important to know where good ideas come from. It's important to recognize what you think is an interesting idea when you see it.

That presents a problem, of course, because I just said that no one in Hollywood really knows what a good idea is until we see it out there in the world.

But I do know what I think is a good idea, an interesting idea, when I see it.

A TV series built around catching a terrorist, where the good guy is racing the clock in real time. That's an interesting idea.

A movie about how one man—one very smart and also very

strange man—came to shape the FBI for forty years, and thus shape crime fighting and America itself. That's an interesting idea.

Jim Carrey as a lawyer who can't tell a lie for twenty-four hours. That's an interesting idea.

Tom Hanks as a Harvard professor who needs to find the Holy Grail in order to clear himself of murder charges and in the process uncovers the deepest secrets of the Catholic Church. That's an interesting idea.

All these ideas worked out really well—I thought they were good ideas, we brought together a team behind each one of them, and that team made good movies and TV shows.

We've had interesting ideas that didn't work out that well. How about Russell Crowe as a washed-up 1920s boxer who makes a tremendous comeback and becomes world champion? That was the movie *Cinderella Man*, which wasn't a big hit with moviegoers. But it's a good movie.

How about a movie dramatizing David Frost's four interviews with disgraced president Richard Nixon? It also wasn't a big hit with moviegoers. But *Frost/Nixon* is a good movie—it received five Oscar nominations and five Golden Globe nominations.

You may or may not like those TV shows or movies. The important thing is that I thought they were worthwhile ideas when they came to me; I recognized them as interesting. I worked passionately to develop each of them. I didn't just think they were interesting ideas; I believed they were, and then I acted like they were interesting ideas.

So how did I know they were worthwhile?

It's a question of taste.

They were good ideas—in my opinion. But my opinion about something like a movie or a TV show isn't the same as the opinion of a person buying a ticket and a bucket of popcorn to see *Liar Liar* or *Cinderella Man*.

My "opinion" about this kind of storytelling is based on decades

of experience—listening to people talk about movie ideas, reading their pitches, reading their scripts, seeing what happens between idea and script and screen. My opinion is based on understanding, over and over, the work necessary to create movies and TV shows of quality—and trying to understand why quality sometimes matters to popularity, and why it sometimes doesn't.

My opinion is based on something people outside show business never see—all the things I say no to. Because I say no as much as anyone. The stories that we get pitched and don't make are as important a measure of taste as the ones we do. We are trying to make movies we love, as I tried to make clear in the conversation I had about the stalled movie. We're trying to make movies with a sense of good taste about them.

I do think I have good taste in movies. But it is clearly my own sense of taste about them. Steven Spielberg has good taste about movies, James Cameron has good taste about movies—but their movies look nothing like our movies.

If you have good taste, three things are true. First, you have the ability to judge the quality of something, whether it's music or art, architecture or cooking, movies or books. Second, your sense of whether something is worthwhile is individual—you bring a perspective to your judgments. And third, there is also something universal about your judgments—your taste can be understood and appreciated by people who aren't as experienced as you, whose sense of taste isn't as well developed as yours. Your good taste is educated; it has a splash of individuality about it, and also a certain breadth of appeal.

That's what taste is, in fact: an educated, experienced opinion that you can articulate and with which other people can agree or argue.

What I think is a good idea comes from applying my many years of experience—my taste—to the ideas that come my way. It's a little more complicated than that, of course—I may think something is a

good idea that isn't commercially viable; or I may pick the occasional project that's just fun, that doesn't really hit the top of the curve in terms of taste but is very entertaining.

So to find interesting ideas, to have good ideas, most of us need curiosity.

And to recognize those ideas with real confidence, you need good taste.

And to develop that sense of taste—of personal style and experienced judgment—you also need curiosity.

That's where my sense of taste comes from, in large part: curiosity—and experience.

If you've only ever heard one song, say, "Gimme Shelter" by the Rolling Stones, you can't have a well-developed sense of music taste. If your experience with art is only seeing Andy Warhol—or only seeing Andrew Wyeth—you can't have an evolved sense of taste about art.

You may say, "Hey, I really liked that song." Or "Hey, I really didn't care for those paintings by Andrew Wyeth." But that's not taste—that's opinion.

Developing a sense of taste means exposing yourself to a wide range of something—a wide range of music, a wide range of art—and not just exposing yourself, but asking questions. Why is Andy Warhol considered a great artist? What was he thinking when he did his art? What do other people think of his art—people with well-developed taste? What other art was being produced at the same time as Warhol's? What are his best pieces? Who thinks his art is great? What other artists did Warhol influence? What other parts of the culture did Warhol influence?

Obviously, it helps to like what you're paying attention to, because developing a sense of taste requires commitment. There's no point in developing a sense of taste about hip-hop music if you really don't like listening to hip-hop music; the same is true of opera.

The point of all that curiosity isn't to persuade you to have the

same opinion as anyone else about Andy Warhol. It's to give you a framework for understanding his work. You still have your own reaction—you can say, "I understand the importance of Andy Warhol, but I don't really like his art. It's not to my taste."

And the point of all that curiosity isn't to turn something fun—like music—into a chore. We all know people who are totally immersed in contemporary music. They know every new band, they know every new style, they know who produces who, they know who influences who. Music aficionados like that make great playlists. They do it precisely because they love music. Their curiosity flows so naturally that it's a passion.

Taste is opinion framed by the context of what you're judging. And taste gives you confidence in your judgment. Taste gives you confidence that you understand more than what you simply like—you understand what's good and what's not. It's taste that helps give you the judgment to assess something new. To be able to ask, and answer, the question, "Is that a good idea?"

For me, the dozens of curiosity conversations I've had are the foundation for developing a sense of taste about music, art, architecture, and about popular culture in general. They give me an informed filter for assessing what comes my way—whether it's movie ideas, or a conversation about developments in particle physics, or electronic dance music. I don't think it gives me a "better" filter—my taste is my own. But it definitely gives me a more informed filter. I'm always talking to people with deep experience—and deeply educated taste themselves—about the things I care about. That curiosity gives me confidence in my own judgments.

There's one small caveat to using curiosity to develop good taste. Not everyone gets a sense of taste about art or music or food driven by their own curiosity and energy. If you grow up with parents who care about opera, who fill the house with classical music or modern art, poetry, or fine cuisine, you may well arrive at adulthood with a very well-developed sense of taste about those things. Especially as a child, you can develop taste based on immersion. That may be the best way to develop a sense of taste, in fact, but it's not an opportunity most of us have. And it's certainly not an opportunity we get to choose.

Curiosity equips us with the skills for openhearted, open-minded exploration. That's the quality of my curiosity conversations.

Curiosity also gives us the skills to zero in on the answer to a question. That's the quality of a police detective driven to solve a murder. That's the quality of a physician determined to figure out what disease is causing a patient's set of oddly contradictory symptoms and test results.

And curiosity gives us the skills to better relate to people, and to better manage and work with them in professional settings. That's the quality of my asking questions in the office. I'm not quite having an open-ended conversation with Anna Culp or our other executives about the state of our movies in production, but I'm also not pursuing specific answers with the relentless zeal of a police detective. Those kinds of conversations are a kind of accountability curiosity— open to hearing what's going on, but asking questions with a specific purpose in mind.

I think developing a sense of taste about something—or more broadly, a sense of judgment—falls into this third quality of curiosity. It's about being curious, but with a purpose or a goal in mind. I'm not asking about the progress on our movies because I'm idly interested in how things are going. I'm doing my part to move things along with the goal of getting those movies made, made well, made on budget, made on time. I'm doing it while deferring to my colleague's judgment and autonomy, but we both know that although I'm asking questions, I'm using them to hold her and the movie itself accountable.

Taste works the same way. You take your experience and your

judgment and your preferences, and you apply them with openness but also some skepticism to whatever comes your way—ideas, songs, meals, an acting performance. You're using taste and a skeptical curiosity to ask: How good is this thing I'm being asked to consider? How enjoyable is it? Where does it fit into what I already know?

Your good taste can discover things that are thrilling. It can save you from mediocrity. But it is skeptical. Using your judgment always involves raising your eyebrow; it means starting with a question mark: How good is this thing—how interesting, how original, how high-quality—given everything else I know?

There is one more quality of curiosity that we haven't touched on yet, and that's the quality of curiosity that the astronomer and author Carl Sagan refers to in the opening quote of this chapter: the value of curiosity in managing our public life, our democracy.

Democracy requires accountability. In fact, accountability is the very point of democracy—to understand what needs to be done in the community, to discuss it, to weigh the options, to make decisions, and then to assess whether those decisions were right and hold the people who made the decisions accountable for them.

That's why we have a free press—to ask questions. That's why we have elections—to ask whether we want to retain the people who hold public office. That's why the proceedings of the House and Senate and the courts are open to all, as are the meetings of every city council, county commission, and school board in the nation. It's why we have three branches of government in the United States, in fact—to create a system of accountability among Congress, the presidency, and the courts.

In a society as complicated as ours, we often outsource that accountability. We let the press ask the questions (and then criticize the press for not asking the right questions). We let Congress ask the questions (and then criticize Congress for being either too timid or too destructive). We let activists ask the questions (and then criticize them for being too partisan).

Ultimately, the accountability has to come from the citizens. We need to be curious about how our government is functioning—whether it's the local high school or the VA health-care system, NASA's International Space Station or the finances of Social Security. What is the government supposed to be doing? Is it doing that? If not, why not? Who, in particular, is responsible—and do we have a way of getting them to do what we want, or should we fire them?

The way American government is designed assumes our curiosity. It doesn't have the skepticism itself built in—that has to come from us—but it has the *opportunity* for the skepticism built in.

Curiosity is as powerful in the public sphere as it is, for instance, at work. The very act of showing up and asking questions at a local government hearing is a vivid reminder that the government is accountable to us, and not the other way around. The questions communicate both authority and a sense of our values—whether we're standing at the lectern at the school board meeting, or raising a hand at a candidate forum, or watching the House of Representatives on C-SPAN.

The connection between the personal curiosity we've been discussing and this more public curiosity is very simple: it's the habit of asking questions, of constantly reminding ourselves of the value of asking questions and of our right to ask questions.

In fact, it's not just that democracy permits curiosity. Without curiosity, it's not democracy.

And the opposite is also true. Democracy happens to be the societal framework that gives freest rein to our curiosity in every other arena.

7

The Golden Age of Curiosity

Perhaps one day men will no longer be interested in the unknown, no longer tantalized by mystery. This is possible, but when Man loses his curiosity one feels he will have lost most of the other things that make him human.

—*Arthur C. Clarke*[1]

We were driving in the car one afternoon with the windows open. It was 1959—I was eight years old. We stopped at a traffic light, and suddenly there was a bee buzzing around, in and out of the windows. It was making me nervous. I didn't want to get stung by the bee.

I couldn't wait for the light to change, for the car to get moving again. But all of a sudden I had a question: Which moves faster—a car or a bee? Maybe the bee would be able to keep up with us, even after my mom pulled away from the intersection.

We eluded the bee that afternoon, but the question stuck with me. Which moves faster—a car or a bee? I tried to puzzle it out, but I didn't come to a satisfying answer. As an eight-year-old in 1959, I could do nothing with that question but ask a grown-up. So I did what I often did with my questions: I asked my grandmother. She was kind of my own personal Google—not quite as omniscient as the Internet seems to be, but much more understanding and encouraging.

She liked my questions even when she didn't know the answers.[2]

I've been curious for as long as I have memories of myself. I was thinking of myself as curious before I was thinking of myself as anything else. It is my first personality trait. Sixty years later, I think of myself as curious the way some people think of themselves as funny, or smart, or gregarious.

For me, being curious defines not just my personality, not just the way I think of myself; it has been the key to my survival and my success. It's how I survived my reading problems. It's how I survived a bumpy academic career. It's how I ended up in the movie business; it's how I figured out the movie business. And curiosity is the quality I think helps distinguish me in Hollywood.

I ask questions.

The questions spark interesting ideas. The questions build collaborative relationships. The questions create all kinds of connections—connections among unlikely topics, among unlikely collaborators. And the interesting ideas, the collaborative relationships, and the web of connections work together to build trust.

Curiosity isn't just a quality of my personality—it's at the heart of how I approach being alive. I think it has been the differentiator. I think it's one of the reasons people like to work with me, in a business where there are lots of producers to choose from.

Curiosity gave me the dream. It, quite literally, helped me create the life I imagined back when I was twenty-three years old. In fact, it's helped me create a life much more adventurous, interesting, and successful than I could have hoped for at age twenty-three.

Everyone gets to use curiosity to chase the things that are most important to them. That's the wonderful way that curiosity is different from intelligence or creativity or even from leadership. Some people are really smart. Some people are really creative. Some people have galvanic leadership qualities. But not everyone.

But you can be as curious as you want to be, and it doesn't matter when you start. And your curiosity can help you be smarter and more creative; it can help you be more effective and also help you be a better person.

One of the things I love about curiosity is that it is an instinct with many dualities. Curiosity has a very yin-and-yang quality about it. It's worth paying attention to those dualities, because they help us see curiosity more clearly.

For instance, you can unleash your curiosity, or it can unleash you. That is, you can decide you need to be curious about something. But once you get going, your curiosity will pull you along.

The more you limit curiosity—the more you tease people with what's coming without telling them, as the streaming shows *White Lotus* and *Succession* do so well—the more you increase their curiosity.

Likewise, you can be intensely curious about something relatively minor, and the moment you know the answer, your curiosity is satisfied. Once you know who won the $1.5 billion Mega Millions jackpot, the instinct to be curious about it deflates completely.

You can be curious about something very specific—like whether a bee or a car moves faster—curious about something to which you can get a definitive answer. That may or may not open up new questions for you (how do bees manage to fly at twenty miles per hour?). But you can also be curious about things to which you may never know the answer—physicians, psychologists, physicists, cosmologists are all researching areas where we learn more and more, and yet may never have definitive answers. That kind of curiosity can carry you through your entire life.

Curiosity requires a certain amount of bravery—the courage to reveal you don't know something, the courage to ask a question of someone. But curiosity can also give you courage. It requires confidence—just a little bit—but it repays you by building up your confidence.

Nothing unleashes curiosity in an audience like good storytelling. Nothing inspires storytelling, in turn, like the results of curiosity.

Curiosity can easily become a habit—the more you use it, the more naturally it will come to you. But you can also use curiosity actively—you can always overrule your natural pacing of asking questions and say to yourself, *This is something I need to dig into. This is something, or someone, I need to know more about.*

Curiosity looks like it's a "deconstructive" process. That seems almost obvious—by asking questions about things, you're taking them apart, you're trying to understand how they work, whether it's the engine in your Toyota Prius or the personality of your boss. But, in fact, curiosity isn't deconstructive. It's synthetic. When curiosity really captures you, it fits the pieces of the world together. You may have to learn about the parts, but when you're done, you have a picture of something you never understood before.

Curiosity is a tool of engagement with other people. But it's also the path to independence—independence of thought. Curiosity helps create collaboration, but it also helps give you autonomy.

Curiosity is wonderfully refreshing. You cannot use it up. In fact, the more curious you are today—about something specific, or in general—the more likely you are to be curious in the future. With one exception: curiosity hasn't inspired much curiosity about itself. We're curious about all kinds of things, except the concept of curiosity.

And finally, despite the proliferation of misinformation, and misleading information, we still live at an extraordinary moment—when we, as individuals, have access to more information more quickly than anyone ever has before. It is a "golden age of curiosity"—if you choose to appreciate it that way. Some places are using this to significant advantage—companies in the worlds of artificial intelligence and biotechnology are vivid, instructive examples. The energy and creativity of people pushing the boundaries, sometimes in uncomfortable ways, comes from asking questions—questions like "What's next?" and "Why can't we do it *this* way?"

And yet, curiosity remains wildly undervalued today. In the structured settings where we could be teaching people how to harness the power of curiosity—schools, universities, workplaces—it often isn't encouraged. At best, it gets lip service. In many of those settings, curiosity isn't even a topic.

But just as each of us can start using our own curiosity the moment we decide to, we can help create that golden age of curiosity in the wider culture. We can do it in some simple ways, by answering every question our own children ask and by helping them find the answers when we don't know them. We can do it, within our own power, at work in a whole range of small but invaluable ways: by asking questions ourselves; by treating questions from our colleagues with respect and seriousness; by welcoming questions from our customers and clients; by seeing those questions as opportunities, not interruptions. The point isn't to start asking a bunch of questions, rat-a-tat, like a prosecutor. The point is to gradually shift the culture—of your family, of your workplace—so we're making it safe to be curious. That's how we unleash a blossoming of curiosity and all the benefits that come with it.

Robert Hooke was a brilliant seventeenth-century English scientist who helped usher in the era of scientific inquiry—moving society away from religious explanations of how the world worked toward a scientific understanding.

Hooke was a contemporary and fierce rival of Isaac Newton; some have compared Hooke's range of interests and skills to Leonardo da Vinci's. Hooke contributed discoveries, advances, and lasting insights to physics, architecture, astronomy, paleontology, and biology. He lived from 1635 to 1703, but although he's been dead more than three hundred years, he contributed to the engineering of modern clocks, microscopes, and cars. It was Hooke, peering through a microscope at a razor-thin slice of the bark of a cork tree, who first used the word "cell" to describe the basic unit of biology he saw in the viewfinder.[3]

This range of expertise is astonishing today, in an era when so many people, even scientists, are so specialized. The kinds of discoveries and insights made by someone like Hooke are thrilling. But what is really humbling is that scientists like Hooke didn't just revolutionize how we understand the world—from the motions of the planets to the biology of our own bodies. They had to *be* revolutionaries. They were fighting contempt, mockery, and two thousand years of a power structure that set strict limits not only on how each member of society could operate, but also on what was okay to ask questions about.

As the scholar of curiosity Barbara Benedict explained when I talked to her, "One of the things that made the seventeenth- and eighteenth-century scientists really extraordinary is that they asked questions that hadn't been asked before."

Hooke, she pointed out, "looked at his own urine under the microscope. That was hugely transgressive. No one had ever thought to look at urine as a subject of scientific examination."

Benedict is a literary scholar—once the Charles A. Dana professor of English Literature at Trinity College in Connecticut—and she became captivated by curiosity because she kept coming across the word, and the idea, while studying eighteenth-century literature. "I came across the word 'curious' so often in every text I got a little irritated," Benedict said. "What does it mean when you call someone 'the curious reader'? Is that a compliment or not?"

Benedict was so intrigued by the attitudes about curiosity she kept bumping into that she wrote a cultural history of curiosity in the seventeenth and eighteenth centuries, titled simply *Curiosity*.

In fact, says Benedict, before the Renaissance, official power, the kind of power that kings and queens had, along with the organization of society, and the limits on what you could ask questions about were all the same thing. They were interwoven.

Powerful people controlled information as well as armies. Rulers controlled the story.

In that setting, curiosity was a sin. It was a transgression. It was "an outlaw impulse," as Benedict described it in her book.[4] Curiosity, including scientific curiosity, was a challenge to the power structure of society—starting with the monarch himself. It was a challenge to two millennia of "wisdom"—"I'm the king because God said I should be the king. You are a serf because God said you should be a serf"— that culminated in the American Revolution.

Curiosity—asking questions—isn't just a way of understanding the world. It's a way of changing it. The people in charge have always known that, going all the way back to the Old Testament and the myths of Greece and Rome.

In some places, curiosity is considered almost as dangerous today as it was in the late 1600s of Robert Hooke's era. The Chinese government censors the entire Internet for a nation of 1.4 billion people, three-quarters of whom are online.[5]

And everywhere, curiosity retains a little aura of challenge and impertinence.

Consider what happens when you ask someone a question.

They might respond, "That's a good question."

Or they might respond, "That's a curious question."

Often, the person who says, "That's a good question," has the answer ready—it's a good question, in part, because the person knows the answer. They may also genuinely think you've asked a good question—a question that has caused them to have a fresh thought.

The person who says, "That's a curious question," on the other hand, is feeling challenged. They either don't have an answer at hand, or they feel the question itself is somehow a challenge to their authority.

So why hasn't the Internet done more to usher in a wider golden age of curiosity?

I do think the questions we ask by typing them into an Internet search engine are a kind of curiosity. You can search the question "Which moves faster—a car or a bee?" and find a couple of helpful discussions.

But the Internet runs the risk, as Barbara Benedict puts it, of being turned into a more comprehensive version of the pope. It's simply a big version of "the machine with all the answers."

Yes, sometimes you simply need to know the GDP of Ukraine or how many ounces are in a pint. We've always had great reference books for things like that—the *World Almanac* used to be a definitive source.

Those are facts.

But here's the really important question: Does having all of human knowledge available in the palm of our hands make us more curious or less curious?

When you read about the speed of bees flying, does that inspire you to learn more about the aerodynamics of bees—or does it do the opposite? Does it satisfy you enough so you go back to Instagram?

It was Karl Marx who called religion "the opium of the people."[6] He meant that religion was designed to provide enough answers that people stopped asking questions.

We need to be careful, individually, that the Internet doesn't anesthetize us instead of inspire us.

There are two things you can't find on the Internet—just like there were two things Robert Hooke couldn't find in the Bible or in the decrees of King Charles I:

You can't search for the answer to questions that haven't been asked yet.

And you can't Google a new idea.

The Internet can only tell us what we already know.

In the course of a business meeting, people in the movie business will often say, "That's good enough."

They'll say, "That script is good enough." "That actor is good enough." "That director is good enough."

When someone says to me, "That's good enough," it never is. It means exactly the opposite. It means the person, or the script, *isn't* good enough.

I'm sure the same thing happens in every line of work.

It's such an odd expression that means exactly the opposite of what the words themselves mean. It's a way of saying, "We're going to settle here. Mediocrity will do just fine."

I'm not interested in "good enough."

I think part of my reservoir of determination comes from all those decades of curiosity conversations with people who themselves didn't settle for "good enough." Their experiences, their accomplishments, are a reminder that you cannot live by curiosity alone. To have a satisfying life (and to make valuable use of curiosity), you also have to have discipline and determination. You have to apply your own imagination to what you learn. Most important, you have to treat the people around you with respect and with grace, and curiosity can help you do that.

For me, the most valuable kind of curiosity is the kind where there isn't a specific question I'm trying to get the answer to. The most valuable kind of curiosity is the truly openhearted question—whether to a Nobel laureate or the person sitting next to you at a wedding.

And I've come to realize over time that you archive curiosity—that is, you archive the results of your curiosity; you save up the insights and the energy it gives you.

There are a couple of ways of thinking about the kind of open-ended curiosity I've been so determined to pursue since I was in my twenties. Those conversations are like a mutual fund—a long-term investment in dozens of different people, personalities, specialties, themes. Some of them will be interesting at the moment we're having the conversation, but not afterward. Some of them aren't even interesting while we're doing them. And some of them will pay off hugely in the long term—because the conversation will spark a broad interest, and a deeper exploration, by me; or because the conversation will get tucked away, and a decade later an idea or an opportunity or a script will come along and I'll understand it completely, because of a conversation I had years before.

But just like with the stock market, you don't know in advance which conversations will perform and which won't. So you just keep doing them—you invest a little bit of effort across a wide range of time, space, and people, confident that it's the right thing to do.

I also think of the conversations as an artist might. Artists are always watching for ideas, for points of view, for artifacts that might be helpful. An artist walking along the beach might find a dramatic piece of driftwood, eroded in an interesting way. The driftwood doesn't fit into any project the artist is working on right now; it's just compelling on its own. The smart artist takes the driftwood home, displays it on a shelf, and in a month or in a decade, the artist looks up, notices the driftwood again—and turns it into art.

I don't have any idea where good ideas come from, but I do know this:

The more I know about the world—the more I understand about how the world works, the more people I know, the more perspectives I have—the more likely it is that I'll have a good idea. The more likely it is that I'll understand a good idea when I hear it. The less likely it is I'll agree that something is "good enough."

When you know more, you can do more.

Curiosity is a state of mind. More specifically, it's the state of having an open mind. Curiosity is a kind of receptivity.

And best of all, there is no trick to curiosity.

You just have to ask one good question a day and listen to the answer.

Curiosity is a more exciting way to live in the world. It is, truly, the secret to living a bigger life.

PART TWO

Introduction to Part Two

On September 17, 2019, I was lucky enough to publish my second book, *Face to Face: The Art of Human Connection*, about the value, the importance, and the joy of meeting people in person—and the incredible, simple power of actually looking people in the eye while you're talking to them.

On March 12, 2020, not even six months later, COVID-19 took dramatic hold of the U.S.—Thursday, March 12, was the day all Broadway theaters went dark, the day the NCAA canceled 2020's March Madness college basketball tournament; it was the day San Francisco canceled in-person public school, the NHL suspended its season, and Major League Baseball suspended spring practice. The day before, Harvard canceled in-person classes, and Tom Hanks and Rita Wilson announced from Australia that they had caught COVID. That Thursday was the day most of us realized the world had changed dramatically—and that our own lives were about to be upended as well.

The one thing we wouldn't be doing much of: meeting each other face to face. For months and months and months, at least until the vaccines became available.

Together, with incredible speed, adaptability, and everyday sacrifice, and with a lot of help from Zoom, we figured out how to keep the world running. One thing we discovered: on Zoom, you can't actually look someone in the eye.

As I write this in the spring of 2023, the world is a very different place, and our day-to-day lives have changed again. Some things we learned to do remotely—especially some routine work meetings—we're still doing that way. Zoom turned out to be efficient and effective.

But the one thing we learned from the pandemic, more than any other, is that people want to be with each other in person. Having almost all in-person contact stripped away for more than a year showed us with incredible vividness how important being with each other is. We need it, we enjoy it, we value it, we crave it.

I'll be honest: I came to really miss the office. I missed the people, I missed the hubbub, I missed the possibility of surprise. I missed seeing how everyone was dressed and what mood everyone was in. I missed the fun. I did three thousand Zoom calls during the pandemic, and we got a lot of work done. But here's the thing: I don't remember any Zoom calls that were *fun*.

We survived on Zoom. But to read each other's energy and body language, we need to be together—to sit at the same dinner table or conference table, to look each other in the eye as we talk, as we listen, as we react. To thrive, we need to be together. And part 2 of this book is the story of how I came to understand that, well before COVID-19, and how I try to keep it in mind in every interaction I have.

In chapter 3, I talked about my childhood difficulties with reading, what was actually an undiagnosed case of dyslexia. Once I got to the University of Southern California, the stakes were raised and the pressure to do well intensified. College was an entirely different playing field, and I had to be even more resourceful to master what I wanted—and needed—to learn in order to do well out in the world after I graduated. Building on the habits I started to develop as a teenager, I became laser focused on my professors and found ways to connect with them beyond the traditional confines of the lectures. I would corner them after class and make sure I went to their office hours (my favorite) so we could discuss the material they were teaching. Being able to ask questions in an intimate environment where we could look at each other face to face brought the subject matter to life for me in new ways.

Study groups had similar benefits. In face-to-face gatherings with my peers, I learned both from what was being said and what wasn't. People became my human guidebooks and cheat sheets. I grew adept at listening to them and reading their nonverbal cues, from their expressions to their body language. I noticed that when I focused on someone, they could feel I was interested in them and were more apt to keep talking and sharing with me. During these conversations, I asked questions that made what we were learning in class more personally relevant—things like "Why do we care about this lecture on physics? How does it apply to real life?" Or I asked probing questions about their thoughts and feelings—things like "Why did you do that?" and "How did that affect you?" Sometimes we would spar, sometimes agree, but the back-and-forth exchanges were far more interesting than the one-way communication method of a lecture. Through these, I absorbed as much information as I could, nurturing my intellect and starting to expand my world. Not to mention that I enjoyed them immensely!

In my junior year, I decided to take an advanced chemistry class with some of the smartest kids in the school. After the first class, I realized that I might be in over my head. However, as the semester went on, I noticed that I was asking more insightful, more thoughtful questions than most of my classmates were. I could see the respect in my professor's eyes when I asked him what he thought were the most unsolved mysteries in chemistry, and I remember the exact moment when it occurred to me: *Maybe I'm one of the smart kids.* Amazingly, the more I connected with others, the more I got out of my education and the more confident I became. It was like I had a superpower that was just starting to emerge.

Once I recognized this skill, my life legitimately started to change for the better. I know it sounds trite, but it's true. And that pretty much explains how I got here, thinking about how these curiosity conversations have really worked—what made them so impactful. I quickly realized that it was the ability to connect with someone—to look them in the eye and signal to them that I wanted to actually listen to them and learn from them. Figuring out how to connect has probably been the most important skill I've learned in life, and I use it every day: in negotiations, on movie sets, with friends, and especially in new situations. Human connection is my antidote to living a life that would have been more defined by my learning disability. Instead, I found these skills and they've made my life so full.

What I know about connection comes from my own experience and instincts. There is compelling research, however, to back up my personal truth. Harvard researcher Dr. Robert Waldinger, for instance, has found that "people who are more socially connected to family, friends, and community are happier, healthier, and live longer than people who are less well connected." Other studies show that good relationships appear to protect our brains, helping our memories stay sharper longer. This suggests that staying connected should be just as important as exercise or a good diet when it comes to taking care of ourselves.[1]

When I read these kinds of studies and think about the profound impact the ability to connect has had on me, I can't help but worry. In today's world, it's become too easy to overlook this key ingredient to our health, happiness, and success. Everything is always go, go, go. We don't take the time to really see the people in front of us; we are not patient enough to stick with the gradual process of building meaningful relationships. Instead, the modern impulse is for quick, transactional communication. I find this to be especially true in business, where people can be more interested in "getting ahead" and "getting it done" than getting to know one another—what motivates someone else, what they care about. In fact, as we learned during the pandemic and the years afterward, getting to know one another in person is almost always the most effective path to getting anything done, both in the near term and the long run.

Technology only exacerbates the problem. Think of how often

you've seen a couple out at dinner scrolling through their Instagram feeds, both engrossed in their phones instead of each other. Or parents tapping away at their screens while their kids vie for their attention. Or a room full of executives looking at their email instead of paying attention to the person presenting. Every day we seem to take another step away from the vital practice of interacting with the people right in front of us. Now, I'm the first to acknowledge the benefits of having a mobile computer in our hands, and yes, I am known to post breakfast videos from my backyard. But the more preoccupied we become with devices and the more social media monopolizes our attention, the more we seem to be sacrificing real connections for virtual ones, and the rewards of these mediated relationships just aren't the same.

Despite the fact that we're more "connected" than ever before, isolation and loneliness are increasingly serious issues for many of us. In one study of Americans ages nineteen to thirty-two, the top 25 percent of social media users were *twice* as likely to report feeling lonely as the people using it least. Sure, loneliness existed long before the Internet and social media, not to mention the long months of lockdown in 2020, but we seem to have reached a new level of alienation. Nearly half of all Americans today say they are lonely,[2] and in the U.K. the problem was severe enough to warrant the appointment of the first "minister for loneliness."[3] I would venture to say that people today are starving for genuine relationships, a sense of belonging, and the feeling of being known and understood.

A major reason we are becoming so bad at forming connections is because we are losing the ability, the opportunity, and the desire to look others in the eye. The more we attend to our devices rather than the people in front of us and the more we send messages via text, email, and social media rather than meeting and talking face to face, the more comfortable we become looking down at our screens rather than up at one another. And the loss is huge. Research now tells us that babies who don't have sufficient eye contact are at more risk for neural and brain disorders, and that children and adults who are denied eye contact tend to have more psychological problems.[4] But I don't need these studies to tell me what I already know. All I have to do is think about how much I missed out on in elementary school, when I spent all my time trying *not* to look at my teacher.

We, of course, use many tools during face-to-face contact that help us communicate more clearly and navigate relationships. For me, however, eye contact is far and away the most critical. It's like the Wi-Fi of human connection. Just as Wi-Fi connects us to endless information on the Internet, making eye contact opens up endless possibilities. One look is enough to capture someone's attention, spark engagement, ignite attraction, and create a bridge to real connection. In addition to making me a more focused, active listener, being able to look someone in the eye puts me in a mindful state and makes me more self-aware. It gives me internal power and confidence. And that draws people in.

No one wants to open up with someone who is looking at everyone and everything else in the room. No one wants to keep sharing with someone fixated on their phone. Looking someone in the eyes with genuine interest signals to them that you are present with and for them. And that is the starting point for respect and validation. It signals that they matter. It is the jumping-off point for everything that is essential in a meaningful relationship—curiosity, trust, intimacy, empathy, and vulnerability. When we look someone in the eyes, really look at them, we are telling them, *I see you.* We are recognizing their humanity. And they, in turn, have the chance to recognize ours.

Although this might sound like it's only relevant to personal relationships, I can tell you firsthand that it makes a huge difference in *all* kinds of relationships. In fact, your ability to make eye contact can be the determining factor in whether or not you get a job, earn the trust of your coworkers, or get the green light on a project you're pitching. It can make or break your career. Yes, a thing as small as looking someone in the eye is that powerful. After all, whether or not we're at the office or in some other professional context, we're still human.

In a world where our attention is too often focused downward or elsewhere, simply lifting your eyes to meet another's gaze can be transformative. Today, whether in business or socially, I am surprised and struck when someone makes really good eye contact. When a person looks calmly into my soul and is genuinely interested in my existence, it feels unique and real. And I remember them for it. In our chaotic world of perpetual busyness and distraction, eye contact just might be the ultimate differentiator.

Try this quick experiment and you'll start to understand what I mean. For one day, put your phone away—out of sight—in every in-person meeting, at every meal, and during any conversation. Look each person you interact with in the eye. As you hold eye contact with them, focus on what they are saying. Be present and listen. Notice how your interactions change. Be aware of how it makes you feel. And watch as it makes others feel more respected, heard, seen, and valued. Chances are, they will reciprocate.

One of the best things about eye contact is that it's completely democratic. The ability to look someone in the eye doesn't require money or special equipment or membership in any elite club. It's not about who you know or what you do. With a little intention, courage, and practice, anyone can do it. That doesn't mean it's easy. It wasn't until I was well into my twenties that I was able to (almost) regularly look people in the eye and feel comfortable and calm. I'm so glad I pushed through the awkwardness to get there, though, because it has made all the difference. This simplest of behaviors—the one step of looking another person in the eye—has changed everything about how I show up in the world, how I get filled up, and how I give back.

As humans, all of us seek deep, soulful, genuine connection with other humans. It's what it means to be alive. I view every interaction in my life, even and especially the smallest—whether it be with the person standing next to me in line for coffee or disentangling their dog from mine at the park—as an invitation to connect. Throughout part 2, I'll tell you stories about how those connections have transformed my life. Without exception, all of the stories I write about have one thing in common: no matter where I was or who I was with, every connection was made possible by a face-to-face interaction and a look in the eye. Choosing to see another person is a simple, split-second decision we make multiple times, every day. I hope that reading about my personal experiences will inspire you to prioritize face-to-face encounters in your own life and encourage you to start looking up and truly *seeing* each other. Make the choice, and watch how your life starts to transform in the most profound ways.

8

Do You See Me?

What we're all striving for is authenticity, a
spirit-to-spirit connection.

—Oprah

As discussed in part 1, for more than forty years, I have been tracking
down people about whom I am curious and asking if I can sit down
with them for an hour. I have no other motive than to learn something from them that will broaden my mind and alter my understanding of the world. It's also important to me that my conversation
partner benefit as well, so I try to ask thought-provoking questions
that might ignite insights for them too. In addition, I am sure to
bring some kind of gift or some knowledge they would find useful or
interesting. For example, when I met with George W. Bush, I gave
him a baseball cap with the logo from my show *Friday Night Lights*,
which was set in Texas. When I met with Dr. Dre, I came ready to
tell him about the theme song to *Exodus*, thinking he would enjoy it
because his own music contains beautiful and spectacular melodies.

Today, as a movie and television producer, I look for people who
are experts in anything *other* than what I do, hoping to find what
moves and inspires them. I love getting to know the heartbeat of
people from all types of backgrounds—from spies and Nobel laure-
ates to athletes and tech entrepreneurs. I've been honored to meet

with artistic giants like Andy Warhol, Catherine Opie, Jeff Koons, and Mark Bradford, as well as heads of state including Barack Obama, Ronald Reagan, Margaret Thatcher, King Abdullah II bin Al Hussein of Jordan, Mohammed bin Salman, and Benjamin Netanyahu. I've picked the brain of iconic investor Warren Buffett, Spanx creator Sara Blakely, and so many others. I've enjoyed scores of curiosity conversations with interesting and accomplished strangers, some of whom I now call friends.

In one such memorable encounter, I sat in my living room with rapper-activist Sonita Alizadeh. At seventeen, Sonita wrote and recorded a rap song protesting forced marriage after learning her family intended to sell her off as a child bride for $9,000. The song went viral, and she became a hero to the many girls facing this oppressive life sentence. With lyrics like "I scream to make up for a woman's lifetime of silence," the song became an anthem in her home country of Afghanistan.[1] With long black hair and big, beaming eyes, she exudes a calm confidence considering all she has been through in her life. As a child, Sonita and her family fled from Afghanistan to Iran, to escape the oppressive rule of the Taliban. Instead, she had to scrub bathroom floors to support herself and her family while also managing to teach herself how to read and write. Listening to the radio as she cleaned, she became enamored by the music of Iranian rapper Yas as well as Eminem. In rap music she discovered an outlet for self-expression and began to write her own songs about child labor. Haunted by the memories of her many friends in Afghanistan who had disappeared one by one from the classroom to be sold off as child brides, she could no longer remain silent. Though it is illegal in Iran for women to sing or rap, and incredibly dangerous to speak out, she would hide her lyrics in her backpack. When she heard about a contest in the United States to write a song to get Afghan people to vote, she entered her song and won the $1,000 prize. She sent the money to her mother, who had moved back to Afghanistan.

Soon after, Sonita wrote a rap song called "Brides for Sale" (later retitled "Daughters for Sale") to give voice to all the children facing forced marriage. She played the video for me, sharing in a soft yet serious voice that she was just ten years old when her own mother first considered selling her to a man.

In the video, Sonita speaks out against this practice dressed in a white wedding dress, her body adorned with painted-on bruises and a bar code across her forehead. She pleads into the camera not to be sold. The video went viral with over 1.5 million views to date and earned her a full scholarship to a music school in Utah.

With her deep and compassionate eyes, Sonita told me that she does not resent her mother for trying to sell her; she understands that this was how the older generation was raised. Instead of hanging on to the past, Sonita is looking forward, trying to change tradition and shift culture through community education. Although there is a lot of suffering in the world, she says, there is also a great deal of hope when you put your voice to work for the change you want to see. Sonita's composure and emotional intelligence really struck me. She was still in high school yet spoke with the wisdom of someone far beyond her years. As I sat next to her on the couch listening to her story, I sensed a deep knowing in her.

After we finished our conversation, we made our way to the dining room to have a meal. She was staying at our home that evening, and my wife, Veronica, and I thought it would be nice to spend time getting to know her as a family. After dessert, Sonita sprung up from the table to go throw a football around the yard with my son Patrick, just like any other teenager. Our time together opened my eyes to a long-standing tradition that subjects millions of girls to a devastating life of violence and servitude. I walked into that conversation having no idea about the life experience of a girl in Afghanistan or Iran, and she gave me a bird's-eye view into the factual elements of not only what life is like—being expected to submit to a lifetime of rape and forced labor—but most important, what it feels like to live in fear and have the courage to rise from oppression. She gave me a whole new understanding of human grace, resilience, and, most of all, hope.

Another memorable conversation I had was with award-winning journalist and "flow" expert Steven Kotler. It was inspired by my experiences of flow state over the years.

I was just starting to film my surf movie *Blue Crush* on the North Shore of Oahu. Absorbing the surf culture up close, through the eyes of the locals, I found the sport to be irresistible. It was exhilarating to watch and mind-blowing to imagine that the incredibly intense waves of the North Shore are completely created by nature. I would watch surfers eagerly and fearlessly race into twenty- to fifty-foot waves and come back exhilarated. I wanted to experience it but had never tried to surf before. So it was then, at age forty, that I decided to learn. I befriended a local named Brock Little who had surfed the biggest paddle-out wave in the world. He was stoic and cool without pretention, and known to be fearless in surfing, fighting, dirt biking, and anything he took on. We immediately had chemistry. He was a natural at teaching—he knew everything about surfing and water safety—and I'm a natural-born learner. We got to work.

He taught me the very basics of how to stand up on a board as well as the physics of the ocean so I could pick the perfect wave. As my instructor and friend over the years, Brock saved my life many times when we've been out on the water. I often pushed the limits of my abilities because I felt safe with him.

As I became a better surfer, I started to experience flow state. Flow state in surfing is easier to understand when you think of these big-wave surfers like Brock, Laird Hamilton, Keala Kennelly, and Makua Rothman . . . think about any one of them navigating and waiting to intersect with a forty-foot towering wave with enough power to destroy a building, and then being able to mount their board with millisecond precision that has to all be intuited in a flow state to survive the wave. It's literally impossible to measure all the variables in that single moment. You have to be in flow state not to die.

When I would catch the right kind of wave, I became completely immersed in the moment as I stood up, super aware but no longer worrying about how to balance the board or where to position my feet. It was like slow-motion euphoria, and like nothing I had ever experienced. That fleeting fifteen seconds was so exhilarating and euphoric that I would fly to Indonesia or Hawaii to experience it as often as I could. I became increasingly curious: *Could I transport the ingredients and format of flow state into other endeavors, like playing tennis or one-on-one curiosity conversations, which feel timeless when they're good?* Since I didn't have the answers, I reached out to Steven.

We met for dinner at Giorgio's, an intimate Italian restaurant in Santa Monica, right off the Pacific Coast Highway. Steven walked in, and I immediately liked him. He gave off a fresh, almost vibrating energy. He sat down and we ordered a bottle of red wine. Conversation came easily. Steven was highly alert, so much so that he barely blinked as we spoke. He defined flow as moments of total absorption, when we are fully energized, focused, and immersed in the process of our activity and achieving optimum performance. In these moments, everything else, including space and time, seems to disappear. He was describing exactly those rare moments I felt when surfing, and more recently on the tennis court.

Steven went on to explain that "the zone" or "flow state" is one of the most desirable states of being on Earth. It's also one of the most elusive. Seekers have spent centuries trying to reproduce the experience in a consistent and reliable way, but few have succeeded. One exception is action-and-adventure athletes like surfers, skiers, and climbers who regularly take on terrifying obstacles from towering cliffs to gravity-defying waves. I was curious: *What do these athletes know that I don't? What is their "inner game"?* Steven told me that during a flow state, the brain produces a cascade of performance-enhancing chemicals, such as epinephrine and dopamine, which tighten focus and lower signal-to-noise ratios.[2]

After we finished our entrées, Steven shared that the reason he started to research flow was because he had been struck with Lyme disease. For three years, the disease had completely disabled him, leaving him bedridden and in pain. The disease was also making him extremely paranoid. He would find himself hallucinating. His short- and long-term memory were gone, and he couldn't read, write, or even recognize the color green. He said it was terrifying, that there's nothing worse than watching yourself go crazy. He was thirty years old and thought about ending his life.

One day, a friend prodded Steven to go surfing in the hope that it would lift his spirits. The activity left him so physically exhausted that he could barely get out of bed for the next two weeks. But as soon as he felt better, Steven did it again. And then again. Each time he surfed, he entered into an altered state of consciousness. He explained that this flow state flushed all the stress hormones out of his system and pumped his body full of performance enhancers. It reset his nervous system and ultimately helped cure his Lyme disease.[3] I was riveted.

For weeks following that evening at Giorgio's, I spent my early-morning time digesting YouTube videos, articles, interviews, and anything interesting I could find on flow. This led me to think about the overall concept of altered mind states, and I started reading Michael Pollan's book *How to Change Your Mind*, about the effect of psychedelics on our consciousness. I've never tried drugs, yet I was curious about what he had to say about how they can positively affect our well-being. It's not unusual for curiosity conversations to take me on these kinds of journeys of exploration, with each meeting whetting my appetite to learn more.

Every curiosity conversation is different. I always prepare for them as best I can, but what I've found is that the key to a fulfilling interaction depends on much more than showing up with a list of questions. In fact, while it's important to be prepared, it's even more important to show up with the capacity for wonderment and openness—a beginner's mind, really. Approaching these meetings with no end point in mind is what makes them *conversations* rather than rigid, agenda-driven interviews. When you enter into conversation with someone, you *must* pay attention to what they are saying if you want the exchange to go anywhere. And paying attention starts with the eyes.

The basic habit of looking other people in the eye is the starting point for *why* my curiosity conversations work and why they are so exciting. If curiosity is the engine that gets me in the room with another person and propels the conversation, eye contact is the ignition point. It is the first step in truly getting to know someone and creating a real connection.

In a curiosity conversation, looking at someone with calm, centered, interested eyes helps me focus, listen, formulate questions, and move the discussion forward. It also sends a message that is critical to the success of the conversation. It says, *I am present.* When you show someone that you are paying attention to them with your eyes, you are also communicating that you sincerely want to get to know them. You are taking the time and energy to focus on them because they matter; their knowledge, thoughts, insights, experiences are of value. There is not one person on earth, regardless of their industry, status, or passions, who doesn't crave that kind of validation, whether they admit it or not. In my experience, when you are able to give people that, they are more likely to talk openly and honestly about who they are and why they do the things they do. And often they will want to know about you too.

We've all heard the truism that love isn't a one-way street. In fact, no connection, even one made between strangers, is. Think about your own experiences at work or at home. If your daughter comes home and you tell her all about your day without asking anything about hers, the moment is likely to fall flat. The same is true if you are talking to someone who wants to tell you everything about their life but expresses no interest in yours.

A one-way soul grab never works. It has to be mutually fulfilling. The best curiosity conversations are the ones where both people are engaged, contributing, and learning from each other. We're absorbed in each other's eyes, listening, empathizing, and, sometimes, even reaching a place of vulnerability and trust. There is a give-and-take, which fosters intimacy.[4] When that happens, there is (almost) nothing like it. I often find myself thinking, *Wow, this is like being on the most fantastic date.* When I feel the chemistry of a real connection, I don't want it to end.

Although eye contact was always key to my curiosity conversations, I wasn't practicing it consciously or even aware that I was doing it in the beginning. It wasn't something I thought about and certainly wasn't an approach I'd adopted in my everyday encounters. It never even crossed my mind to do so. Until Ron Howard called me out.

In my twenties, after doing the law clerk position at Warner Bros., I knew I wanted to become a producer, and I went to work for a hot-tempered television VP named Edgar Scherick. Scherick offered me a deal I couldn't refuse: "Whatever you can sell, you can make." So, I sold a TV movie. It did really well and led to other well-received projects, including the prestigious series on the Ten Commandments I mentioned earlier. I used my success to leverage an exclusive contract with Paramount. As I said, that's where I met Ron Howard at the time he wanted to branch out from acting and direct movies, and I wanted to produce them. And so our partnership began. Together, we cofounded Imagine Entertainment, where we've been partners for the last forty years.

Even back in his twenties, Ron always had exceptional communication skills. One day, in his kind way, he shared an observation with me.

"Do you realize you seldom look other people in the eye when we're meeting with them?" Ron asked.

It was 1980, and we were sitting in my office on the same Paramount lot where we met. We had just spent time with the writers

Lowell Ganz and Babaloo Mandel, who would later go on to write *Night Shift*, *Splash*, and other movies with us. I had been multitasking, as was my habit during meetings back then. I would read something or jot down a list of what I had to do that week while others were talking. I wasn't thinking about it. It's just what I did.

In 2023, I know that multitasking when people are trying to talk to you isn't good. It's not only disrespectful, but it sucks the air out of the room. At the time, however, I didn't immediately grasp what Ron was trying to tell me.

"What do you mean?" I responded.

"Were you really listening to what Lowell and Babaloo were saying?"

"Of course," I said. "I heard every word of it."

"Maybe," Ron said, "but you weren't *looking* at them. If you don't look at them when they're talking, it hurts their feelings."

"But I heard everything," I said.

"It doesn't matter," he said. "If you don't look people in the eye when they talk, they don't feel respected."

This struck me. I distinctly remembered being on the receiving end of this sort of behavior. At the outset of my career, I'd met one of the most powerful agents in Hollywood. He never looked me in the eye; instead, he looked right through me or right past me whenever I saw him or tried to talk to him. It made me feel like a nobody because I could tell that he didn't care one bit about what I had to say. We've all had that experience, of meeting someone at a party who looks over our shoulder while they talk to us. It never feels good. But it wasn't until Ron pointed it out to me that I realized I might have sometimes been doing this myself! I couldn't help but wonder if my actions were making people feel the way I had felt with that agent.

The influence of that tip-off from Ron can be seen in *Night Shift*, the first movie we made together. The hero of *Night Shift* is Bill Blazejowski, played by Michael Keaton. Bill is a young guy who, after being fired from a series of jobs, comes up with the idea to operate a prostitution ring while working the graveyard shift at the New York City morgue. Although this particular venture wasn't one I'd undertaken, Bill's story was inspired by my early struggles with keeping down a job. Drawing on the advice from Ron, I decided to give Bill an exaggerated trait—a severe inability to maintain eye contact. Every time a new hustle popped into his head, Bill's eyes would bounce around wildly. It was clear that his mind was somewhere else, not focused on whomever he was with in that moment. He was a hustler who didn't yet know that eye contact equals respect. It was an odd characteristic for a character in a comedy. But for me personally, it was a friendly reminder to correct my own behavior.

Ron's feedback also had a direct impact on my interactions with others. From the moment he pointed out my lack of eye contact, I resolved to always look at others during meetings. As soon as I did, something magical began to happen. The meetings no longer felt plainly transactional. I felt more in sync with people than I had in the past. I was able to gain insights that I wouldn't have picked up if I had been looking away, like how much belief they had—or didn't have—in a project. People could tell I was paying attention and they felt respected. As a result, they had more respect for me and more genuine interest in what I had to say. There was a new sense of reciprocity.

If this all sounds familiar, it's because it is. It's the same thing that happens during my curiosity conversations. I naturally go into those conversations eager to learn from and about another person. That eagerness shows in my rapt gaze, and the door to connection opens up from there. It hadn't occurred to me to think about all of my face-to-face encounters this way. Now, of course, it seems like the simplest thing. Everyone wants to feel seen, heard, respected, and valued—not just the people I invite to sit down with me for a curiosity conversation. And the truth is, every person has the potential to teach us something new or show us a new way of looking at the world. All we have to do to unlock that potential is to acknowledge them through our eyes and invite them to connect.

9

Take a Chance on Connection

Staying vulnerable is a risk we have to take if we
want to experience connection.

—*Brené Brown, The Gifts of Imperfection*

Oprah Winfrey is arguably the most gifted communicator in the
world. Her empathetic eyes combined with her perceptible warmth
serve to disarm even the most closed-off interviewees, who inevitably open up and share their innermost feelings and life stories with
her. It's a phenomenon I've experienced firsthand.

I got to meet Oprah Winfrey at just the moment when I needed
to meet her. I was feeling a little low, and Oprah was exactly the kind
of warm, reflective, and honest person I needed to talk to.

It was early 2007. I had never crossed paths with Oprah, despite
all her impact on TV and the movies.

I was talking to Spike Lee, and I knew they were friends. "I want
more than anything to meet Oprah," I said to Spike. "Will you help
me?"

Spike laughed. "Just call her, man!" he said.

"I don't know her," I said. "I don't think she'll call me back."

Spike laughed again. "She knows who you are," he said. "Just call
her."

Spike gave me the push I needed. I called Oprah.

The next day, I was meeting with Jennifer Lopez. In fact, JLo was in the office singing a beautiful Spanish ballad for me.

My assistant knocked on the door, cracked it open, and said in a stage whisper, "Oprah's on the phone. It's Oprah herself."

I winced. I looked at Jennifer. I said, "JLo, it's Oprah herself. I have to talk to her. Let me take that call."

Jennifer graciously stopped singing. But she wasn't smiling.

I picked up the phone. "Oprah!" I said. "I can't begin to tell you how much I'd like to meet you. I'll go wherever you are." I explained my curiosity meetings in just a sentence.

And in that wonderfully reassuring Oprah voice, she said, "I'm happy to meet you, Brian. Of course I know who you are." And then she said something nice about one of my movies. "I'm going to be at the Hotel Bel-Air in LA in just a couple of days," she added.

And that's how I came to be sitting outside ten days later, on the morning of January 29, 2007, in the courtyard of the Hotel Bel-Air in Los Angeles, waiting to have breakfast with Oprah Winfrey.

I was feeling low because I was going through a relationship crisis. I had to make a major life choice.

Oprah came down to breakfast with her longtime best friend, Gayle King, a major talent in her own right as a journalist and television anchor. We had huevos rancheros. We talked about life, about relationships, about what is really important and how to hold on to it—not just in the moment, but in the long term.

Who better to have that kind of conversation with when you're feeling emotionally bruised and uncertain?

Oprah has that deep well of common-sense wisdom. Oprah also knows how to listen. She reminded me that life is the process itself, not the individual moments—that there's fallibility, that of course there is both happiness and unhappiness.

"I'm always trying to solve life myself," she said.

We talked for almost two hours. It became evident that Oprah had a lot of things she had to attend to. Gayle was ready—she was dressed in a business suit. Oprah, on the other hand, had to go back to her room to get ready to tackle her day. She'd come to the poolside breakfast wearing her pajamas. And that was exactly the comfort level of our conversation—as if we'd both been wearing pajamas.

That morning, somehow I trusted Oprah right away. I felt like I already *knew* her. I found myself pouring my heart out to her, divulging feelings I had never shared with anyone else. There was something about the quality of Oprah's attention, the way she leaned in and held my gaze that made me feel like she saw me and she cared about me. Not only did she play back the things I said, she had a gift for helping me synthesize and clarify my thoughts and feelings. She would say things like, "So, in other words, it sounds as though you must believe *this*, based on how you were feeling about *that* . . ." Oprah helped me understand *myself* better. Connecting with her was an incredibly powerful experience that has never left me.

Years later, when Oprah invited me on her show *Super Soul Sunday* to talk about my first book, a similar thing happened. I was used to doing press for movies and TV shows I'd produced, but the publicity tour for the book was much more personal. Because the book was about my own life experiences, talking about it made me feel vulnerable and uneasy. Now I was being asked to be the sole focus of an hour-long show about diving deep into your own soul. Oprah often does interviews for the show at her home in Montecito, and driving there, waves of anxiety washed over me.

When I arrived at my destination, the gate opened, and we pulled up the long driveway. As soon as I saw Oprah, dressed in a bright green shirt, walking across the lawn toward me, my nerves just melted away. I immediately felt comfortable and safe. I could breathe. The feeling didn't come from any words she said. It came from the way her face lit up as our eyes met in greeting. I felt understood.

In her 2013 commencement speech at Harvard University, Oprah explained her observations about human beings this way:

I have done over thirty-five thousand interviews in my career, and as soon as that camera shuts off, everyone always turns to me and inevitably, in their own way, asks this question: "Was that okay?" I heard it from President Bush. I heard it from President Obama. I've heard it from heroes and from house-wives. I've heard it from victims and perpetrators of crimes. I even heard it from Beyoncé in all her Beyoncéness . . . They all want to know one thing: Was that okay?[1]

Deep down, all of us have doubts and insecurities. We use peo-ple's eyes as a gauge to see whether we can trust them. When we find openness and attentiveness there, we are more likely to let ourselves be vulnerable and share. When we feel listened to, we feel under-stood and validated. When we feel understood and validated, we like a person. When we like a person, we trust them. And when we trust them, we're more inclined to bare our essential and authentic selves. In order to form deep and meaningful bonds that transcend small talk and cookie-cutter conversation, we have to get to this place.

A big part of the reason people open up when face to face with Oprah is because they can see sincere interest and concern in the way she looks at them. Oprah is unreservedly herself, and she makes oth-ers want to be the same in her presence. I have a tremendous admira-tion for Oprah in this regard and strive to approach others with honesty and authenticity.

I find that if I'm not pushing myself to be as true and raw as I can be when I am face to face with someone, then I'm not maximizing the moment for them or me. If I'm guarded and just skimming the surface with them, then I might as well not be there. If I'm hiding my authentic self by trying to impress or be something I'm not, then I am denying both of us the chance for a true soul-to-soul connec-tion.

Meeting another person's gaze can feel awkward, frightening, even embarrassing at times. Being "real" with another person isn't always comfortable either—many times it's not. But I have learned that if we want to form connections in our lives that actually mean something, we have to make ourselves vulnerable.

Before the proliferation of cell phones, when I would arrive early to an event or when I found myself alone with a stranger (in an elevator, say), I felt compelled to speak to them, or at least to acknowledge their presence. I think we all felt this way. But these days, we're more apt to look down at our phones, getting lost in the scroll of our social media feed or our mounting inbox, because we're not sure how to start a conversation, or whether the other person even wants to engage in a conversation with us at all.

It takes a bit of courage to take a chance on a connection. After all, our interest, attention, or gaze may not be reciprocated. And because we, as humans, are all insecure in some way, we often assume that we are the reason why: *Is it the way I look? Maybe I'm not interesting. Or important enough. Or smart enough.* But usually that's not the case.

Sometimes people just aren't in the frame of mind to want to connect. It's not the right time or circumstance. Or maybe we need to work on our technique a little more. Research suggests that the ideal length of time to hold a person's gaze if you want to form an authentic connection is seven to ten seconds (three to five if you are in a group).[2] Any longer than that can turn people off and start to feel creepy. If someone isn't responding to you, you might want to consider whether you crossed the threshold. Did your glance turn into a stare? Did you stand too close? Maybe your energy felt forced. Maybe you came across as wanting something. Next time you're in a similar situation, try to do something differently.

The other possibility, of course, is that your attempt to connect isn't catching, because the other person is awkward, shy, or insecure. Maybe they aren't comfortable being vulnerable because of the environment they grew up in or bad experiences in the past. You may never know why they are hesitant to receive your offer of a connection. But I've found that if you can push through the uncomfortableness, there's a good chance that you'll eventually get that spark that you're looking for.

When I first decided to make the film that would eventually become *8 Mile*, I knew only that I wanted to make a movie about hip-hop. I'd gotten to know some of its iconic figures—Slick Rick, Ol' Dirty Bastard, RZA, Chuck D—pretty early on, and by the time the nineties rolled around, I was fully aware that hip-hop sat at the very center of life for young people in America. One night I debated a prominent *New York Times* journalist, who insisted that hip-hop was simply an inferior, niche culture, one among many, that wouldn't last long. This seemed ridiculous to me. If history has taught us anything, it's that what is cool with the kids now will be mainstream tomorrow. It was clear to me that the dominant culture of the youth generation was on a trajectory to become *the* dominant culture. The *Times* journalist thought he was on the inside looking out, when, in fact, it was the other way around. But he was far from the only one who didn't get it.

Disconnected from what was actually happening in society, most establishment voices at that time couldn't see how important hip-hop was and wouldn't give it the respect it deserved. This frustrated me, and I wanted to change it. So I decided to make a movie that would convey the power of the hip-hop movement. A film in which hip-hop itself would be the protagonist. Instead of starting off with a story, I started with a theme and a strong point of view.

After hearing what I had in mind, Dr. Dre and Jimmy Iovine introduced me to Marshall Mathers (Eminem). I had never met him before, but I was intrigued. He'd had a hit record, but he wasn't a superstar quite yet. I was drawn to what I knew about his underdog background and to his original and groundbreaking music. Eminem's music brought together a unique combination of ingredients: the voice of the inner city; the humor and irony of his alter ego, Slim Shady; and pop culture. I thought it was brilliant.

As I mentioned in chapter 2, when Eminem came into my office, he seemed defensive at first. He greeted me with a steely-eyed, icy glare. There was no warmth at all. He sat down on my couch and did the best he could not to look at me—or connect with me on any level—for the better part of thirty minutes.

Maybe you've encountered versions of this, moments where the person you're with won't emerge, not even briefly, to accept the attention you are offering. Looking back, I recognize that he didn't have anything against me personally. He was a social introvert, which is ironically common with extremely gifted artists.

The minutes dragged on painfully. I tried everything I could to infuse the room with positive energy and make Marshall feel safe enough to let his guard down. I struggled to show him my soul and make clear my intentions. I wanted this movie to portray hip-hop in its most authentic form, and I was deeply interested in Marshall's perspective. But no matter how hard I tried to engage him in conversation, no matter how specific or inviting the questions I asked, he simply wouldn't respond. It was excruciating. Finally, he'd had enough. He heaved up off the couch.

"I'm out."

I could've just let him go. It wouldn't have been the first—or the last—time a meeting fell flat, with no connection established. But I made a split-second decision. I jumped up and made a last plea.

"C'mon." I looked him straight in the eyes and paused. Then, and I'm not sure where this came from other than desperation, I said, "Talk! Animate!"

My move could easily have backfired, or come off as too aggressive, because he looked at me, at first, like he was angry. To my surprise—and relief—however, he sat back down and started talking. He told me about where he was from and how he got his start as a rapper. The conversation lasted for almost an hour, and the story he shared with me that day essentially became *8 Mile.*

I later found out that the word "animate" derives from the Latin "anima," which means life, soul, or spirit. I could've picked any word that day with Marshall, but somehow, instinctively, I chose the one that said I was looking for his soul. And it was enough to get him to see me too.

There is no one clear path or prescription to connecting with someone. It doesn't always happen right away. Sometimes it requires patience. Other times you just have to try and break down the wall, like I did with Marshall, and see what happens. Sure, you might ruin any chance of forming a connection. But is that really worse than playing it safe and leaving with no connection made?

Marshall didn't entirely open up to me during that first meeting. But at least he was willing to stay and talk. And that was enough to lay the groundwork to gradually build a deeper connection.

Eminem and I made *8 Mile* together and he ended up winning an Oscar for best original song. In fact, "Lose Yourself" was the first hip-hop song ever to win an Oscar. My love and respect for hip-hop has only deepened over the years, showing up in my work through the series *Empire*, the scripted drama series *Wu-Tang: An American Saga*, and the documentary *Made in America* with Jay-Z. Hip-hop is now the most popular genre in the world, making a profound impact throughout the culture, from sports and technology to media and fashion; finally there is no dispute that hip-hop is *the* dominant culture of our time.

10

The "Key" to Serendipity

The beauty of a woman must be seen from in her
eyes, because that is the doorway to her heart, the
place where love resides.

—*Audrey Hepburn*

In November 2012, I ended a relationship that I had been in for a
few months. I thought I might take a break from dating for a while.
My neighbor Barbara lived a few doors down from me in Malibu
with her husband, Roy. I'd known her for over a decade. She's a confident, beautiful Italian woman who brings a certain fierceness to
everything she puts her mind to. She had seen me go through my
share of bad relationships and breakups and suggested we go out to
dinner to catch up. I was looking forward to it because Barbara
knows me so well; in fact, we often warmly greet each other with the
likes of "Hi, brother," or "Great to see you, sister!"

Along with Barbara's best friend, Max, who was visiting from
Italy, we headed to Capo, a restaurant in Santa Monica. Capo is a
coveted reservation in this beach town. I love the food there—my
favorites are the branzino cooked over a wood-burning fire and the
grilled chicken Caesar salad—and the place itself is rustic and cozy
yet elegant. We were having a good time over dinner, enjoying a
great bottle of Barolo. Just as we finished our entrées, I noticed an

incredibly attractive woman in a red dress walk in. Her wavy blond hair bounced off her shoulders as she turned her head to look at the room. I couldn't quite make out her ethnicity, just that she had an exotic look about her and a radiant life force. As luck would have it, she started heading toward our table. I couldn't take my eyes off her.

"Hi, Veronica!" Barbara called out. She stood to hug and greet her friend. Veronica's eyes seemed to twinkle as she broke into a bright smile. Then, Barbara introduced me. As a show of good manners, I popped up and shook her hand. Our eyes met for a quick moment and I instantly felt an attraction. An unexpected warmth rushed through me.

"Would you like to have a glass of wine with us?" I asked, hoping for a yes. She blinked and politely declined, saying she didn't want to interrupt our dinner.

"I just came by to get my key. Barbara and I went out last night to celebrate my birthday and I forgot it in her purse."

"We just finished dinner; you're not interrupting at all," I said. "Please, join us!"

She took the empty seat, which happened to be next to mine, and we all started talking. It was a few weeks before Christmas, so we chatted about our vacation plans. I was heading to St. Barts with some friends, and she was heading to Pennsylvania to see her family. The conversation was easy and fun, and when Veronica started laughing at a joke, I noticed her mouth. And the shape of her lips. I was so drawn to her I felt like kissing her. We had only known each other for five minutes, yet everything and everyone else in the room seemed to disappear. I was magnetized. I had never felt this way with anyone.

At the end of the evening, we walked out and stood facing each other at the valet. Her eyes were lit with an inner happiness that I've come to learn is exactly what she is all about. I immediately asked for her number and called her the very next morning. We've been to-gether ever since. (After all these years, by the way, I still don't believe that Veronica was just stopping by to get her key back from Barbara. She'll never admit it, but I would venture to say that serendipity and "planned serendipity" might be very close cousins!)

My friend Whitney Wolfe Herd is the charismatic founder and CEO of Bumble, a social network that allows people to make connections in all areas of their lives, from the romantic to the professional. Today, Veronica and I have a lot of friends who have turned to apps like Bumble in order to break out of their patterns and meet people they wouldn't cross paths with in their usual social circles. "It's pretty incredible," Whitney says, "that a swipe and a few keystrokes could possibly change the course of your entire life by leading to a powerful and inspiring human connection in the real world."

Whitney is right. I have seen long-lasting, real-life connections come out of online meetings. But however great Bumble or any other social network may be, virtual interactions can only get you so far. Swiping left or right is transactional. You can't find trust, authenticity, or intimacy using Google. And exchanging texts and emails doesn't give you a chance to really connect spirit to spirit with someone. If what you want is a meaningful relationship that goes beyond the surface, at some point you have to get to know a person face to face. Only then can you read their eyes, body language, and vibe to get clues about their character, what they're really thinking, and whether there is something special between you. This is especially true when it comes to romance.

Personally, I have found that true love always starts with the eyes. A little bit of eye contact with the right person is like a drug. It ignites all our other senses. This is what happened the first time Veronica and I locked eyes. Even though it was a brief look, it was a look that revealed a mutual curiosity. When we see curiosity in the eyes of another person, it validates us. It feels great to know that they want to know more about us, that they see something worthwhile in us. If the chemistry is there, we want to return that feeling. With our eyes—and our body language—we tell the other person that we see them too, and we also want to know more. The desire to connect encourages vulnerability. We begin to open up to each other, and as we do, we find out whether we can trust the other person. If we can, then we become even more vulnerable. We feel safe to expose what's inside—our deepest fears and secret dreams. It's a cycle that begins with eye contact and leads to the most fulfilling of connections, the kind in which you come to know another person completely and you, in turn, are known.

To this day, Veronica and I can have a whole conversation across the room from each other at a party. She can tell just from my eyes when I find something funny and I can tell when she is put off by something. Just the other night we were at a dinner party—the kind where they split up the couples to shake up the conversation. I looked over at Veronica and she widened her eyes in a certain way that she does. One of the guests was telling a very long-winded story about his political views. I had to catch myself from laughing out loud because I knew exactly what she was thinking. I could see that she was ready to jump ship and head home. Using our eyes, we share the inside joke or the story in our head. We get exactly what the other is thinking and always have a lot of laughs about it on our way home.

After all this time, I still can't take my eyes off her.

11

Together We Rise

No matter how brilliant your mind or strategy, if you're playing a solo game, you'll always lose out to a team.

—Reid Hoffman

I have long been a fan of Spike Lee's films. My appreciation of his work started with *Do the Right Thing*. I was blown away by the film's invention, politically progressive substance, and visual style, with its striking and original color palette. Right away, I wanted to work with him. But another seventeen years would pass before we partnered on a movie.

Spike and I first met in 1990 at the Oscar Nominees Luncheon, where Spike was being honored. It was relatively early in both of our careers. Though young filmmakers, we had both been nominated for Oscars in screenwriting—me for *Splash* in 1984 and him for *Do the Right Thing* then. I told him how much I admired his work and how stunned I was by *Do the Right Thing* in particular. The respect was mutual, and we expressed interest in working together. At the time, however, we couldn't find a subject that aligned for us. Spike was looking for an origin-of-hip-hop movie; I didn't have the right story for it. And so, the years passed.

In the decade after meeting Spike, I noticed that his projects in Hollywood occasionally ended in some friction. This isn't completely uncommon for gifted filmmakers with strong creative visions. Great artists are nonconformists by nature and tend to resist the homogenizing forces that are rampant in the movie business. Clashes ensue. I don't like things to end badly. That's why early on in my career, I developed a rule. There were always four or five different teams of people on a movie (directors, stars, producers, and writers would lead their respective groups). If I concluded by fact or intuition that things might end poorly for one of those leaders, it would temper my enthusiasm to work with them. So, I considered what I'd observed about Spike seriously.

Eventually, I took on some projects that he seemed interested in pursuing. One of these was *American Gangster*. Spike came in for a meeting. Sitting on the couch in my office, Spike explained his vision for *American Gangster* with exceptional clarity. His ideas were thoughtful and precise, as I'd expected they would be. However, his version didn't align with the way I had envisioned the movie.

"Let's keep trying to find something to do together," I said. I walked him out, trading the usual platitudes.

Just as the elevator arrived, Spike reached back behind him and pulled out a script. To this day, I have no idea where it came from.

"Brian," he said, "*this* is something else. This is something I'd like to do with you."

The script was *Inside Man*, which Imagine owned.

Before I could respond—just before the elevator doors closed between us—Spike reached out and grabbed my hand. For the first time that day, he looked me directly in the eyes. Anyone who knows Spike, or has ever shared eye contact with him, knows the unique character of his gaze—it is patient, deeply sincere, transparent. "I promise you," he said, "this relationship will have a good beginning and a great ending, and that this will be a fantastic experience for you." Now, how he knew to say that—I'd certainly never *told* Spike what my hesitations were—I'll never be quite sure.

Up to that moment, I'd simply meant to say good-bye. But one of my life axioms is to be open to spontaneity, so I embraced the possibility of *this* moment.

Technically speaking, *Inside Man* wasn't even available. We had already hired a director on the project. And yet, whatever I might have thought was impossible to do a second ago was instantly negated. I couldn't say yes fast enough. I hired him right on the spot.

Spike did direct *Inside Man*, and the project was one of the most positive experiences in my career, not to mention a box-office smash. Critics and audiences alike loved it.

Making movies is a tough business, which is why I prefer to work, whenever I can, with people I can connect with in an authentic way. I get excited about collaborating with someone not just because I respect their talents, but also because I sense that the perspective and intention they bring to the work will make the project better.

When I finished watching the HBO television series *The Night Of*, I knew I had to meet the lead actor, Riz Ahmed. In this haunting crime drama from writers Steve Zaillian and Richard Price, both of whom I'd worked with in the past on two of my movies (Steve as the writer of *American Gangster* and Richard as the writer of *Ransom*), Riz delivers a mesmerizing performance. I was awestruck by the transformation he was able to achieve as Nasir Khan, an American Muslim railroaded by the criminal justice system. At the start, Nasir comes off as gentle and naïve. But after he is sent to prison, he is forced to adapt to life behind bars. By the end of the story, the innocent, doe-eyed boy becomes a hard-faced, streetwise man. John Turturro, who plays Nasir's lawyer, delivers a line to the jury that sums it up perfectly: "What I see is what happens when you put a kid in Rikers and say, 'Okay, survive that while we try you for a crime you didn't commit.'" For his performance, Riz, who is British Pakistani, made history twice over, becoming the first actor of Asian descent and the first Muslim to win an Emmy in a leading role.

Sometimes I read about someone—an actor, writer, director—or see their work and reach out to them about a specific project. Other times, there is no existing project. I will set up a meeting with an artist just because their talent struck me and I want to better understand who they are and what they're passionate about. Connecting with them gives me a chance to decide whether they are someone I'd like to collaborate with in the future, and in getting to know them, I get a better sense for what kinds of projects might grab them or be a good fit. The meeting I planned to have with Riz was this second kind.

As you have probably guessed by now, I have had thousands of meetings in my life with all different people who communicate in all different ways. Some of them have been easy to get to know. Others are naturally more difficult to connect with. There are certain people who can close the door on you even when you are focused, attentive, and asking good questions; they might respond with a one-word answer or look generally uninterested. For this reason, I always try to go into meetings (and curiosity conversations) with some background about the person with whom I'm sitting down, and some knowledge of topics that might be stimulating or relevant to them.

While this type of preparation may seem forced, I see it as necessary work for nurturing a relationship. When I enter a meeting with a potential collaborator, I always assume they are wondering, *What does this person have to offer me? What can he add to the conversation? Where do our shared interests lie?* Everyone sizes someone up before going into business with them. If I am fluent in another person's areas of interest, they are more likely to feel that I understand them on some level. That feeling of *Oh my gosh, I relate to you. I get it! I feel that too!* is what often ignites the desire to collaborate—in both directions.

Before meeting with Riz, I did my homework. What I learned is that being a talented actor is just one of many things that make Riz a superstar. He has also channeled his creative and intellectual energy into tackling racial profiling, lack of diverse representation in the media, and anti-immigration rhetoric.[1] As a student at Oxford, Riz had felt like an outsider among the wealthier white crowd. He managed to break into the black-tie social circuit by starting a weekly "club" night, at which he was the MC. It became one of the most popular events at the university and kicked off Riz's music career. Today "Riz MC," as he is known to his music fans, is half of a critically acclaimed hip-hop group called the Swet Shop Boys, which uses irreverent humor and sharp satire to protest social injustices. Riz, who also advocates on behalf of Rohingya and Syrian refugee children, was named one of *Time*'s "100 Most Influential People" in 2017 and won an Oscar in 2022 for best live-action short film.

Riz chose a small, unassuming restaurant on the west side of Manhattan for our meeting. When he walked in, his distinct energy and presence was palpable. I knew right away that he would have something of substance to say. As we started to talk, I looked into his soulful eyes, and I could feel the enormous power of his humanity. Infuriated by the world's indifference to the plight of refugees, he made a passionate and cogent case for why we need to stand up for these people, who, like any of us, are just trying to survive and make a better life for themselves and their families. "We're all in this together," Riz said.

Before we even had a chance to talk about creative work, I felt connected to Riz. I was attracted to his spirit and certain that we could create something meaningful together. A project did, in fact, arise. Unfortunately, because of a competing commitment, Riz ended up having to bow out. There's no other way to put it—I was heartbroken. This wasn't the first time a project with someone didn't work out, and it wouldn't be the last, but I took this one especially hard. Riz had offered a bridge to a kind of authentic humanity and selfless purpose that isn't always easy to come by in Hollywood. I do believe in karma, the kind where good things are born from pure intentions, and have a feeling we will work together in the future.

Although it might sound counterintuitive, the best professional decisions I make tend to be the ones based on personal connections. If I trust in someone, if I am impressed and inspired by them, whether or not there's empirical evidence, then I am willing to take the chance that the other pieces will fall into place.

In the early 1980s Eddie Murphy was on fire. He made his big-screen debut in *48 Hrs.* with Nick Nolte in 1982. The following year, he appeared in *Trading Places* opposite Dan Aykroyd. And the year after that, he starred in the megahit *Beverly Hills Cop*, which in 1984 was the highest-grossing comedy of all time. I was dying to meet him.

In 1987 I got my chance. That year, Eddie was touring with his tremendously popular stand-up concert, *Raw*. (As of 2022, *Eddie Murphy Raw*, the live-audience recording, was still the number one stand-up film of all time.) Eddie invited Michael Keaton to the show, and Michael, whom I knew well from making *Night Shift* together, invited me. After the performance, we went backstage. I remember waiting a long time for Eddie to emerge. But when he did finally come out, he did it in fabulous fashion—decked out in a now-iconic purple leather suit. He was well worth the wait. Eddie had a gigantic presence and magnetic charisma. Everything about him was shocking, original, and brave. He radiated a brash confidence and, even offstage, was brilliantly funny. You couldn't help but like him.

At the time, Eddie had an exclusive producing and acting agreement with Paramount. But I got the sense that the studio and Eddie were politely fed up with each other. Eddie had lost trust in the system and felt underutilized.

Experiencing his dynamism in person that night after *Raw*, I was more excited than ever to understand who Eddie was as an artist and a person. I called Skip Brittenham, the powerful entertainment attorney who repped him (who also happens to be my neighbor and tennis partner), and asked him to arrange a meeting.

With Hollywood stars like Eddie, many people—even big directors and high-powered executives—avoid making eye contact. I wasn't going to make that mistake. Sitting across from him, I leaned in and caught his gaze. *Who*, I wanted to know, *is the real Eddie Murphy? What really matters to him?* He had a sharp antenna for disingenuous intentions. But from the look in my eye, my body language, and my tone of voice, Eddie could tell that I didn't want anything from him. He gradually opened himself up to a connection, and out of that initial sit-down, a friendship began to develop.

As we got to know each other, it became clear that Eddie and I had the same goal: to create the highest-caliber movies with the very best stories. Eddie, being a true savant across multiple art forms—comedy, music, and film—had endless ideas, and we would spend hours talking through them. One day, Eddie shared an idea for a movie that eventually became *Boomerang*.

In *Boomerang*, Eddie plays Marcus, a hotshot, cocky advertising executive with a reputation for being the ultimate player and chauvinist. At one point, he has his assistant send flowers to nine different women with a card that reads "Only thinking of you." When a company merger places him under a beautiful new boss, Jacqueline, played by Robin Givens, Marcus sets his sights on her. Marcus and Jacqueline become involved, and he quickly realizes that she is a female version of himself—noncommittal and conniving. Suddenly *he* is the subject of gossip at the office, and all the finger-pointing and snickering is about *him*. For the first time in his life, he is the one who gets played. It was a prescient idea; in the early nineties, movie and television plots were often centered around the male "player" as the person of power, and the woman as the one getting hurt. Now the tables were turned.

Our cast, which included Halle Berry, Chris Rock, Martin Lawrence, Eartha Kitt, John Witherspoon, and David Grier, was vibrant and talented. *Boomerang* was a hit and went on to become a cult classic. Over thirty years later, people still laugh about their favorite scenes and quote their favorite lines: *When I seduce you . . . if I decide to seduce you, don't worry. You'll know.*

Several years after *Boomerang*, Eddie and I made another comedy together. The movie *Bowfinger* was already underway with Steve Martin, who wrote the script and named it after his favorite bistro in Paris. Steve had created the role of lead action star, Kit Ramsey, with Keanu Reeves or Johnny Depp in mind. But I thought, *This should be*

Eddie! He would be so brilliant as Kit! I asked him to take a look. Eddie accepted the part immediately . . . and thought it would be interesting and challenging if he played two roles. Not only did he want to play Kit, but he also wanted to play a new character—Kit's look-alike, Jiff. Steve loved the idea, so we went with it.

To date, I've made five movies and a television series with Eddie that were all either creative or artistic successes, or both. None of it would have happened without an initial connection between two human beings. The most successful creative relationships—like any good relationships—start from a place of authenticity and pure intentions. This means showing up in our truth, with no ulterior motives, a genuine curiosity about the other person, and respect. When two people approach each other in this way, the outcome is almost always valuable for everyone involved. That first face to face between Eddie and me led to a deeply trusting relationship in which we see and bring out the best in one another.

These days in Hollywood, many studios, media platforms, and networks create algorithms and financial models that they hope will produce low-risk, breakout hits. As executives try to come up with a perfect formula to satisfy the audience at the lowest possible cost, story and character development can suffer and a project can quickly lose its soul. In this system, it's easy for an artist to get broken down.

For me, the most predictable path to creating a hit show is to build and nurture true and trusting relationships. With any artistic collaborator, whether the actor, the writer, the composer, or another creative, I make it my goal to get to know them as a person and to understand what they want to communicate and why. If I find I can trust in them, I give them the space, freedom, and support to express what they feel in an honest way, from the soul. This lifts up the artist and, more often than not, results in storytelling that ignites a powerful emotional response in viewers, which is the ultimate goal of any film or piece of art.

12

Trust in the Vision

Your vision will become clear only when you can look into your own heart. Who looks outside, dreams; who looks inside, awakes.

—Carl Jung

People ask me all the time how a good movie is made. What *really* happens behind the scenes? They're usually interested in the juicier parts about stars and parties, so I'm never quite sure how to answer. The truth is that movies are often much less glamorous than people think. In fact, underneath all the polish, they can be unbelievably complex and challenging to bring to fruition.

As a film and television producer, my job is to nurture a creative idea from inception all the way through to its realization on-screen. Being a producer is very much like being an entrepreneur starting from zero every time. There are no guarantees and countless obstacles. It's a risky business. For each new project, you need to build a strong case that will be attractive to everyone from funders to actors to audiences—all kinds of people with different mind-sets, different concerns, and different ideas. Needless to say, it requires *a lot* of negotiation. Given all this, there are two things that are absolutely crucial for me to see a project through successfully—a clear and compelling vision that I believe in and the ability to form strong connections with others.

The idea for a film or television show can come to me anywhere at any time. Sometimes it is rooted in something personal; sometimes it's about an overarching universal human theme. Two of my first movies—*Splash* and *Night Shift*—were very personal to me. They were therapeutic at a time when I was a single twentysomething trying to work out things in my life. My futile search for true love inspired *Splash*, a rom-com (romantic comedy) about a man falling in love with a mermaid. The idea for *Night Shift* was born out of my almost superhero-like ability to get almost any job . . . and then lose it. I thought, *What would be the worst possible job that I could find myself in?* A night shift worker at a morgue running a prostitution ring seemed like a terrible—and hilarious—answer.

Whatever the idea, I ask myself some important questions about the story at the onset: *What is at the center of the story—a concept, character, theme, mission, or deep personal passion? What thoughts or feelings do I want the story to stir up for my audience? Why would they be drawn in by it?* But perhaps the most important questions are: *Why does it exist?* and *Why does it matter to me personally?*

A Beautiful Mind tells the story of John Nash, a schizophrenic who earned a Nobel Prize in economics. As I've mentioned, I made the film to help destigmatize mental disability, or any kind of disability. It was a mission that mattered to me deeply. My son Riley, now thirty-six, has Asperger's. Back when he was in elementary school, I was watching him from the fence and saw a bunch of kids hide his lunch tray while he was getting a drink. He came back to the table and was disoriented and confused as they all laughed. It broke my heart in pieces, and I wanted to do something about it. I was determined to tell a story that would be a vehicle to create empathy and compassion for those who are different.

Author Simon Sinek, who delivered one of the most watched TED Talks of all time, says, "People don't buy what you do; they buy why you do it. And what you do simply proves what you believe."[1] Making a movie or a TV show is not a solo affair. It takes studio backing, financiers, and a whole team of committed people—writers, directors, actors, production—working together. If I don't believe in the vision, or I can't articulate it in a compelling and persuasive way, then how can I expect anyone else to believe in it or commit themselves to it? How can I attract the most talented and interesting people to the project?

Sometimes, I'll come across a script or book I love for its plot or characters, but the message or purpose of the story is not immediately apparent or compelling to me. When that's the case, I will often try to find out what the writer intended, or work on it together with the writer until I truly believe in the vision. If I don't believe in it, then I don't want to do it. Because I know that no one else will believe in it, either. They'll just go through the motions to make the movie. And it will be shitty. We've all seen those movies.

Finding people who share my vision and convincing them to come on board is only half of the equation, of course. I couldn't do either of those things effectively, let alone make a successful film, without trust. People have to trust that I am authentic and genuinely believe in the project. They need to trust that I am going to hold up my end of the bargain, and I need to trust them to do the same. We need to be able to come together, face to face, look one another in the eye, and know that we are in it together, willing to do what we have to do to see the film through. Whether or not you are able to build trusting relationships will make or break not only a movie, but pretty much any big idea that you want to bring to life. One of the most powerful examples of this from my own life is the backstory of how the movie *American Gangster* got made.

Nick Pileggi caught my eye in the early nineties. Nick was married to the late Nora Ephron, and the two of them were toasts of the town—more specifically, literary toasts of New York. Nora was a superstar screenwriter first and then became a director. Nick was a renowned journalist specializing in American crime. When he came to my attention, he had just cowritten the script for *Goodfellas*, based on his nonfiction book, *Wiseguy: Life in a Mafia Family*, and would soon pen the screenplay for *Casino*, based on his book of the same name.

I was impressed by the scope of Nick's knowledge on twentieth-century crime, and enthralled by his ability to foster rapport with so many Mafia bosses and organized crime figures. Somehow, he—a journalist, no less—had gained enough trust to earn entrée into that usually impenetrable world. So, naturally, I reached out to see whether he would have a curiosity conversation with me. He agreed and suggested we have dinner at Rao's, an Italian restaurant in Harlem that is notoriously difficult to get into.

Since it first opened in 1896, Rao's has occupied the same corner of East 114th Street and Pleasant Avenue. It wasn't until the seventies, however, when owner Frank Pellegrino took the helm, that it morphed into a true New York landmark. After Mimi Sheraton penned a glowing three-star review in the *New York Times*, the demand for reservations at Rao's went through the roof. It was more than the ten-table (technically four-table, six-booth) hangout could handle. To deal with this newfound fame, Frank came up with a novel idea—a time-share system of sorts. He assigned each of his customers a regular night—some weekly, some monthly—and a table. The original eighty-five regulars essentially "owned" their tables for the night—even if they finished dining early, the table would not be reset—and for life. When an "owner" dies, their family often inherits their table. As a result, it's nearly impossible to dine at this New York establishment. The likes of Celine Dion, President Bill Clinton, Hank Aaron, and even John Gotti had to have an "in" to dine here.

When I walked into Rao's, I felt like I had walked straight onto the set of *The Godfather*. Christmas lights (that apparently stay up all year long) hung on paneled walls along with photos of Sinatra and Frankie Valli. It was unusually bright inside, with a jukebox along the wall and a bar at one end—dark-stained, oak-paneled wood with a red leatherette pad where Nicky the Vest (so-called because of his rumored collection of over a thousand vests) held court. Far from fancy, Rao's was a homey throwback with a rack for coats near the men's room. It was a place where everyone seemed to know everyone and knew exactly what they wanted to eat. (At Rao's, you don't get a menu unless you ask for one, and asking didn't seem advisable.) I had no idea what to expect of Nick, or what he would be like, but the sense of familiarity and exclusivity of the place seemed conducive to establishing a genuine connection with him. I was happy he had chosen this spot to meet.

Just then, Nick walked in wearing a dark shirt and jacket. He was tall (about six feet), balding, and wore big, round tortoiseshell glasses. There was an intellectual quality about him and a quiet, unaffected way that was compelling to me. Immediately, I liked this guy.

We sat down at a booth, and the conversation was effortless. It turned out we had a mutual and intense interest in each other's crafts and worlds. I was eager to talk about Nick's writing and learn more about the crime world he knew so well. I knew he could feel my sincerity and interest by the way I listened and asked questions that made him think. He was an animated listener himself and responded by telling the most entertaining stories; I would reciprocate with some of my own from Hollywood. We were both intrigued by the complex characters who became leaders of organized crime, and the personalities of the enforcers, or lieutenants, beneath them.

Nick had an easy, instinctive charm—I could see why gangsters would open up to him. Even in the rare times when he raised his voice to punctuate the punch line in a story, he didn't intimidate. He spoke openly and kept eye contact. The warmth of his eyes drew me in, but not all the way. At a certain point, they were guarded. Of course, that made sense. Nick was talking about crime and the Mafia. Everything was confidential. I got the sense that this meeting was a kind of test. That he would be gauging how far he could go, how much he could say to me, whether or not he was going to continue the conversation or excuse himself. I intuited that he had very clear, inflexible values and boundaries, and I respected him for it.

Eye to eye all night, jumping from casual and funny to deep and intense conversation, we were simultaneously processing one another as the stories flowed. I felt a trust with him that I can't quite describe. I understood why it had seemed, from the moment he walked in that night, that Nick was beloved by every person in the restaurant.

With a final farewell and a genial handshake, Nick and I ended the evening agreeing to stay in touch. I could tell that it was not one of those empty "keep in touch" moments. Over an Italian family-style dinner and a bottle of Chianti, we had created a bond that, in my experience, usually takes years to form. We both thoroughly enjoyed the conversation, and each other. I knew that we would see each other again. Every year or so after that, Nick and I would get together to have coffee.

It was ten years after Rao's that Nick reached out to me with some urgency. He called me to say he had a story that he thought could be a movie. He had read the *New York* magazine article "The Return of Superfly," written by Mark Jacobson. It was the story of Frank Lucas, the biggest and most powerful heroin dealer and gangster in America during the seventies.

Raised poor in rural North Carolina, Frank moved to New York in 1946, where he saw a quick way to make money. He started robbing bars and jewelers, becoming more bold and brazen with each ensuing crime. He quickly realized that dealing dope was how real money was made on the streets. Frank started earning his stripes by going against both the Italian Mafia and the Black crime syndicate. To break up their heroin operations, he decided to go directly to the source—the poppy fields of Southeast Asia.

In a move that was both outrageous and risky, Frank flew to the Mekong Delta during the Vietnam War and made his way through the jungle to meet face to face with Luetchi Rubiwat. Rubiwat, known by the nickname 007, was a legendary Chinese drug kingpin, who controlled all the heroin in the Golden Triangle, which comprises the borders of Thailand, Burma, and Laos. Frank struck a deal with him to guarantee shipment of heroin directly into the U.S., cutting out the middlemen. And that's how he single-handedly modernized the heroin trade and ended up the head of the largest drug empire in America . . . at least for a while. Eventually Frank was busted: a forty-year federal term and thirty-year state term.[2] He was released in just a few years, though, after providing cooperation that led to over one hundred arrests.

After reading about Frank, Nick was intrigued. He secured special permission to visit him in prison and spent time getting to know him. "I know this guy ran the narcotics things," Nick told me, "but there was also a charm. He and I got to be friendly and when he got out of prison, I said to Frank, 'You are a story.' By then, he trusted me totally and I trusted him. At this point, we hadn't really sold anything yet, and he said he needed money to pay the tuition for his kid at Catholic school. It was ten thousand dollars. So, I wrote him a check for ten thousand dollars. My wife, Nora, said, 'Are you out of your mind?!'"

I was riveted and immediately asked to meet with Nick and Frank at my office in LA. Just days later, across a long, shiny oval table in our conference room, I first laid eyes on one of the most notorious gangsters in American history. You could tell he was a boss. He had a commanding presence and charismatic air about him that made his mythology almost instantly believable.

I have to admit that the idea of meeting with a ruthless drug kingpin—let alone going into business with one—was a bit nerve-racking. Frank had spent a fair amount of time in prison, most recently seven years for heroin trafficking, and though he'd never actually served time for any violent offenses, the man had admitted at least once to being a stone-cold killer, although he later denied it.[3] But my curiosity was greater than any qualms I had. My desire to learn more about Frank was insatiable. It would not let up, and I had to keep peeling back the layers to see what was there. *What is he like? Will his story hold up face to face? Can it translate well to film? Where is the redemption in his narrative?*

Once they were both seated, Frank set his sights right on me. I held his gaze with a strong, discerning look as he began to tell his story. At one point, I leaned forward and asked point-blank if he ever killed anyone. Although he didn't exactly admit to murder, he did offer up a shockingly graphic description of events that took place, including acts of disturbing violence. At the same time, he was also telling me about his devotion to his family and his deep and abiding loyalty to his mother.

It hit me that Frank was telling me his story of survival. The story of a semiliterate Black man who was able to teach himself not just how to survive, but how to be successful in the face of poverty and brutality. It was a story with a theme that was larger than the specific details of Frank's life. At the core of it was the American dream and the human capacity for resourcefulness. I knew I had to make this movie. No question. No thinking. I bought the story right there in that room.

Next we had to hammer out the terms of our agreement with Frank. Naturally, he was always after more money. Given who he was, maybe he was always going to be squeezing us a little, trying to extract as much as he could. I pointedly looked him in the eyes and directly stated, "Look, I have a very good record of getting movies made. Believing in me and believing that the movie will get made will create the most remunerative income stream to you. You'll get the option payment now, a purchase payment later, and then bonuses for performance." He signed the deal with us. And he ended up earning every single payment.

About a decade after *American Gangster* was released, Nick, who was then in his eighties, reflected on that fateful meeting, where all three of us committed to the long road ahead and got into business together: "I never had a doubt about you, Brian, ever. You're the person who truly committed to the project. I don't know what Frank would have wound up doing. By committing yourself, flying us out, Lucas began to trust me because I said, 'We're going to get this thing made as a movie.'"

Now, Nick realized that a Hollywood deal doesn't necessarily mean that a movie actually gets made, but from getting to know each other, and thanks to that first connection at Rao's, he believed in me. And I believed in him. I knew enough about Nick's values that if he believed in this story, then it was going to be good. In fact, much, much better than good. What I didn't know at the time was that I was about to embark on making the most difficult movie of my career.

With Frank on board, my next step was to find the best screenwriter in the world. Nick and I were both convinced that Steve Zaillian, who had won an Oscar for writing *Schindler's List* and had written other Oscar-nominated screenplays, was the one. Through Nick's personal friendship with Steve, I was able to make contact and convince him to read the Superfly article. He didn't immediately bite. It took him six months to really focus, and another three years of me constantly calling him, explaining the vision, and sending him research materials, to get him to commit. But—finally—he agreed to write the screenplay. And once he did, he was all in.

In order for Steve to write the most authentic and captivating script possible, I knew that he and Frank would need to get to know each other. Frank barely trusts anyone, but he did trust Nick. And since Steve and Nick are friends, it made sense to have him serve as a liaison. I hired Nick to spend a few months helping writer and subject connect with one another. Eventually, Frank became reasonably comfortable around Steve, and vice versa. Frank illuminated the shadowy gangster underworld for Steve and granted him rare insight into the power dynamics at play there. For his part, Steve, with some help from Nick, turned in a stunning script. Every word he had written was genius; all of his ideas were elevated: strikingly original and sophisticated, surpassing any of our expectations.

I now set out to create a list of master filmmakers to direct, and I started at the top: Ridley Scott. Director of *Alien*, *Blade Runner*, and *Gladiator*, Ridley agreed to read the script because Steve Zaillian wrote it, and they knew each other well. Ridley flat out turned me down. He said he liked the era in which the film was set, but he couldn't do it. I then asked a few other directors, but none of them had a great take on the movie. We continued to develop the script and after almost a year, I went back to Ridley. Once again he said no; he was still unavailable. So I finally gave in. I hired a different director.

My next challenge was convincing Steve to trim down the script. The completed screenplay he had turned in was 170 pages . . . that's 50 pages more than the maximum a script should be. Anything over 120 pages gets too expensive to make. As originally written, Steve's script would have been a $150 million movie. In the early 2000s, that was an exorbitant amount. We had to cut the script to cut costs. Steve, however, felt strongly that it should stay as it was. I held my breath and took the bloated script to the studio. The studio firmly replied, "*No way.*"

At this point, it was becoming extremely difficult to get this movie made. But once I have faith in a project, I am wholly committed to it. Regardless of any challenge to my vision, whether time, economics, scale, or relevance, I need to see it through to the end. That meant I had to get this script that I was in love with, for a movie that I deeply cared about and believed in, down to a budget that the studio would green-light. When I had exhausted all my other options, I knew that the only thing left to do was to fire the greatest and most accomplished screenwriter in modern film history. I told Steve I would have to let him go. Not surprisingly, he was upset with me, and I thought I had burned that bridge for life.

I found a writer, Terry George, who could also direct the film. He said he could cut the script down to 110 pages, which he did, and Universal Pictures (accountable to their owner, General Electric) finally gave the green light. They agreed to make the film for a budget of $80 million, just over half of the previous estimate. Unfortunately, to achieve the lower cost, we would have to remove the scenes to be shot on location in Southeast Asia, and to me, that was a deal-breaker.

Frank's trip to the Mekong Delta carried extremely high stakes. That he went so fearlessly into such a dangerous situation in a completely unknown land was critical evidence of his will, tenacity, resourcefulness, and desperation. The trip was essential to the theme of the film and the authenticity of the story. There was no way I could look Nick Pileggi in the eyes and say, "Yeah, I think it'll be great," with this pivotal part of Frank's life missing. Nick trusted me with our shared vision, and I wasn't about to break that trust. So, as difficult as it was to fathom at this point, I decided that we were going to have to go back to the drawing board. I told the studio that I could not make the film without shooting in Asia.

I needed Steve back on the movie. He understood the vision. And his work was incomparable. It took lots of apologizing and lots of pleading, especially when the studio was refusing to green-light the budget we needed, but ultimately his belief in the project prevailed. I would reestablish trust with him and together we would figure out how to pull it all off.

Around that time, I hired Antoine Fuqua, a stylish commercial director who had recently directed Denzel Washington in his Oscar-winning performance in *Training Day*. In my mind, Denzel was the only person who could play the complex and multidimensional Frank Lucas. Denzel was intrigued, and because he trusted both Antoine and me (we first met when he was up-and-coming and not yet a big star), he said yes to the part. With one caveat. A man of morality, Denzel made it a condition of his involvement that we include Frank going to prison in the film. He felt that the audience should see Frank paying the price for his brutality and criminality. Prison is also where Frank finds redemption, cooperating with the authorities to help bring about the biggest crackdown on corruption in the history of the New York City Police Department.

American Gangster was a "two-hander movie," so to speak—meaning it had two key roles. Richie Roberts was the highly principled and determined DA who ultimately brought down Frank Lucas and then, ironically, after going into private practice, was hired to be Lucas's defense counsel. From there, the two became friends. I had to get somebody just as talented as Denzel to play Richie. I approached Benicio del Toro with the role. In appearance, Benicio was not the most obvious choice (he is Puerto Rican, whereas Richie was a New York Jew), but he is such a powerful and convincing actor that I thought he was the right creative choice.

Now I was building the movie with Steve, Antoine, and two huge stars. Everything seemed to be coming together. But then, with just four weeks to go before shooting was scheduled to start, the studio suddenly fired Antoine. With $35 million already spent in preproduction, including period wardrobe and props, Universal Pictures deemed Antoine fiscally irresponsible. They didn't want to see how high the costs would go once production started. So they decided to pull the plug on the film and absorb the loss. In shock, I went right to the head of the studio, who politely said, "Brian, we adore you, but don't say the words 'American' or 'Gangster' to us ever again."

That night, the pain of the shutdown really hit me. I loved everything about this movie—the era, the music, Frank's ingenuity, the universal theme of surviving and succeeding against all odds. I loved that it was simultaneously a gangster movie *and* a movie about the American dream. Grappling with the reality that it might not get made was tough. But the following morning, I got in the shower and said to myself, *I've already been deeply affected by this story. I believe in this film. Steve and Nick believe in this film, and they are counting on me to get it made. Today, I'm going to restart* American Gangster. *I don't care what the studio says. I'm going to find the people I need and convince them.* I had no idea how I'd do it, but I knew I could. Twenty years before, I had been persistent enough to make *Splash*, an impossible mermaid movie. I wasn't about to drop this movie easily.

Three weeks later, I was serendipitously at a Hollywood party where Ridley Scott happened to be as well. I saw him across the room and immediately beelined over to him. This time I stopped, took a breath, and focused my eyes directly on his. "Ridley, I know you've said no on *American Gangster* several times in the past, but please, would you take another read?" To my surprise, he said okay. The way he looked at me made me think it might be different this time. I was so hopeful I started to meditate on it. It was all I could think about. *When is Ridley going to call?*

Within the week, he called. He said, "I'll do it. I'll make the movie. Do you think your friend Denzel will come back?"

I said, "One hundred percent." Of course, I didn't know, but I had to say so—and I had to believe he would. Everything was on the line. I immediately went to meet with Denzel. He respected Ridley's work and had had a great experience working with his late brother, Tony Scott. Most important, he still believed in the vision for the movie.

Denzel was back, but I still had to get somebody to play Richie Roberts, as Benicio had committed to another movie. Who else had his creative force? While making *A Beautiful Mind* with Russell Crowe, we developed a relationship of strong mutual respect. I knew he would be incredible as Richie. But how to convince him was another story. The role of Richie Roberts in *American Gangster* wasn't nearly as remarkable as the lead in *A Beautiful Mind* or *Gladiator*.

Russell and I met up to discuss the part. Having already read the script, he looked at me intently and he said, "The character is undeveloped; it's not there right now." I wasn't surprised; not only brilliant and well-read, Russell is also extremely street-smart. I knew him to be vigilant in pushing to make a better movie. I looked back at him and said with conviction, "We'll get it there. I'll dedicate myself to getting it there. Trust me—I'll use all my time and energy and resources to make it happen with you, and to fulfill this promise."

I shared my vision and belief in the story and told Russell that Steve Zaillian would work with him to create dialogue and a character that he could personally believe in. I was asking Russell to take a huge risk in committing to a movie before the character was acceptable to him. The fact that he took it was a testament to the trust that he had in me, trust that I had started to build during our first project together. Now Denzel and Russell, two of the most respected actors in the industry, were on board for the leading male roles.

Just when I thought we were actually ready to shoot, we hit yet another snag. The studio has a green-light committee that approves a film's budget, and it's a one-time event, no negotiation. They had approved the new iteration of *American Gangster* for $112 million— but Ridley Scott kept insisting it would cost $120 million. We had come this far, so I wasn't about to let a small percentage in the budget derail the movie.

I invited Ridley to my office, and when this strong, fearless, uncompromising director (he is known as "the General" for a reason) sat down on the L-shaped couch, instead of sitting catty-corner to him on the couch, which is what I would ordinarily do, I sat on the coffee table directly in front of him. With our knees touching, I looked at him and said, "Ridley, please listen to me. The studio's green-light committee will only allow us to start if we agree to the $112 million." This time, I was able to get through to him, and he agreed. We were finally in business!

(Ironically the movie cost $120 million in the end. After agreeing to the original $112 million, Ridley later gave the studio the option for additional shots. They wanted those shots in the movie and so agreed to the higher budget. Funny how these things work out sometimes.)

Since we were filming in Manhattan, I decided to relocate my entire family to New York for one year, new schools and all. I've produced almost one hundred movies, possibly more, and I've never done that for a project; I knew I could better control films by *not* doing that. But this was a project where I had a pact with five people who were important to me—Nick, Steve, Ridley, Denzel, and Russell—and I was going to honor that pact. Being present in New York would serve as a reminder of the commitment we had all made to *American Gangster.*

Making it in Hollywood is like flying a Cessna through the fog. You often can't see where you are, but you have to keep going if you want to maybe arrive safely someday. Being a producer is far from a straightforward art or science. There were a million reasons why *American Gangster* should never have seen the light of day. But it did get made. In fact, it received many nominations and awards and went on to become one of the top-grossing gangster movies of all time.

I am convinced that the reason *American Gangster* exists is human connection. I never would have met Frank Lucas had it not been for that agenda-free dinner at Rao's with my now long-standing friend Nick Pileggi. And Frank would never have trusted me or Steve to tell his story if he hadn't first established trust with Nick. I am sure I would not have been able to get Ridley to direct had it not been for the goodwill we had developed prior to any movie and the trust he had in Steve as a scriptwriter. Denzel would not have been attracted to the project had he not had trust in me and Antoine. And so on. Through trust in each other and a tenacious belief in a shared vision, we brought *American Gangster* to life despite every challenge that came our way.

In some ways, there is nothing comparable to making a movie. But in other ways, I think it's like any other big undertaking. If the principal of a school wants to roll out a new student-leadership program, they must sell their vision to the students and teachers whose collaboration is imperative. A product manager for a new app must be able to articulate the product vision with passion and conviction, and then work cross-functionally with developers, finance, marketing, and sales to deliver it. A restaurant owner can only execute a new concept once they understand the story they want to tell.

Whatever business you're in, getting from idea to reality usually takes a group effort. And the best efforts are made when the group trusts in the vision and in each other.

13

What Do Your Eyes Say?

> You are responsible for the energy that you create for yourself, and you're responsible for the energy that you bring to others.
>
> —*Oprah*

Hierarchy is alive and well in Hollywood. The creator, executive producer, or showrunner (essentially, the lead writer) of a program is the most powerful and valued person in the television ecosystem. In the movies, it's the creative producer, or producer, who nurtures the idea to life and has the most decision-making power. In either business, you *start* at the bottom of the food chain—in the mail room, fetching coffee on set, or like I did, driving papers all over town for signatures. Even if you have insane writing talent, rarely can you just break into the industry. You have to work your way up and be willing to put in the time. More often than not, making a name for yourself takes patience, persistence, luck, and a clear understanding of who is in charge.

Despite this rigid power structure, there are those individuals lower down the ladder who seem uniquely capable of getting Hollywood to pay attention. They're not the producer, director, or top executive in the room, but somehow they are able to signal that what they say matters. Some will say ego plays a big part in it. But I believe that eye contact is the real key. A big display of ego easily comes across as arrogance or pretension and can put people off. In contrast, the right kind of eye contact can be magnetic, a powerful source of attraction. It is essential for asserting presence, projecting confidence, showing your humanity, and connecting with others—all qualities that in my observation make a person stand out as unique and worth my attention.

Julie Oh is a talented young executive—now on her own—who brought exactly these characteristics when she pitched me an idea during her almost five years at Imagine. Her pitches were always impassioned and crisply delivered. She communicated her resolve about a project with confident, unflinching eyes and kept her gaze on me throughout our conversation, so that she could see whether she was reaching me. If I was fidgeting or look confused or unconvinced, she would pause to ask whether I had a question or comment. When we encounter someone like Julie, who has (or appears to have) confidence, we're naturally attracted to their energy and want to hear what they have to say.

Many people that I've met in the highest positions of power have mastered eye contact so distinctly and skillfully that I absolutely believe it has helped them achieve their status. Leadership isn't always about strength, position, or circumstances. Being a great leader starts with looking people in the eye. After all, if you can't connect with people, you can't convince people of your beliefs. If you can't convince people of your beliefs, they won't follow you. If they won't follow you, you can't become a leader. Eye contact matters.

In 2005 I went to the White House to premiere the movie *Cinderella Man*. While I'd been to the White House before, this was my first encounter with President George W. Bush. I had no idea what to expect. He'd always presented as likable, with easy, Texan sensibility and style, but I didn't know what this would amount to in person. Would he be friendly or obligatorily polite? Would my conversation with him just be pro forma, like with other politicians I've met or know of?

The presidents I'd met to date had certainly impressed me. Bill Clinton, for example, really is as charismatic in person as his reputation suggests. He has a way of making you feel singled out even in a crowd. When I met him, I was struck by the sheer intensity of how he seemed to focus on just me. He looks straight at you, zeroing in on you with his eyes, making you feel the full weight of his interest in you and you alone. It's like being hypnotized. Even if you wanted to resist it, you wouldn't stand a chance.

Barack Obama, whom I first encountered in his office in Washington, DC, on the very same day I was to meet George W. Bush, had a completely different way about him. At the time, being a junior senator from Illinois, he was far from the height of his achievements. As the person who was ninety-ninth in seniority as a member of the minority party, he had the smallest office, situated farthest from the Senate floor. Still, you could feel the energy, purpose, and intensity in his eyes. Even though his office was the most crowded one I'd ever seen—it was jam-packed with his constituents, people spilling out into the hallway, carrying manila envelopes or bags of groceries—Obama seemed fully present for our conversation, completely engaged in a way that seemed almost, but not quite, relaxed. I could feel a certain deliberate edge. Not quite a calculation—he wasn't sizing me up—but rather a slight and subtle caution, perhaps just the natural outgrowth of his status as a politician.

So here I was at the White House to meet with George W. Bush. When we shook hands, I was stunned by how warm and inviting his eyes were. They were completely with mine, not rushing away. He was president of the United States, which meant he was incredibly busy. Yet his eyes signaled to me that he was fully present in the moment, patiently waiting to hear what I had to say. He came across as refreshing and completely unpretentious. He wasn't drilling into me or weighing my importance. He wasn't fishing for anything or trying to serve an agenda. He was just . . . with me, in a way that was altogether genuine.

Since he has a deep love for Texas, we talked about *Friday Night Lights*, which I filmed in Odessa, Texas. I shared what I had learned about that culture and he shared what it was like to grow up in it. As we talked, Bush maneuvered himself to my side so that we were standing shoulder to shoulder. Every time I would reposition myself to face him, he would immediately walk around to stand next to me again. Then he'd gingerly nudge up against me in a way that said, *Brian, it's all good*. He didn't do it to avoid looking at me—in fact, he turned his head in order to maintain eye contact. I got the impression that literally standing shoulder to shoulder was a way for him to connect in a more egalitarian way, even though he was the president.

Though we might think of making eye contact as a discipline or a good habit—one that we can all learn—not everyone's eyes communicate in the same way. Each of us has our own style that uniquely identifies us. Almost like a fingerprint. The indelible mark of who you are. Clinton, Obama, and George W. Bush were all leaders of the free world, but they each have their own way of applying eye contact. In each case, how they look at you tells you something about who they are or who they want to be as individuals and in relationship to others.

When people look you in the eyes, they almost instantly decide whether they want to hear what you have to say, whether they trust you to be their leader, or whether they want to know you better. So it's worth reflecting on what your eyes are saying. Are they conveying what you want to convey? If you're warm and welcoming, do your eyes convey that? Does it take more time for people to get to know you because your eyes say something different than you intend? If you're not sure what your eyes are communicating, ask a family member or good friend how you come across. Then practice and adjust until the message you're sending with your eyes reflects who you are, who you want to be, and how you want to show up in the world.

We were deep into casting on my television series *Empire*—a show full of drama, conflict, bling, and very catchy music—and looking for "Cookie." Cookie Lyon is the outspoken wife of the show's protagonist, Lucious Lyon, a former drug dealer turned hip-hop titan. The storyline of *Empire* goes like this. After seventeen years in prison for taking the fall for her husband, Cookie gets released. She will stop at nothing to claim her half of their multimillion-dollar recording empire—an empire that Lucious had built in her absence using $400,000 from the drugs she sold before her conviction. Meanwhile, all three of their sons are vying for the position as head of the company, so they wage war for control of Empire (think William Shakespeare's *King Lear* in the world of hip-hop).

As the family matriarch, Cookie is a complex character who shatters the stereotype of what a Black female ex-convict should be like. She is a take-no-prisoners hustler but an immensely stylish one, with faith, humanity, and at times, deep compassion. She's a fierce, intelligent, loving force of nature. A charmer who is flawed. When casting for her role, we looked for someone who could embody all these things. We wanted someone who had the strength and footing to challenge Lucious but who would also possess a smart and bold femininity that audiences weren't accustomed to seeing. Just minutes into Taraji Henson's audition, we knew that she *was* Cookie. We immediately offered her the role.

I didn't meet Taraji in person, though. Not right away, and not for a while. I saw some of the first dailies—the unedited, raw footage—from the pilot, and simply from that I could feel the truth and potency of her presence. Her wide and sultry dark eyes were ablaze with force and intensity one minute, gentle and concerned the next. Cookie is always on the move, creating some kind of drama or situation, jumping from one show-stopping scene to the next with complete ease. Her energy has an explosive quality that is completely addictive to watch. Her "no filter" mouth says exactly what she wants, leaving zero room for misunderstanding. In the pilot episode, Cookie emerges from jail dressed in an eye-popping leopard ensemble and struts into the Empire record label offices. She belts out, "I'm here to get what's mine." She doesn't need to prove her worth; she demands the respect of everyone around her. When she swaggers into a room, you *feel* her. If you've seen *Empire*, you know exactly what I mean. Taraji embodies Cookie like no one else could.

Draped in fabulous furs and drenched in attitude, Taraji brought Cookie to life in a way that was much bigger than the character was written. Bursting out of the confines of the show, she was alive in social media, and celebrated on magazine covers, blogs, and talk shows. Women admired her: she's loud, savvy, wise, humorous, extremely blunt, unapologetic—and a feminist. I mean, what's not to love? *Vibe* magazine described her as "fierce, caring and extremely powerful. Her wardrobe is filled with fur, animal prints, gold and sparkles. After only one premiere show, women are asking how to look like Cookie."[1] Cookie had permeated the culture.

A few months after the show debuted, Taraji and I were able to find time to get together. I was excited and curious about what she would be like in person. It's rare to meet an actor whose style and persona off-screen much resemble their style and persona on-screen. Taraji is an exception to the rule. As soon as I saw her walk into the room, I knew immediately that she *is* as big of a presence in real life as her character is on the show. Maybe even more so. She radiates a kind of compelling energy that attracts your attention.

"I'm Brian," I think I said. Honestly, I don't know what I said. She has an unmistakable fearlessness in her eye that nearly took me off-balance. I caught myself by quickly referring to a technique in my head that helps me regain composure. I have a few of these techniques, and in this situation, I thought of a rubber band snapping my wrist. This visualization jolts me back to the immediate present moment (I've used it when meeting powerful politicians and heads of state too). It allowed me to regain my footing so we could continue our conversation.

Taraji is whipsmart, creative, and gregarious, a straight-talker who, like Cookie, doesn't hesitate to tell you what she really thinks. I don't see her as someone who ever vacillates. And I found her immensely witty; she's quick to the joke and fun. We were able to establish a real connection that day, one that has since evolved into the great relationship we have now, one grounded in mutual trust and respect.

14

It's Universal

That's what storytellers do. We restore order with
imagination. We instill hope again and again.

—*Walt Disney*

"Tell me a story!" It's something we have all said or heard from our
kids at some point in our lives. Stories are as old as the rock drawings
of the cavemen and as modern as movies like *Black Panther* and the
Star Wars franchise, which use cutting-edge CGI (computer-
generated imagery) to create new worlds. Stories make life infinitely
more interesting. Through them, we can pretend to be someone else
or escape to someplace far away. We can even do the impossible, like
fall in love with a mermaid or travel through time. Stories contain
lessons that open up our hearts and minds. They confer plausibility
on everything from faith and science to love.[1] In stories, we find
meaning.

As human beings, we are social creatures, and one of the most
powerful tools of connection we have is a well-told story. Stories not
only give us a reason to interact and engage with others, but they are
also how we learn about ourselves, others, and their experiences of the
world. We share stories wherever we go, when running into a friend
on the street or gathered around the dinner table. We remember sto-

ries, and they tie us together. It gives me a deep sense of fulfillment when people tell me how much a story in one of my films or books resonated with them and made them feel validated or not alone.

Of course, there is also a flip side to this. Stories are subjective. There are many ways to tell the same story and infinite stories to be told. Not everyone is moved by the same stories, and not every story speaks to every person. This is one of the biggest challenges that the movie business, the television business, and any other business that trades in stories has—because the corporations financing media content (meaning TV, films, videos, music, and the like that are directed at the consumer), like most companies, are risk-averse.

The paradoxical result of this conflict is that these story-driven industries are some of the toughest to break into for a storyteller with an original, creative vision. Which leads me to my point: if you want to make a living as a storyteller in Hollywood, you *must* learn the art of the pitch. And that art is all about making connections. None of my movies or shows would have seen the light of day if I hadn't been able to successfully pitch them.

The story or pitch meeting is a ritual that every writer, from the gazillion-dollar screenwriter to the lowly essayist, will sooner or later experience. Here's how it works. You come up with a movie or television idea and go in and pitch it to different studios or potential buyers in order to get funding or distribution. It's a cutthroat environment. Studios sometimes hear thirty to forty pitches per day and select, at most, one or two. I am very familiar with the process. Even today, I continue to pitch stories I believe in. Alongside all my successes, I have endured countless rejections over the years.

When I wanted to make *Splash*, I was turned down once, then twice, then so many times thereafter that I literally stopped keeping track. As I mentioned in chapter 4, *no one* wanted a mermaid movie. I walked out of literally hundreds of meetings where the executives not only said no but seemed to go out of their way to humiliate me by pointing out how stupid the premise was. Illustrating the defini-tion of "insanity" to a tee, I kept on pitching it basically the same way—it was a mermaid movie—expecting a different outcome.

Then one day I had a conversation with a friend that changed everything. He asked me how I came up with the idea of a mermaid falling in love with an average, hardworking guy from Long Island. I told him that *Splash* was inspired by my personal search for love in Los Angeles, a place where everything—including relationships—seemed superficial. I started to fantasize about what my dream girl would be like . . . *What if she were kind and generous? How would she look at me? What would it feel like?* Then I thought about how we would meet and what would make her unattainable. (Giving her a mermaid tail seemed like a sufficiently large obstacle.)

As I was talking, I stopped dead in my tracks. Suddenly I under-stood what I had been doing wrong in pitch after pitch—I had been trying to sell the studio execs on a story. But stories, as I've explained, are subjective. Anyone can argue against a specific story for any rea-son. It's much harder to turn down a universal theme, an experience, or feeling that almost every human being can relate to. With crystal clarity, I realized that I needed to reframe *Splash*.

My next pitch was with Disney. I went in and did everything dif-ferently. Rather than starting off by saying it was a story about a man who falls in love with a mermaid, I pitched it as a story about the universal search for love. Hasn't every person at some point felt that finding love was more elusive than meeting a mermaid? Would any one of the execs in the room dare to insist that love doesn't matter? I spoke with a conviction of personal experience that every other per-son in the room could relate to on some level. The studio finally bought *Splash*. Audiences loved it and I received my first Oscar nom-ination for cowriting the screenplay.

Now when I pitch a movie or television project, I always begin with an inarguable, universal theme, something that is essential to the human experience. My protagonists have goals that we all, as a species, want and root for—things like love, family unity, self-respect, and survival against the odds. Here are some examples.

Genius is a scripted docudrama series on National Geographic that dramatizes the stories of the world's most recognized thinkers and innovators. The first season of the show focused on Albert Einstein. Ostensibly, we were telling the specific story of a single person—a rebellious young man, an unexceptional student, and an unemployed father who unlocks the mysteries of the atom and the universe. But the pitch starts with the theme at the heart of the story: the struggle for self-realization and the courage to challenge established thinking.

Parenthood, a television series that tells the story of three generations of one family—the Bravermans—living in Berkeley, California, is really about the complexities and idiosyncrasies that exist within all our families. We all look across the street thinking the family over there is perfect, but what we come to realize is that none of them are. Similarly, while *Arrested Development* focuses on the dysfunctional Bluth family, it too is ultimately a celebration of love within families. However imperfect they may be, we want to see them stay together! Why? It makes us feel happy and secure.

I am convinced that this approach to pitches—looking for the common human thread in the story and opening with that—accounts in large part for my ability to "sell" my ideas in an ultra-competitive, high-stakes business that is generally wary of outside-the-box thinking. A universal theme increases the opportunity for the viewer to connect and relate to the narrative and is, therefore, the central ingredient in creating a transcendent event that brings the viewer to a heightened emotional state. That's what the best movies do, and when it happens, it inherently reduces the risk for the investor.

When you give the person you're pitching a theme that they can relate to and believe in, they will feel more connected to the story. But it is also absolutely crucial that they feel connected to you, the person doing the pitching. Over my many years of doing this, I've learned that it starts with being attentive and plugged in from the moment you arrive in the room. Rather than walk in reciting your opening in your head or tapping away at your phone, enter the room open and eager to establish a relationship.

Most meetings begin with a few minutes of small talk, but we've all been in that awkward situation where a few minutes threatens to continue on for eternity. The person leading the meeting doesn't know when or how to switch gears, and you can see the other people becoming increasingly impatient. Try to get ahead of that impatience. Don't be afraid to take the reins of the conversation. You don't want to waste any more time than is necessary. In fact, I always ask, in a light and casual way, when the people I'm meeting with need to be out of there.

Even before you start to speak, let your eyes initiate the pitch. Be sure to direct your pitch *to* someone by catching their gaze. If you are pitching to more than one person, as is often the case, look at each person in turn. If you focus only on the most senior person in the room, others are likely to disengage. Given that the person in charge will usually ask for the opinions of the others in the room after you leave, keeping everyone engaged is highly advisable.

We've all had that excruciating experience when the people we're speaking to avoid our eye contact, glance down at their phones, or appear to glaze over. If you are attentive to your audience throughout the pitch, you will pick up on the signs that you are losing them early enough to reel them back in. This might require tightening up your story to focus on the highlights, or disrupting the moment with a quick, personal example—"For instance, yesterday I was talking with my daughter and she said a similar thing happened with her and her friends . . ."

Be aware that different people will react to your pitch in different ways and at different times. Their eyes, their body language (nodding, smiling, laughing), and their words ("That's so true!") will tell you whether it is sticking and with whom. More important, these signals will tell you when what you're saying is reaching their hearts as well as their heads.

Reading the audience throughout my pitch, I work to build excitement and momentum. When I can tell that everyone "gets it," I wrap up quickly. I always want to leave them wanting more. I don't try to force a decision on the spot or wade into logistics unless they take it in that direction themselves. If I already have other buyers interested in that show or movie, I simply say, "Let me know as soon as possible." Then I'm out.

I remember a pitch meeting a few years ago with a decision maker whom I respect but find very hard to read. His demeanor is almost stoic, and he rarely offers a word to help you unlock what he's thinking. From the start of the meeting, I was uncomfortable. The room was dead quiet and the energy was completely flat. There was no buzz to tap into or build on. How was I supposed to whip up excitement for the project under these circumstances? There was only one way to find out.

I cast off any doubts and inhibitions I was feeling and flew into an impassioned case. I gave it everything, delivering my pitch authentically and with conviction. By the end, I felt confident that I had connected with everyone in the room—almost everyone, that is. I walked out of the room that day still uncertain as to whether I had forged a connection with the one person whose decision mattered most. True to form, he wore one of the best poker faces in the business throughout the pitch.

To my surprise, later that night, I received a rare call from the decision maker. He wanted to tell me how much my story had affected him. By tapping into my own passion for the project, I had managed to connect with this person whom I'd only ever known to be dispassionate. Hearing that my pitch had reached him on such a profound level felt really good. Whatever he decided about the series, I still felt that I had succeeded. Life is about people, and when I feel like I'm connecting with someone I deeply respect, it matters as much as, or more than, selling a project. I find it deeply satisfying.

15

In the Public Eye

Courage is what it takes to stand up and speak; courage is
also what it means to sit down and listen.

—*Winston Churchill*

All of us have heard this question hurled at us at some point: *What
are you looking at?* The fact is, not everyone wants to be looked at, or
looked at by a certain person, or looked at in a certain way.

Back in my school days, when I didn't yet understand my learning
disability, I was extremely self-conscious. It wasn't just my teachers
that I didn't want looking at me. I didn't want *anyone* looking at me.
If I thought I felt someone's eyes on me or caught them glancing in
my direction, I would get defensive and lash out. This led to a fair
number of altercations, earning me a reputation as someone who
didn't turn down a brawl.

Consequently, it seemed like there was always someone who
wanted to pick a fight with me. When I was fourteen, it was a tough
kid from Texas—Jack Jones—who challenged me in the middle of
the cafeteria, right in front of everyone (usually the custom was to
meet out by the handball courts, where at least the audience would
be a little smaller).

"Let's do it right now, man," he said, standing up.

As the other students turned to looked at me, I felt the heat rising up through my body. I didn't want to fight Jack. But I didn't feel like I had a choice either. If I backed down, the others might think of me as a coward. If I didn't, chances were high I'd get my ass kicked.

"All right," I said. "Let's go." And indeed, I got my ass kicked.

Now that I'm an adult, I know that when we worry about what other people think, we are giving up our own power and that sometimes *not* giving in to insult or antagonism is the best way to convey our strength. I've also been able to shed the self-consciousness that plagued me as a kid, which is fortunate, given that I now have a career that puts me at the center of attention nearly every day.

Today, whether I'm leading a pitch, speaking at a conference, on the set of one of my movies, or appearing on camera myself, I'm regularly in the spotlight with all eyes on me. There is one thing that has allowed me to find comfort there and even, most of the time, enjoy it: establishing intimacy with the audience through connection. But how do you create intimacy—a feeling much more easily achieved face to face—with an audience of dozens, hundreds, or even thousands of people?

Back in 2002, I was at the Oscar Nominees Luncheon at the Beverly Hilton Hotel alongside Will Smith. Will had been nominated for his performance in Michael Mann's film *Ali*, and Ron Howard and I had both been nominated for *A Beautiful Mind* (Ron for best director and both of us for best picture). The luncheon was a strange event: It was designed to be informal and relaxed. In reality, it felt more uncomfortable than the awards themselves.

You might imagine a ballroom full of Hollywood insiders who all know one another flitting from conversation to conversation with ease, swapping compliments and accolades, and generally having a good time. But the opposite is true. Many of us know each other by reputation only, and it's more than a bit intimidating to have the eyes of your most respected peers on you. Add in the unspoken awareness of competition (we are, after all, there competing for the same awards!), and it's no day at the beach. I was a little nervous just being at the luncheon, so I couldn't help but be impressed when Will Smith spontaneously stood up and addressed the room.

"Hey!" he said with a huge smile. "Isn't this a blast?! Aren't we all excited to be here?! It's great to see everybody!"

In that moment, one person single-handedly changed the entire dynamic of the room. By recognizing our shared uneasiness, Will connected with me and everyone else at the luncheon who thought they were alone in their discomfort. As Will spoke, we laughed and clapped away the tension. By the time he sat back down, the mood was lighter. Everyone had loosened up. More than Will's words—truthfully, I don't even remember most of what he said—it was his outgoing nature and carefree manner that made the difference. He was effervescent, the embodiment of ease and self-assurance. (You never would have known that he was the underdog that year, with *A Beautiful Mind* and *Training Day* favored to win over his own film.)

Now, you might be thinking, *Well, he's Will Smith. Of course he was charming and confident.* But I know lots of celebrities—many more than you'd think—who also appear to be sure of themselves yet who are shy and uncomfortable when it comes to speaking in public or before a large audience. I have no idea how Will was feeling internally in that moment, whether he was uncertain or anxious. What I do know is there are few who would have taken the risk that Will did. It took courage to attempt to connect not just with a single person, but with a whole room full of people, not knowing whether or not they would be receptive.

When I have to speak in public, I remember how Will carried himself at that lunch and the way it transformed the mood in the room. We all know someone like that, I think: not necessarily someone famous, but someone who, for whatever reason, seems to have easy access to the most relaxed, least-rehearsed parts of themselves. As you prepare for a speech or presentation, it can be helpful to visualize that person. You might even picture them *while* you are speaking. In your mind's eye, see how they stand, how they move, how they make you feel when they look at you. As you imagine them, don't imitate them, but try to internalize their presence and make it your own.

In 1996, our movie *Apollo 13* had been nominated for an Academy Award for best picture. In the weeks leading up to the awards ceremony, I'd been assured by many people that it was the odds-on favorite to win, and so while I won't say I "expected" to win, I certainly felt we had a good chance. Just in case, I'd taken my time to write a well-considered acceptance speech.

As I sat in the theater on the evening of the Oscars, I felt overwhelmed. Although it wasn't the first time I had been there, I was still affected by the knowledge that I was surrounded by nearly every important person in the business and part of a live broadcast that would be watched by a good thirty-five million viewers around the world. That's a lot of eyes. My pulse was definitely elevated.

I tried to stay calm, but when the time came to announce best picture—always the last award of the evening—I was on the edge of my seat, vibrating with nervousness. *Is this it? Are we going to win the Oscar?* Sidney Poitier, always a tremendously elegant and deliberate speaker with extraordinarily sharp enunciation, would read the winner. My anxiety was at an all-time high.

"And the Oscar for best picture is presented to . . ." Sidney opened the envelope. I clearly saw his mouth shape itself into a B. Since the producer is the one who goes up to accept the award for best picture, I immediately leapt to the conclusion that he was starting to say my name. *Brian*, I thought. *Presented to Brian Grazer!* I jumped excitedly out of my seat and actually started walking toward the stage.

"Braveheart!"

I stopped dead in my tracks. I tried to sneak back to my seat unnoticed—walking backward in slow motion—but of course, people were cocking their heads back to look at me. A few rows away, the head of a major studio looked at me and held his thumb and index finger to his forehead in the shape of an L, the universal symbol for "loser." I was mortified! I collapsed back into my seat and sunk way down. It felt like the world was closing in on me.

I was on the aisle. Ron, who directed *Apollo 13*, was sitting next to me; and next to him was Jim Lovell, the astronaut played by Tom Hanks in the movie. Suddenly I felt Jim grab my arm. He leaned across Ron and looked me in the eye.

"It's okay," he said. "I never made it to the moon either!" It was a gracious thing to say, and it made me feel better. It grounded me.

Years later I was up for another Oscar. That night things were a little different. Even though the odds—again—seemed to favor *A Beautiful Mind*, I didn't want to take anything for granted. I had a list of names in my pocket—people to thank if we did win—and some light talking points, but not much more. I guess I didn't want to jinx anything by being too prepared.

The awards finally rolled around to best picture, and Tom Hanks walked out to present. There I was again on pins and needles. But this time I didn't move a muscle. The live camera flashes on each nominee as they're announced, so I kept a calm face—well, as calm as I possibly could. Tom opened the envelope. And then he said, "The Oscar goes to *A Beautiful Mind*, Brian Grazer and Ron Howard, the producers!" With adrenaline pumping through my body and everyone cheering, I got up and took a few steps. Russell Crowe hugged me and whispered a few encouraging words.

I may not have looked like it as I climbed up to the stage, but I was actually shaking. I wanted to give everyone who contributed to the movie some love, so I pulled the little piece of paper from my pocket and looked at it. But as we all now know, reading is not my strength! I couldn't focus. Anxious thoughts ping-ponged through my head. *What if I trip over my words, or speak too long and get cut off by the music?*

At that moment, I looked up and scanned the crowd. My eyes found five actresses sitting in the front row: Angelina Jolie, Nicole Kidman, Renée Zellweger, Julia Roberts, and Sandra Bullock. I suppose that sounds like an imposing quintet—five women of astonishing talent, accomplishment, and beauty—but as it happened, I knew all of them. And by looking at each of them in turn, I was able to regain some degree of control. Just as Jim Lovell had in my less-triumphant moment, these formidable women—who also happened to be my friends and peers—were there to lend support. As I struggled to keep my list of names on my paper in order, I could see them rooting for me. Their eyes said, *You can do it*. I broke off from my planned speech and made an off-the-cuff remark.

"I am *so* nervous," I confessed to the sea of people in front of me. "I know it's imperceptible."

It certainly wasn't. The audience laughed and the room opened up. It broke the ice for me completely. If I hadn't been able to connect with those familiar faces in the front row, who knows how things might have gone?

That night, I used a trick that has served me well in countless other public-speaking situations. I narrowed my focus from a giant group to an individual (or individuals in this case). That allowed me to establish an intimate connection under circumstances that were anything but. And that connection was my lifeline. This approach might sound simple, and my experience might seem a little rarified—not everyone has the terrifying good fortune to have to speak on live television—but the principle is the same no matter who you are or where you are speaking, be it at a sales meeting or at a birthday party.

A few years ago, Veronica and I asked our son Patrick, who was then fourteen, to introduce us at the World of Children Awards, where we were being honored. Now, Patrick is a pretty poised kid, and it wouldn't have been obvious to most people, but as his parents, we could tell he was nervous about it. This would be his first time speaking in front of a crowd, and it wasn't going to be a small one.

On the night of the event, we were all sitting at a table up front. It was the entire family, including his aunt and uncle and many of our friends. I noticed that the ink on Patrick's note cards had been smudged by his sweaty palms. Then I heard him whisper to Veronica. He wanted to know whether he could quietly practice his introduction with her one last time. So sitting there at the table, they blocked out their surroundings and got focused. Veronica reminded Patrick to speak slowly, to take natural pauses, and most important, to look up and connect with the audience. She told him to find our faces in the crowd and he would feel us rooting for him.

The time came and Patrick walked up to the podium. Seeing him look so poised in my light gray suit and favorite skinny black tie, I started to tear up. Veronica and I watched him take a deep breath and scan the front row for us. As soon as we locked eyes, he felt safe and started to speak.

"I'm so glad that my dad and Veronica asked me to come up and say flattering things about them . . . in front of three hundred people!"

The audience laughed, and Patrick burst into a big smile. He continued to speak slowly and surely, pausing, looking up, and smiling. He was a natural!

Sometimes you have to speak in front of an audience where the kind of personal connection I found at the Oscars and Patrick found at the dinner isn't available. In those cases, the next best thing is to *forge* a connection with someone in the audience. You might, for example, focus on the person directly in front of you and imagine you're speaking only to them. Or you might challenge yourself to find a way to get the attention of a particular individual in the group.

A few years ago I was invited to speak at the Microsoft CEO Summit outside of Seattle. The audience would include other speakers, among them Jeff Bezos, founder and then CEO of Amazon; Warren Buffett; Muhtar Kent, then CEO of Coca-Cola; Rex Tillerson, then CEO of ExxonMobil and former secretary of state; and

Bill Gates himself. These were the business equivalents of the Holly-wood elite I had been face to face with at the Academy Awards. And once again I found myself a little jittery. To make matters worse, be-fore I went onstage to speak, I was warned by someone that Gates would be sitting in the front row. He had a habit, I was told, of checking his phone during these speeches. So even though he would be following along with my speech, it would appear that he wasn't paying attention to me. I shouldn't be offended; it's just how it was.

The gauntlet had been thrown down. If Gates was so hard to en-gage, I was determined to engage him. But how would I do it?

As it happened, Gates was up right before me. In his speech, he mentioned that there were portions of the world where a dominant part of the population still contracts polio. Well, I seized upon this piece of information. Jonas Salk, who developed the first polio vac-cine, was one of my childhood heroes, and meeting him had been one of the most important encounters of my life. Onstage with Arianna Huffington, founder and CEO of Thrive Global and founder of the *Huffington Post*, interviewing me, I decided to tell the story.

"Bill," I began, "you mentioned polio, and I have to tell you, Jonas Salk was a hero of mine ..."

That got his attention. He looked up and I caught his eyes. Even though I was on a large stage talking to a large audience, it was as if I were talking directly with Gates.

The story went like this: When I first started my curiosity con-versations, as I related in chapter 5, Salk was among a short list of people with whom I had a fervent desire to talk. I was a nobody at the time, and he was one of the most famous medical researchers in the world. But I was persistent, and eventually his assistant told me I could maybe meet Salk for a moment—nothing more—after he gave a talk at the Beverly Hills Hotel.

I was overcome with excitement and scared that I would miss my chance—that I would be late, get lost, or wouldn't be able to find the room. So, even though I wasn't feeling well when I woke up, I arrived at the hotel two hours early. When I saw my childhood hero across the lobby, I began walking to meet him. With every step toward him, my panic grew. I moved closer and closer until I was finally face to face with him. Then, right as I was about to shake his hand, I threw up. I nearly fainted!

Dr. Salk knelt down beside me to see what he could do—he was, after all, a medical doctor. He cradled the back of my head and signaled the waiter for a glass of orange juice to stabilize my blood sugar. He may have been the man who cured polio, but he behaved as a regular doctor in that moment. He looked in my eyes—and, however out of it I was, I managed to look back. We became friends and remained so until the day he died.

As I told this story, I made sure to keep my eyes on Gates. I couldn't help but notice that he didn't look down at his phone once.

16

Listen Up!

When you talk, you are only repeating what you already
know. But if you listen, you may learn something new.

—*Dalai Lama*

I was set to have lunch with my old friend Jimmy Iovine. Jimmy and
I have known each other for many, many years; in fact, we produced
the movie *8 Mile* together. Jimmy is the co-creator of Beats head-
phones with Dr. Dre, but his career actually began as a recording
engineer for John Lennon. He went on to found Interscope Records,
where he signed U2, Tupac, Lady Gaga, Gwen Stefani, Eminem,
50 Cent, and countless other recording artists. Jimmy is an icon in
the industry. He's the type of guy who's very connected to the culture
and seems to have a vivid and original insight on just about everything. He and I are close, so we get together whenever we can, and
our conversations are always juicy and interesting.

One day we made plans to go to The Palm—a power-lunch spot
in Beverly Hills owned by my friend Bruce Bozzi—and had decided
to invite Mark Wahlberg as well. I've known Mark, too, for a long
time—I offered him his first leading role as an actor in a film I produced called *Fear*. He started his career as a recording artist with
Jimmy at Interscope—so we all knew each other. It was shaping up
to be a fun afternoon.

The morning of our lunch, I was sitting at the kitchen table when my phone rang. It was David Geffen. David is a legend, unprecedented in his successes in multiple artistic arenas—music, film, *and* Broadway.

"Brian, what are you doing?" David said. "Would you like to have lunch today?"

I've known David the longest of all—more than forty years. When Ron Howard and I produced our first film together, *Night Shift*, David had offered a powerful moment of validation when he stood up at a packed screening with the entire executive team and both chairmen of Warner Bros. in attendance and declared that he loved the movie. This single act gave both the film and my early career a tremendous amount of propulsion.

"I'm having lunch with Jimmy and Mark Wahlberg," I said. "You want to join us?" David and Jimmy are also close friends.

"Sure," David said. "That sounds great."

A few minutes later, I got a text from Jimmy.

Bono is coming.

Unlike the other guys coming to lunch, Bono wasn't someone I knew well, so I was excited for the chance to spend some time with him.

One o'clock rolled around, and David, Jimmy, and I arrived at The Palm first. We were seated at a cozy booth—my favorite one, actually. Then Mark and Bono arrived and squeezed in with us.

The booth was designed for four people, so we were packed in tight. Our legs were even touching. This immediately made the gathering more intimate than it would have been at a big table where everyone was spaced out. It was a setup conducive to conversation and connection. I liked that.

Often, when I am spending time with really interesting people, I feel compelled to reciprocate. That's my habit when approaching curiosity conversations: to not only take but give back right away with a story or gift of information. On this day, I decided on a different approach. Rather than dive headfirst into conversation, I concentrated on giving my full attention to the guys I was with. I wasn't mute, but I also didn't feel the need to return every story with a story.

I was especially interested in what Bono had to say. He is, after all, one of the most talented rock stars in the world, not to mention a dedicated humanitarian, whose work has touched millions of people living in extreme poverty and with HIV/AIDS. There was so much I wanted to ask him: *What is his unique view on the world? What's most meaningful to him? What's top of mind for him right now?* But I didn't want to disrupt his flow. So I limited my questions to a couple and focused on conveying my desire to know more through my eyes.

Although I knew some about Bono's work in Africa and around the globe, hearing him talk about it firsthand gave me a new and deeper understanding of its enormous scale. *Wow*, I thought to myself, *this guy is working on a higher purpose at a higher level with all these governments to help alleviate poverty and AIDS.* I was impressed and moved. Even more than that, I was inspired.

Through my movies and work with nonprofits, I had long been doing purposeful work. But listening to Bono stirred up all kinds of new ideas about how I could use my own position, talents, and resources to effect positive change in the world. In fact, that lunch was one of the things that helped inspire my latest initiative—a global content accelerator, called Imagine Impact.

The way Impact works is that thousands of writers from all over the world apply to participate in a boot camp of sorts, modeled after the famed Y Combinator start-up accelerator in Silicon Valley that made seed investments in Dropbox, Airbnb, Reddit, DoorDash, and many others. The twenty-five or so people chosen for Impact receive hands-on mentorship from the brightest and most accomplished creators in the industry. Once they have gotten their projects to the finish line, they are then given the opportunity to pitch them to Hollywood buyers. Godwin Jabangwe, a talented writer from Zimbabwe who had twelve dollars in his bank account, had been selected for the first Impact class. He pitched his animated family adventure musical called *Tunga*, and a four-way bidding war ensued. Netflix won and bought it for $350,000. The musical was inspired by the mythology of the Shona culture of Zimbabwe, a culture Godwin was raised in as a child. It tells the tale of a young African girl named Tunga, who, after the death of her father, learns from her elders how to save her village from drought by summoning rain.[1] Impact not only gives writers like Godwin a chance to build careers in an industry that is notoriously difficult to break into but also gives global audiences the chance to hear from new and important voices that we might otherwise miss out on.

I woke up that morning with just an easy lunch on my calendar. I could never have predicted where it would lead or what it would inspire.

Sometimes we need to participate equally in a conversation to make a meaningful connection. But not always. Listening can be just as powerful as talking, if not more, when it comes to establishing a bond with another person. When we are talking with someone, we often spend more time thinking about what we are going to say rather than paying attention to what's being said. Stephen Covey, the legendary author of *The 7 Habits of Highly Effective People*, said, "Most people don't listen with the intent to understand; they listen with the intent to reply."[2] People feel valued when they are listened to, which fosters feelings of trust and respect. In return, when you give someone your full, undivided attention and show them that you want to hear more . . . they will usually give you more. This is especially useful to remember when you are entering a conversation that you are unprepared for or want to connect with someone whose base of knowledge is different from yours. We become wiser and more knowledgeable when we are willing to really pay attention. Good listeners give themselves opportunities to understand other people's viewpoints and widen their own. Not to mention, it's a differentiator; great listeners are not so common!

In 2004, Ron Howard and I purchased the film rights to the book *The Da Vinci Code*. Right around that time, I took my daughter Sage to see Prince in concert. He was playing a small, private show at a (now-closed) venue called Club Black in Lower Manhattan, and I thought it would be fun for the two of us to see him together. I'd met Prince once before, just briefly. I was doubtful that he'd know who I was, let alone remember me.

Once Sage and I had passed the bouncers, we filed into the club, where Prince was standing at the door, greeting people. We were in line in front of various celebrities he seemed almost sure to know, people I imagined he would want to talk to. I expected we'd slip by with a cursory hello, but to my astonishment he actually did remember me.

"Brian, hi," he said. "It's nice to see you."

Like any father would be, I suppose, I was proud in that moment. I wanted to impress Sage, and, well, what could be more impressive than this? I wanted to hold Prince's attention, to prolong the moment a bit, so I held his gaze. It worked.

"What are you working on?" he asked.

I told him that I'd just optioned *The Da Vinci Code*. Why not? It was a famous book, a huge bestseller.

"Really?" he said. "Oh my God, that's amazing. I loved *The Da Vinci Code!*"

Now, it might have slipped my mind at the time—or maybe I hadn't known this before—but Prince was famously religious. He was, in fact, a devout Jehovah's Witness. *The Da Vinci Code* is steeped in alternative theories of religious history about things like the Merovingian kings of France and a marital relationship between Jesus and Mary Magdalene. I'd read the book before optioning the rights, so I knew a little bit about these theories, but I hadn't studied them in any depth. Prince, on the other hand, appeared to be an expert on all of it.

"Have you read *The Templar Revelation*?" he asked me. "Or *The Woman with the Alabaster Jar*?"

Had I read them? I'd never heard of them. I felt a little like a high school student who'd just been hit by a quiz he hadn't studied for. I didn't want to make a fool of myself, but I wasn't going to lie either.

"I haven't," I admitted.

The longer I could keep the conversation alive, I thought, the more memorable it would be for my daughter. So I gave Prince the only thing I had to offer at this point: my attention.

I kept my eyes focused on his and said, "Tell me about them."

I didn't know anything about Pierre Plantard (a French draftsman whose theories about the Merovingians have been disproven) or the other topics Prince was speaking about with such mastery. Yet I was able to hold the connection. With nothing more than my eyes and a few sporadic words of agreement, like "fascinating" and "tell me more," I kept Prince engaged and the conversation going. Behind me I could feel people getting impatient. I didn't care. Sage and I still talk about that epic night when one of the greatest artists of all time spent almost ten minutes bonding with me over conspiracy theories!

17

Adapt or Die

> Empty your mind, be formless. Shapeless, like water. If you
> put water into a cup, it becomes the cup. You put water into
> a bottle and it becomes the bottle. You put it in a teapot, it
> becomes the teapot. Now, water can flow or it can crash. Be
> water, my friend.
>
> —*Bruce Lee*

Maybe you swore off texting and driving but couldn't resist that one
last text that caused you to swerve, barely missing another car.
Maybe you missed the opportunity to meet a new romantic interest
because you were in the corner watching the game instead of mingling at your friend's party. Or maybe you've had the embarrassing
experience of being called on to answer a big question at a meeting
when you were lost in thought about plans for the weekend. If any
of these has happened to you, hopefully you bounced back easily.
The point is, it's easy to make missteps, have accidents, or miss opportunities when we're distracted. When it comes to communication, if we are not paying attention to the people around us—or face
to face with us—we are more likely to miss out on key information,
misunderstand intentions, and lose opportunities to gain or keep
trust and respect.

If we want to have the kind of communication that leads to

meaningful connections, it is essential that we stay alert and fully focused. For me, eye contact is key to being present. When I am engaged with my eyes, my mind is less likely to wander. If a conversation
is falling flat—which does happen—and my mind starts to think
about Jon & Vinny's arugula pizza, refocusing my eyes on the person
I'm with pulls me back into the moment and centers me.

The Roman emperor Marcus Aurelius, sometimes called "the
Philosopher," was known for his ability to focus and avoid distraction. Aurelius advised that the best way to concentrate is to imagine
the task at hand to be the last thing you'll ever do. None of us wants
our last living act to be sloppy or less than meaningful. Aurelius also
believed that a simple mantra could bring focus, so you might want
to think about creating your own personal one. Whatever mantra you
pick, saying it to yourself before meeting someone, before a speech,
or before an important project will help prime your mind to keep
distraction at bay.

In a conversation, there's a constant flow of information—
nonverbal information—that we can only glean from reading a person's eyes, expressions, and body language. So, when I am giving
someone my fullest attention, I am able to absorb all sorts of data
that otherwise would have been unavailable to me. Looking into
someone's eyes, I can get a better feel for their emotional state. I can
tell when their eyes light up that they are excited about what I am
asking or interested in what I am saying. I can tell when they start to
shift their eyes away from mine that they are uncomfortable with
where things are going or are losing interest. All of these cues help
me navigate the conversation and connect.

When I am fully attuned, I'm more likely to recognize and seize
opportunities when they arise, whether it's a chance to engage someone new or deepen a relationship with someone I already know.
Likewise, the more attentive I am to the person in front of me, the
better I'll be able to react and respond when the conversation begins
to take an unexpected turn or the nature of the connection we are

forming begins to change. This happens more frequently than you might expect. Over breakfast, a partner shares that he hasn't been happy in the relationship for a while. During a run-of-the-mill meeting, a coworker you barely know reveals that you've always been her trusted mentor.

Here is one of those situations I remember clearly.

After watching *The Man Who Would Be King*, John Huston's film based on Rudyard Kipling's fantastic adventure story, I became curious about the ultrasecret society of Freemasons; all three of the main characters—Kipling, played by Christopher Plummer; a traveling stranger, played by Michael Caine; and Daniel Dravot, played by Sean Connery—belong to this mysterious brotherhood that was rumored to be a managerial elite that controls the world.[1] I wanted to know more.

Many different orders and levels of Freemasonry exist, with the highest order called the 33rd degree of the Scottish Rite.[2] I was eager to meet the two men—a father and son—who were the regional heads of the organization in the western United States for a curiosity conversation. It took some effort, including a number of letters and phone calls to their office explaining my intentions, before they eventually consented to meet me.

On the agreed-upon meeting date, two older, dignified but unnoteworthy-looking gentlemen arrived at my office. The man I understood to be the father was approximately eighty, and his son seemed close to sixty. They spoke with heavy Lithuanian accents. Dressed in their ties and checked suits, they appeared elegant in a pre–World War II way. On the street, I might have mistaken them for jewelers or merchants from a diamond district. Both men were gentle and unassuming in their manner.

I had anticipated that my guests might approach me with skepticism and be on their guard. They were members of a secret society, after all! To my surprise, that was not the case at all. I found them to be congenial and seemingly at ease with me. At the time, if I had had to guess why, I probably would have said that after thoroughly vetting me, maybe they figured I may have something valuable to share and that at the very least, I wasn't a threat to them.

We all sat down on the couch in my office and started to talk. I was honored to be with them and ready to absorb anything they were willing to share. The father proudly explained that Freemasonry (also called "Masonry") is the world's first and largest fraternity, based on the belief that each man can make a difference in the world. To this day, the order is (almost) exclusively male, and its ostensible purpose is to make "better men out of good men."[3] He went on to explain that they believe there's more to life than pleasure or money, and that they strive to live with honor, integrity, and philanthropic values. Intrigued, I asked how the organization got started.

The son jumped in and said that Freemasonry goes back some seven hundred years, with its roots in the medieval fraternities of stoneworkers.[4] Masons were very prominent in early American life—revolutionaries Alexander Hamilton and Paul Revere were members, as were presidents George Washington and Andrew Jackson. In fact, at least fourteen American presidents, including Harry Truman and Gerald Ford, have been Masons,[5] which blew me away. Never having joined a fraternity in college myself, I was fascinated by the idea of these historical luminaries devoting themselves to a shared philosophy and a code of conduct so shrouded in mystery that most people didn't even know it existed. The time flew by as father and son answered my many questions, sometimes in great detail, other times more opaquely (they weren't sharing *everything*).

After a good hour, the father turned to me and said, "Brian, would you ever consider joining us, becoming a member of the Masons?" In that moment, the meeting, which had started as a curiosity conversation, turned into something quite different—a proposal. My eyes opened wide in surprise, as though I had just been given an unexpected compliment. I didn't have to say a word. The look in my eyes and a slight tilt of the head communicated my receptivity to the idea.

He continued, "Well, we've talked about it. And we feel you are an excellent candidate. We just have one question we would like to ask you."

"What's that?" I said. Although I was trying to play it cool, I was super excited. I couldn't believe that they wanted me to be a member of their secret society!

"We need to know if there is any way in which you would ever betray us."

I was a bit startled. It was a powerful question with historical resonance. There is a reason why the Freemasons' membership process includes something called "the third degree" (yes, that's where the phrase comes from).[6] The Masons are no strangers to treachery and have been the subject of their fair share of conspiracy theories. They have been persecuted under various Communist regimes and were directly targeted by the Nazis.[7] It's estimated that somewhere between 80,000 and 200,000 were killed in the Holocaust.[8]

I immediately recognized a shift in the tone of our conversation. Where before, the exchange had been free-flowing and convivial, now it took on a gravity that required a more measured response. When the Masons asked if I would ever betray them, they were not asking lightly. Nor was this a mere formality. It was absolutely critical for them to know my answer, and my answer would have to be 100 percent sincere.

My mind was racing at lightning speed. I wondered whether I *could* betray them and what that would even look like. I was certain I would never overtly violate their trust, but the Masons have a very strict standard of conduct and an elite reputation to protect.[9] What if I messed up inadvertently? *It is* maybe *possible*, I thought, *that I could do something that they would* perceive *to be a violation of their code.* After all, I'm a pretty spontaneous guy who likes his humor and fair share of creature comforts.

As I considered the situation, I glanced at the two men. In their eyes I found trust and kindness. Getting to know them over the past hour, I felt that they were gentlemen of character. They had given me their full attention, looking at me intently throughout our conversation. They were also impeccable listeners, who expressed appreciation for the recurring themes of human courage and empowerment in my work. In short, they had treated me with the utmost respect. I wanted to reciprocate that and honor the connection we had made. Even though I was flattered and tempted by the invitation to join their very exclusive organization, I *knew* what I had to say. In my heart I knew that my interest in the group wasn't fully aligned with their greater purpose. Or *my* greater purpose.

"I'm sorry," I responded. "But I can't do it."

The father looked at me with surprise. He was clearly taken aback by my decision. The son looked at the father to gauge how he should react, and he followed suit. It wasn't exactly a comfortable moment for me, but I knew in my gut that it was the right choice.

If you are sincere, actively listening, and present with the people you are face to face with, a pact forms. By inviting me into their secret brotherhood, the Masons elevated the level of the pact and changed the nature of the conversation—at least they did for me. I had come to the meeting with no agenda beyond learning more about them and their organization. The Masons, on the other hand, came to the meeting as people interested in connecting with power players across a variety of fields—politics, education, industry, technology, and the arts. For them, this was a chance to feel out and possibly recruit a new member.

If I hadn't been paying attention, I could easily have misunderstood the seriousness of their invitation and made a flip decision about something of great consequence. However, because I was attuned from the start, not only listening but also taking in nonverbal cues, I saw the situation for what it was and was able to adapt accordingly.

In hindsight, some of the questions the Masons posed might have clued me in earlier as to the direction in which things were headed. For example, I can see now that when they asked, "Brian, do you believe in God?" they were evaluating whether I fulfilled that requirement of their code. However, the important thing is that I got it right in the end. To this day, I don't know what might have happened if I had accepted the Masons' offer of membership (although I suspect they would have taken issue with my film *The Da Vinci Code*, given the conspiracy theories it revived). What I do know is that I have never regretted my decision to decline.

18

What Words Can't Say

There is a language that is beyond words. If I can learn to decipher that language without words, I will be able to decipher the world.

—*Paulo Coelho*

Years ago, I flew into Hong Kong for business and found myself wide awake in the middle of the night. Terrible jet lag was part of it. But I was also having a hard time turning off my mind. This was in 1986, when Ron and I were in the midst of taking our company, Imagine Entertainment, public. There's always anxiety involved in taking your business public, and my brain was busy trying to process everything we still needed to do. One of my concerns was the need for a larger office space back in Los Angeles. Over the course of two years, we'd gone from being a company of fifteen people to having nine times as many (accountants, production executives, a COO, a CFO, a head of business affairs). Our current office could barely contain us, and I knew the situation would only be getting worse.

Unable to sleep, I got out of bed and stared out my hotel room window. Somewhere out there, shrouded in a dense cloud of fog, was Victoria Harbour. As I looked, a form started to emerge—an imposing skyscraper. At that hour, and under those conditions, both the base and top of the building were obscured, but the center of it rose, gleaming, through the mist. Even then, it was a hypnotic, powerful sight. In the morning, after I'd managed a few hours of sleep and the fog had cleared, I took another look. The building was just as stunning as I'd thought. In the clear light of day, I recognized the distinct style of the architect I. M. Pei at work. I also noted how the building completely dominated the skyline.

Later, down in the lobby, I asked the hotel manager about it.

"That's the Bank of China Tower," he told me. Today, of course, the building is internationally famous, but at the time it was only recently constructed and not even occupied yet. "Everyone in Hong Kong is very upset about it. There's been an enormous uproar among the owners and proprietors of the neighboring buildings, particularly among the feng shui experts."

"Feng shui" was not a widely known term in the U.S. back then, and I had no clue what the manager was talking about.

"What are those?" I asked. "The feng shui experts?"

He explained to me that these were consultants hired routinely by businesses to identify the most auspicious architectural and interior design arrangements: where to place doors, windows, and furniture to harmonize, which things signify trust and the influx of money, and so on. I don't know that I am a superstitious person, but I was fascinated by the concept. Particularly given my preoccupation with our hunt for office space.

I spent the next few days of my trip asking around about feng shui consultants—who were the best and most highly regarded in Hong Kong? It became a matter of urgent curiosity for me that went beyond its relevance to my business. I was dying to know more about this unfamiliar idea.

Eventually I found my way to the people I'd been looking for— two brothers renowned and highly sought after for their expertise in feng shui. Gaining access to them, especially as a Westerner, was difficult and involved a fair amount of ceremony. I was growing increasingly worried that there would be no meeting with the consultants. But then, on the very last day of my trip, it happened.

The two brothers met me in my hotel room. I presented them with an envelope containing a generous donation; this was customary, and they didn't look inside. As I do with any other curiosity conversation, I had prepared as best I could for the meeting. However, I don't speak any Cantonese, and though it was lucky for me they spoke any English, their command of the language wasn't great. I had to rely on my eyes to do a good deal of the communication and paid very close attention to theirs as well. I leaned in and watched them very, very closely as we spoke. To the best of my ability, I asked them about what they did and how they did it. Did their expertise extend beyond the placement of furniture, doors, and windows? How did they know what to do? I still hold the memory of one of the brothers remarking, in his halting but strangely idiomatic English, that they proceeded by virtue of feeling themselves "connected to the source."

We struggled through most of the conversation. Then, just before the meeting concluded, one of them leaned over and took me by the wrists. He studied my hands for a moment, and my arms. Then the other brother did the same.

"Do you have a person in your life," the first brother asked, "with the initials Q. N.?"

I thought for a moment. It was an uncommon set of initials, but I ran a fairly large company and had a lot of other people in my life too. I watched him almost as if I were going to see the image of a particular person reflected in his eyes.

"I'm not sure, but I might," I said. "Yes."

"Be careful," he said. "This person, Q. N., is going to be very dangerous to you in your life."

I instantly believed him. I could feel the credibility of the information coming to me through his eyes.

I thanked them and set off for the airport. All the way there and for the entire flight home, I thought about Q. N. and the look in the brothers' eyes, which flashed with warning and intention.

Back in LA, the logistical headaches awaited. It was great that we'd raised a fair share of capital, but our company still didn't have its offices.

I was thrilled then, when, upon my return, Robin Barris, one of our senior executives, pulled me aside. "We found something. Quinn," she said, naming one of the consultants we'd hired to help with the office search, "found a great spot for us to move into. It's a ten-year lease on a space in Bel Air."

"Bel Air?" It seemed pretty out of the way and largely residential. Most entertainment offices in Los Angeles tend to cluster in a corridor around Wilshire Boulevard in Beverly Hills or Santa Monica.

"How'd he find it?"

Robin explained that Quinn (his name, of course, stood out immediately; his last name, indeed, began with an *N* as well) had heard about the building through a relative.

"Would you look into it a little deeper?" I asked Robin. "I know you say it's a great space, and ten years is a reasonable term for the lease and all that, but it's a lot of money to pay into a space we don't own. Who owns that building?"

I might have known before she did. The people who were to stand on the receiving end of our lease payments were none other than Quinn himself and a college friend of his who had become a real estate agent. Turns out had we locked ourselves into ten years of payments, at the end of the term *they* would have owned the building. We narrowly avoided signing the papers.

"Get rid of Quinn," I told her. "Don't offer any explanation—just let him go."

She did. He left without any argument. He knew he had been found out.

A story like this always feels like it contains shades of coincidence. The brothers' warning to me was not specific, and there are other people with the initials Q. N. in the world. So I'm not going to argue that there was some divine or mystical force at work during that meeting in Hong Kong. But I do believe that information is transmitted—in fact, I *know* that information is transmitted—in many, many ways that transcend the verbal.

That's what the whole discipline of feng shui is about, after all, and that's what my conversation with the two men—which was barely a conversation at all in the conventional sense—was about too.

We spoke with our words but also, more important, with our attention and our intention. Who knows what was "said" in that respect? I believe they understood me better than many people whose English is flawless and with whom I've exchanged words by the bucketful.

I travel quite a bit for both work and pleasure. As was the case in Hong Kong, I rarely know the native language of the places I visit. I mean that both in terms of spoken language and in terms of nonverbal language. On a trip to Israel, for example, I noticed that when our Israeli guide ran into a friend, he slapped each side of the man's face with strong hands. As the two smiled and seemed to enjoy a loud and lively conversation, he shook his friend's cheeks up and down. I noted to Veronica—more than once—that I would have felt assaulted had a friend done that to me.

Knowing that different cultures have different ways of using eye contact and body language to communicate, I strive to be extremely attentive and sensitive to this information when I am in another country. I have to be if I want to form strong, meaningful connections with the people I meet there—and forming those kinds of relationships is to me what traveling is all about.

Several years ago, Veronica and I decided to go to Burma. For years my friend Tom Freston, one of the founders of MTV and former CEO of Viacom, had been telling me I needed to go, but Tom is something of an adventurous traveler. He has frequently invited me to join him in places like Baghdad or Kabul, places that while surely fascinating are not necessarily where I would choose to go on vacation! Still, Tom always has his finger on the pulse when it comes to those rare, off-the-beaten-path gems. And Burma lingered in my mind.

I was working on the movie *Get On Up* with Mick Jagger, who was also a producer, and we spent quite a bit of downtime together on the set in Natchez, Mississippi. One day I asked him where he liked to go most on vacation. After all, Mick Jagger knows a thing or two about how to live. Without hesitation he said, "Inle Lake, in Myanmar. Burma." Well. Now two experienced travelers with impeccable taste were telling me this was the place to go. I figured I *had* to check it out. Veronica, herself an adventurer (she once climbed Mount Kilimanjaro on a whim and had been diving in the Philippines without formal training), loved the idea. She booked the trip the next day, planning it all out with a local travel agent who knew the region extremely well and could ensure an authentic experience. That's always super important to us when we travel.

When we touched down in Yangon (formerly Rangoon), we were met by our guide, a wonderful and wise Burmese woman in her fifties named Kiki. At the time, Myanmar had only recently opened up to tourism, and it was still not an easy place to visit. The country has a volatile political history full of horrid human rights abuses, military regimes, and voter suppression. Kiki, we later learned, had grown up amid this turbulence and terror. Her own father had been thrown in jail for years. Yet she still saw beauty in this country that she loved, and as a guide, she wanted visitors to experience that side of her homeland as well.

We embarked on a nine-day journey with Kiki, culminating in a visit to Inle Lake, our long-awaited destination. One of the most stunning lakes in the world, it's situated in a valley between two mountain ranges. This raw and expansive body of water seemed to reflect the surrounding beauty like glass. Dotted with active villages on stilts and illuminated by Buddhist temples rising from the water, the place was extraordinary. Told that the best way to experience the lake would be by canoe, we chose to travel in a slender, long-tail wooden version used by the locals.

During our three days on the lake, we watched as farmers with water buffalo tilled the rice paddies and residents of stilt villages went about their daily chores. Locals in weathered boats drifted by us, selling hand-carved Buddha statues, tourist knickknacks, and oranges grown in nearby floating gardens. Periodically, we would stop to explore a village, where we would visit a chaotic farmers' market or learn a cottage industry. Young girls and old women hand-rolled cheroots (thin cigars) in the lakeside stalls and grandmothers sold noodles. Small children delighted in a game of sticks.

A woman welcomed us into her family's umbrella-making workshop. She walked us through the intricate and time-consuming process of crafting each piece by hand. We watched closely as her younger daughter, who couldn't have been more than ten years old, made paper pulp from a mulberry tree, while her father cranked a foot-powered lathe to shape the wooden handles. The little girl put flower petals in my hands and guided them through a pool of water to create a design on the wet paper pulp. Different parts of the final product were produced by various family members and assembled in the end to create the most beautiful umbrellas in a rainbow of vibrant colors, patterns, and sizes. I was moved, knowing that we were witnessing cultural traditions and practices that had been handed down from generation to generation.

On our final night at Inle Lake, Veronica and I went out on the canoe at sunset to experience the silence and emptiness of this magical place. We lay back and took in the infinite red and gold layers settling over the water. I was feeling emotional thinking about what we had experienced here. Coming from the world of Hollywood, where people tend to have complex and, at times, questionable motivations, I was delighted by the transparency and realness of our interactions with the Burmese people.

I remembered one morning when we had stopped to talk with an elderly woman in one of the villages. She had been checking us out with a friendly but curious gaze. With the help of Kiki's translation and some deliberate nonverbal signals, we quickly understood that they rarely saw tourists here; the woman was enthralled by Veronica's blond hair. Although we were strangers to her, the woman invited us into her home to share in a traditional breakfast of *mohinga*. The fish-based broth with rice noodles (and lots of condiments on the side!) was absolutely delicious, made all the better by the warmth of our host. There were so many stories of connections like this one. Among all of the connections we made, however, none was as special as the one we formed with Kiki.

For more than a week, Kiki had traveled the country with us, by boat, plane, train, and foot. She had been with us when we visited the Buddhist monasteries in the north, an orphanage deep in the countryside, and a remote village where they still draw water from the town well. She facilitated authentic exchanges with locals and shared her own unique perspectives with us.

The Burmese government is aggressively concerned with how their country is presented to outsiders. So becoming a guide is no easy feat. Kiki had to complete a tremendous amount of work and pass a number of difficult tests to do her job. Not unsurprisingly, she was careful in her historical narration. But when she shared personal stories describing her family and their deep connection to the land, Kiki would truly come alive. Through Kiki's emotional lens, we were able to experience the country in a way we will never forget.

With the trip coming to an end, it was time for us to say goodbye to our beloved guide and new friend. Standing on the tarmac, I moved to give Kiki a hug. It was completely instinctual, the kind of affectionate gesture that is the norm for Americans. To my surprise, she stepped away. Still, she kept her eyes trained on my own.

I backed up out of respect. "I'm sorry," I started to say, but she stopped me with her open and understanding gaze. "I *know*," she said, indicating that it was okay. "I know."

In that moment, I understood: she wasn't refusing the affection, just the embrace. Kiki explained that people in her culture don't hug. Instead, during moments of greeting and parting, moments of emotional connection, they look one another in the eyes, because the eyes, Kiki told us, "are the window to the soul." "We see everything we need to know," she said, "by looking in each other's eyes. Hugging seems almost dishonest."

(In fact, there's some science behind the idea that the eyes reveal the depth and authenticity of affection. It was a French physician named Guillaume Duchenne who discovered that the crow's-feet that accompany a genuine smile are controlled by muscles that cannot be moved voluntarily. Only a genuine smile will reveal those creases around the corners of the eyes.)

The exchange with Kiki on the tarmac was poignant not only because it signified the end of an unexpectedly meaningful vacation, but also because it introduced me to a new and profound way of connecting to another human. As soon as Veronica and I settled in on the plane, we looked at each other, tears in our eyes, and vowed to bring our family back to Burma.

So we did. The very next Christmas, we journeyed back to Inle Lake with our kids. Once again, we experienced the country in a way that was deep and beautiful, only now it was amplified by the fact that we were seeing it through the eyes of our children. This time departing, we all knew. We didn't need to say it. We wouldn't give a hug. We knew to honor the connection with our local hosts by offering gratitude with our eyes, the windows to our souls.

19

Where Life Begins

Life will only change when you become more committed to
your dreams than to your comfort zone.

—*Billy Cox*

Having raised several teenagers, my wife and I came to realize that
eating together is one of the only times that we have a chance for real
conversations with them. To keep this time sacred, she and I decided
we needed a way to create boundaries with our devices during meals,
so all of us put our cell phones in a basket before we eat. It's better
than simply setting our screens down, because the mere presence of a
phone next to a person is distracting in and of itself.[1] This practice
has freed us to have interesting and enlightening conversations with
the kids that are able to stretch to more than just one-syllable answers! It also inspired one of our favorite family traditions.

In an effort to celebrate birthdays in a less materialistic way that
would make each person feel valued by other family members, we
came up with an activity. We go around the table and everyone has to
give a toast while looking the person with the birthday in the eye. If
the person is at the far end of the table from you, or you can't face
them directly, you have to get up so that you can. As you can imagine, the kids hated it in the early days. Patrick and Thomas would
shrink down in their chairs to avoid having to go next. But then little

by little, they became really good at it. These days, they raise their hands to go first!

We taught the kids that the easiest toast or speech is the one that is not made up of a bunch of generic "nice" adjectives, but rather one that comes straight from the heart. We encouraged them to share a story about the person, a memory that would make them feel good. ("Yeah! I almost died when Riley jumped up and danced with the locals!" or "Remember when we were camping and Sage got a fever? Patrick wouldn't let go of her hand all night!") They loved seeing how their toasts could make the family laugh and cry and earn them shout-outs. This ritual has led to some of our most memorable moments as a family. Not to mention, the kids have gotten pretty darn good at public speaking!

When we were on a boat for a family vacation several summers ago, it happened to fall over Father's Day, so the kids prepared toasts for me. Veronica likes to come up with themes and asked them to focus on something I taught them that still sticks with them today. My daughter, Sage, now thirty-five years old, recalled a time when I spoke to her about the importance of disrupting her comfort zone. She said this was one of the things that made her brave enough to abandon her four-year pursuit of a career in photography and instead pursue her dream of becoming a psychotherapist (which she is today); it brought me to tears. It made me feel amazing to know that I have empowered my kids to step outside their comfort zones, because I truly believe that is where the most memorable moments of our lives can happen.

Several years ago, I got a call from my good friend Tom Freston, the friend I mentioned earlier who had recommended we visit Burma. Tom invited me on a last-minute guys' trip to Senegal with a group that included the singer Dave Matthews, and vocalist and guitarist Trey Anastasio from the band Phish. The motivation for the trip was twofold: a reunion concert for Orchestra Baobab, masters of African/Afro-Cuban music that dominated Senegal's music scene in the seventies, and a private concert with Baaba Maal, a remarkable musician and contemporary globe-trotter who had become an African hero in the eighties when his sound brought him to an international audience.

It was sure to be a thrilling adventure. But I wasn't sure. If I went, I would have to clear my entire schedule that week without much notice. It would mean a full day of travel to the other side of the world. And once there, I'd be spending 24/7 with a group of guys who, other than Tom, I had never met before. There were a lot of unknowns and a lot of inconveniences to consider. I could have easily said no with good reason. But I didn't. I said yes. I was curious about the country, the culture, the people, the guys who were going, and these talented musicians who had created so much attention. I'd be stepping outside my comfort zone, but I thought it would be worth it.

As soon as we landed in Dakar, we quickly dropped our bags at the hotel and headed out into the city. We were all anxious and excited to get a feel for this exotic and alluring place. First stop was Dakar's largest market, Sandaga. Lively and buzzy, it was packed with vendors hawking everything you could possibly imagine, from African masks and carvings to local fabrics and exotic fruits. The influence of Senegal's French colonizers also came through. Some of it was touristy for sure, but we liked mingling with the local Senegalese as they shopped for the day's requirements. We watched as suit-clad businessmen knelt down in the middle of the street for prayer, and talked to a woman who convinced us to try a popular street food called *accara*. The crispy black-eyed-pea fritters served with a tomato-and-onion-based hot sauce called *kaani* reminded me of southern hush puppies. Delicious!

The next morning we ventured out of the city to see Lake Retba, otherwise called Lac Rose, a body of water nestled between white sand dunes and the Atlantic Ocean. It was a stunning and memorable visual: a brilliant shade of strawberry pink that gets its color from algae. As we got out of the truck, dozens of village children ran up to us and grabbed our hands. They led us down the beach as their fathers worked to harvest salt from the lake with spades and sticks, and their mothers waited ashore to help haul the filled buckets from the boat to the land. This basic industry would create income for families from surrounding countries such as Mali, Ivory Coast, and Guinea.[2] That afternoon, we traveled to Gorée Island, a UNESCO World Heritage site that was once the largest slave-trading center on the African coast. George W. Bush, Clinton, and Obama have made the pilgrimage there, as did Nelson Mandela. It was a somber reminder of the deep and complex history of where we were.

That evening would be the first of two of the most captivating musical experiences I've ever had in my life. Baaba Maal was performing for the Senegalese aristocracy, and we were lucky enough to be his guests. Sitting on the floor with about seventy-five others, we watched as three priestess singers in long, flowing, colorful Senegalese dresses appeared. Their nearly imperceptible slow-motion moves, which gradually picked up speed throughout the performance, were almost hypnotic. Just then, Baaba Maal himself, wearing a magnificent red robe, arrived with dramatic flair. Instead of a big first number, he broke into a delicate and soulful piece, surprising us with bursts of sudden power. He's a breathtaking performer, and he brought the crowd to a point of mania again and again. The three-hour experience built to a high-energy closing act that left me in a state of complete euphoria.

As the concert finished in the wee hours, we headed outside to feast on a freshly slaughtered goat, a cultural tradition they were proud for us to partake in. There, I met Baaba, and he was as charismatic and exuberant as one might expect after seeing him perform. At the same time, he was serene and thoughtful as he talked about where he came from: he grew up by a river in a rural village named Djoum, as part of the Fulani, a seminomadic people.[3] Having spent a lifetime on the road as a musician, he talked about the feeling of coming back home and how there's nothing quite like it. He said, "You realize you're still you," but with new connections and experiences that become a part of you. I could certainly relate to that.

The next evening we headed over to the reunion of the famed Orchestra Baobab. The concert was at a local venue on the outskirts of Dakar, over an hour's drive from our hotel. It was so dark it felt like the middle of the night as we made our way there. By the time we arrived, the place was hot and crowded, everyone standing body to body. I waded through the audience toward the stage to get a closer look at who was behind this incredible sound, a fusion of Afro-Cuban rhythms and traditional African music that one might mistake for the sounds of the Buena Vista Social Club. As the incredible vocals, drums, congas, and bass guitar of the band played at near-deafening volume, every single person swayed in unison. I was thoroughly immersed in the moment, not caring about anything other than the beat of the music pulsing through my body. It was surreal to feel so connected to a crowd of strangers in a place so foreign. Yet somehow we all understood the universal emotion that comes from experiencing music together.

Disrupting your comfort zone can lead to the most unexpectedly beautiful connections in your life. In fact, what I've discovered over the years is that if I'm not taking a chance on connecting, then I'm missing possibilities that could have enormous internal, and external, rewards. If I'm *not* stepping outside my comfort zone—as often as possible—then I'm holding myself back from opportunities to learn, grow, and see the world differently through the eyes of others. Stepping outside your comfort zone means taking a risk. And sometimes, for whatever reason, the risk won't pay off. But in my experience, more often than not, it does. Being willing to disrupt your comfort zone, I've found, is where life really begins.

20

Venturing into New Worlds

The Sanskrit word *namaste* means "the spirit in me honors the spirit in you." Whenever you first make eye contact with another person, say "Namaste" silently to yourself. This is a way of acknowledging that the being there is the same as the being here.

—*Deepak Chopra*

My world, growing up in the flats of Sherman Oaks (known as "the Valley"), was very small. I rarely ventured outside the three-mile radius that existed between my house and school, the grocery store, and my aunt Helen and uncle Bernie's house. My experience of the world was further restricted by my dyslexia. Where other people find ways to broaden their horizons and expand their views through books, that was not an option for me. With time, however, I discovered that there was a simple and accessible way to expand my borders and live a larger life—meeting people.

We are all trapped in our own patterns of thinking, being, and seeing. In fact, most of us get so used to seeing the world *our* way that we come to think that the world *is* that way. It's totally refreshing to be reminded, over and over, how different the world looks to other people. That's why I am constantly on the lookout for opportunities to connect with people whose experiences, views, and lifestyles are different from my own. Sometimes, this takes the form of arranged curiosity conversations with specific individuals, as I've discussed earlier. But a lot of times, I simply start up exchanges with random strangers—a skateboarder, a bartender, a street artist, an astrologist—who for some reason catch my attention. Whoever they are and however it happens, every time I engage someone new, I have the chance to see the world through their eyes. My life is richer and I am a more empathetic, more compassionate, and wiser person for it. Here are a few stories that have stuck with me.

Over the holidays one year, Veronica and I decided to visit Buenos Aires for the first time. On our last evening there, we had dinner at a modern yet intimate Argentine-Jewish restaurant called Fayer that a friend had recommended. We were early and the place was only about half-full. Sitting side by side on a banquette, we settled in with a bottle of wine and some warm pretzel bread. A magnetic waiter caught our attention. Despite his youthful looks, he could easily have been mistaken for a seasoned maitre d' who charmed every table with an authentic charisma. We noticed the exceeding care he took with the other diners, and when he came around to take our order, we were impressed by the way he answered our questions with meticulous detail and expert understanding.

We expressed our admiration and in doing so, opened up a conversation. We learned the waiter's name—Eduardo—and found out that only four years before he had been walking door-to-door looking for a job in a new city and a new country. Although he had no experience, this restaurant decided to give him a shot. He had been working there ever since.

As we chatted further, Eduardo shared that at age eighteen he made the difficult decision to leave his home in Venezuela. The country was in the midst of an economic crisis with high levels of violence and severe food shortages, so Eduardo believed he had to leave to create opportunity for himself.[1] I asked him what made him think that he would be able to find a job in a foreign country where he didn't know a soul. Eduardo explained that his ability to speak English gave him a leg up in a city popular with English-speaking tourists. *How did he learn English*, I thought to myself. Before leaving home, he told us, he gave himself a crash course playing English-language video games.

As the evening went on, we shared anecdotes back and forth, and with every dish or drink he delivered, Eduardo revealed more personal details of his life. For example, he told us that he could barely stand being apart from his girlfriend, whom he was planning to bring over from Caracas and marry as soon as he saved enough money. He showed us photos of the two of them together and talked about marrying her someday. We knew this guy could do anything he set his mind on. Our connection with Eduardo transformed a nice enough dinner into one we'll never forget.

At least once or twice a week, I would have lunch outside at Bouchon in Beverly Hills, only a few minutes' walk from my office. One day I was sitting alone on a conference call, talking and looking across the restaurant's terrace, which was largely empty, as it was already late in the afternoon. I scanned the tables and my eyes fell on a man who was sitting at the far end of the patio. I noticed he was glancing back at me.

What had caught my eye was not the man's standard-issue black turtleneck and slacks, but his unbounded energy. As he carried on a conversation with another man seated beside him, his face exuded enthusiasm and his eyes blazed with life. There was such an intensity about him that looking at him was almost involuntary. I didn't even realize I was doing it at first.

It took me a minute or two to notice that beside the man was a chair of some sort. Not a wheelchair, exactly—not in the same way I was used to—but a sturdy, well-built wooden conveyance, practically like a *throne*, only with wheels. I also observed that the man's companion kept handing things to him. It occurred to me then that he must be the man's assistant.

As I was wrapping up my phone call, the assistant stood up and *lifted* the man from where he was sitting into the sturdy wooden chair. Suddenly I understood: This man who positively dominated the entire patio with his presence, who seemed so animated, was, in fact, immobile from the neck down.

In one sense, this was a thorny and rather complicated moment. Aren't we all taught to avert our eyes from others' conspicuous differences, to look away out of a sense of modesty or a fear of offending or embarrassing someone? Once I became aware of the man's state, that's exactly what I did. I looked down at my lap, breaking the connection that had formed when our eyes first met. But a moment later, I found myself looking straight at him again. I couldn't help myself. I was just so curious as to who this person was and what he was all about.

I stood up, crossed the terrace, and approached him. He greeted me with a gentle look. He seemed surprised that I'd come over, but not unhappy.

"Hi," I said. "Would you mind if I sat down for a moment?"

Sure, it was a little awkward, but I didn't mind. "My name is Brian Grazer. I have to admit I was watching you while I was on the phone. You just seemed to exude so much energy. But then I noticed that you're . . . paralyzed."

He didn't seem insulted, thank God. He just looked at me.

"I am," he said. "I have been for ten years."

"What is it like?" I said. Now, under a certain set of circumstances, that question might have seemed tactless or insensitive. But we'd shared a connection, a small moment of mutual recognition, and I didn't want to let the opportunity pass to know this man better.

I wasn't asking for novelty's sake. I asked because the risk of *not* understanding what his experiences were like seemed greater to me than the risk of asking and being rebuffed. To the best of my ability, I wanted to understand him. Is this tactless? Might the world not be a more humane place if we attempted to understand each other's circumstances a little more often? I think he saw the sincerity in my eyes.

He told me everything. That his name was Stephen and he worked in private equity. That his paralysis was the result of a progressive condition, a rare form of palsy. He told me about its various complications and how he'd learned to live with them. He had a lot of emotional range and appeared to be very accepting of his situation. I asked him how he spends his time, what he cares about, why he chose the career that he did. I sat with him and asked, and he answered. And he asked, and I answered. Somehow, it just flowed. Finally, I got up. I left our conversation having established a new friendship. We agreed we'd keep in touch, and so we have over the years.

I remember the first time I visited Paris after the terrorist attacks of November 2015 had taken place. In a series of coordinated attacks, 130 people were killed, many of them at the Bataclan, where the American rock band Eagles of Death Metal were playing. I had seen the coverage on the news and read about it in the paper. But I couldn't imagine what it was like for the individuals who called this city home.

Sitting in the back seat of a cab, I looked down at my phone and thought about scrolling through my messages. Instead, I decided to engage my driver, Laurent, in conversation. I asked Laurent about the terrorist attack. How had it impacted him on a personal level? How did it affect his country? He put the car in park and turned around to look at me.

For the next forty minutes, Laurent and I talked, face to face, about the events that had happened and what it meant to be living in the current moment. It was an emotional conversation. I was surprised when Laurent confided that he was ashamed by the attacks. I had expected that he would be sad, frightened, angry—but ashamed? He explained how the terrorists had made the French feel a collective sense of powerlessness. I was moved by his revelation. It both deepened my understanding of the French people and opened a window into another way of seeing current events that I hadn't considered before.

When I was young, I only knew my small corner of California. Today, I have traveled all over the globe. But where I am is much less important than who I am with. Every time I connect with someone, I am transported somewhere new. And the best part is, it doesn't require a ticket or a suitcase or a GPS. All it takes is the curiosity and courage to initiate engagement with another human being, and the willingness to listen and learn with an open mind.

21

In the Blink of an Eye

You have power over your mind—not outside events.
Realize this, and you will find strength.

—Marcus Aurelius

When we were shooting *8 Mile*, I flew to Detroit to visit the production. Admittedly one of my favorites among the movies I've produced, the film is the story of Eminem that emerged out of that fateful meeting in my office. After a few days on set—which was an ice-cold urban landscape in the dead of winter—I realized I needed to get out. I was craving sunshine and warmth. I decided to fly right to the set of another movie I was producing in Hawaii.

Blue Crush was filming at the same time on the North Shore of Oahu. I had never been to this part of Hawaii before, so I was excited to check it out. I only knew what I had seen in other movies and on television: iconic surf breaks like Banzai Pipeline, Sunset Beach, and Waimea Bay. As we were touching down, I looked out the window to see the widest, most pristine beaches and the bluest ocean you could possibly imagine. If Detroit was a frigid nightmare, this looked like paradise. I was completely taken. After driving around for only an hour or two, I decided I wanted to live there— just like that. (This definitely marked one of the most extreme, "in the moment" decisions I've ever made in my life!) I found a house that felt good to me: a big, white Indonesian-style place with a blue-tile roof, right smack on the Pipeline, the most legendary surf break in the Western Hemisphere.

My early days in Hawaii were everything I imagined they would be. I was beguiled by the North Shore's tropical beauty, the lush mountains I could see across Waimea Bay, and the laid-back vibe that pervaded the place. As usual, I had been feeling restless, my mind full of more stories than I could keep track of and too many things to think about, not least of which was the other movie I was making back in Detroit. I felt like I had found the perfect antidote, a world that seemed, on the surface at least, perfect—gorgeous, vibrant, and calm. I felt welcome.

We were using a local crew on *Blue Crush*—we'd hired only native Hawaiians, which is rare for productions there—in part because we wanted to integrate as seamlessly as we could within the community. So I was surprised when one day I came to the set and noticed someone hanging around who didn't appear to belong there. He was physically imposing and had a hardened look about him. Although his interactions with the crew seemed friendly and familiar, in my eyes, this stranger was the definition of intimidating.

I soon discovered that this man—let's call him Jake—had arrived with the express purpose of "helping us with some of our permitting and safety issues." He was actually a member of a group called the Da Hui, also known as the "Black Shorts" for the dark surf trunks they wore. The Da Hui organization formed on the North Shore in the mid-1970s with the intent of protecting the Pipeline against an incursion of mostly South African and Australian surfers. For Hawaiians, respect is an important concept, particularly when it comes to the ocean, their coveted natural resources, and their cultural heritage. As foreigners flocked to the area, crowding the waves, and big corporations started to commercialize a sport invented by their ancestors, some Hawaiians felt disrespected.

Groups like the Da Hui were determined to repel these outsiders and reclaim control of the ocean and sport that were so essential to who they were as a people. They would swim out into the water to disrupt competitions and demand that other surfers make way for them. They made it clear that they would do whatever they had to to preserve and protect what was theirs. Today, the Da Hui have traded their activist roots for more mainstream endeavors, like volunteering in the community, producing a clothing line, and overseeing water safety at surf contests. But their commitment to defending native Hawaiian culture is as strong as it ever was.

With Jake, the Da Hui had created a sort of extracurricular line item, a fee that wasn't part of the original budget for *Blue Crush*. But after our production team conferred among ourselves, we decided that the easiest course of action was to pay up. This sort of strong-arming happens everywhere. It's the nature of shooting on location, so it didn't bother me too much.

Jake and I got along well; we even surfed together on occasion. Still, there was something about Jake's presence and demeanor that felt threatening to me. And it started to change the way I felt about the North Shore. Maybe my paradise wasn't so idyllic after all. Maybe it wasn't mine to begin with. As my preconceptions began to crack, my sense of security in this place turned to one of uncertainty.

While in Hawaii I was lucky enough to connect and form a friendship with Brock Little, who, as I mentioned earlier, had taught me to surf. Brock was a professional surfer and stuntman, a local who took me under his wing and showed me around. Among the many forces and factions on the North Shore, Brock was a kind of human Switzerland: strong but peace-loving, powerful but nonpartisan, on good terms with everybody. He was friendly with the Da Hui but not exactly a member. Through Brock, I came to know a lot about the regional culture, including proper etiquette out in the water.

When surfing with the locals, especially the more aggressive, alpha-male types, I learned that the one thing you should never do is look them in the eye when you're out on the water. If you mistakenly cut someone off on a wave *without* looking them in the eye, it's one thing—an accident—but if you make eye contact beforehand, it is understood to be personal. Even if it was inadvertent, that look will be considered a show of disrespect and the locals will brand you with the "stink eye." If you're given the stink eye by a member of the Da Hui or another group, within an hour everybody on the North Shore will know, and from what I was led to understand, a broken car window or a trip to the hospital might follow. Whether those were idle threats or real dangers, I didn't know. But I didn't want to find out either.

Sometimes *not* looking someone in the eye can be as meaningful as looking someone in the eye. Whom we look in the eye, when we look at them, how we look at them—all of these things shape our relationships within a given cultural context. In certain parts of the world, an excess of eye contact is considered disrespectful.[1] In Japan, schoolchildren are taught to look at the neck of the person they are speaking with to soften their gaze,[2] and in Iran, eye contact between men and women is strictly inappropriate.[3]

Even closer to home, there are surprising instances where direct eye contact is frowned upon. In the Minnesota Legislature, for example, Senate Rule 36.8 requires that "all remarks during debate should be addressed to the president." The Senate president resides at the front of the chamber, so even if a senator is debating with someone behind them, they can't look at each other. They must face forward.[4] Apparently, this rule was established to promote civility by eliminating eye contact that might amplify aggression between representatives with opposing views.

In other situations, looking someone in the eye can lead you somewhere you don't want to go. When I produced the movie *The Chamber* (based on the John Grisham book) in 1996, we shot it at the Mississippi State Penitentiary—a death-row prison in the state, famously known as "Parchman Farm"—and the warden instructed us never to look the inmates in the eye when we passed. He knew that the inmates would *try* to make eye contact with us. For them, con-nection was an opportunity to get something they wanted but couldn't have. In other words, it was a tool for manipulation.

Out on the water with Jake, I minded my manners, and he never branded me with the stink eye. But the experience of surfing with him revealed a new dimension of the culture to me and led me to think about eye contact in a new way. The eyes can help forge deep, trustful connections between people, but they are also brokers of power. With the Da Hui, you had to use your eyes carefully, to signal just the right amount of deference for the situation.

After we finished *Blue Crush* (which I'm proud to say became a cult phenomenon that helped bring surf culture—specifically *female* surf culture—a little further into the mainstream), I spent a lot of time on the island. I went whenever I could break away and got to know it well. I wasn't exactly a local, but I wasn't what they call a haole, a non-native Hawaiian, either. I was accepted, or so I believed. Until one evening, when I was riding my bicycle along the trail to the same place I always went: past Sunset Beach to a place called V-Land.

V-Land was Da Hui territory, and I was humming along on my bike when two guys stepped out of the bushes and blocked my path.

"Oh, hey, Brian." One of them moved toward me. He was pumped up like a bodybuilder, with tattoos covering his arms and knuckles. "What are you doing?"

I recognized him. I'd met him once or twice before. He was one of my surf buddy Jake's "associates," one of the most feared—and fearsome-looking—members of the Da Hui. He stepped closer to me. I knew immediately that this wasn't a social approach; these guys had something on their mind.

"I'm riding my bike," I said, keeping cool as best I could. The friend stepped forward now too.

"Brian, you haven't paid your taxes."

For a moment I wondered what he was talking about. *Taxes?* Then I realized he was trying to shake me down. Jake wringing us on the set of *Blue Crush* was one thing. But these guys wanted protection money from me personally.

"Oh, no," I said. "I've paid my taxes."

"We don't have any record of that," the tattooed guy said. "It's a new year, and we need new taxes."

I'm usually a pretty hyperactive guy: I thrive on the energy of other people and social situations, but in moments of physical danger—for whatever reason—I slow down. I've been held at gunpoint on two different occasions, and I once was on an airplane when the electricity failed and it seemed likely we'd crash. This moment was a bit like those. My mind became very still.

"You know, we saw your girlfriend over at Foodland," the tattooed guy said. Foodland is a place where all the surfers congregate, the social hub of the North Shore. "She's very beautiful. I hope everything goes good for her. We'd hate for anything bad to happen to her."

Were they actually threatening her? Me? What exactly did they plan to do? This was serious. I had to have the right response. Rather than try to push back verbally or negotiate, I tried a different tack. Just as I had discovered that it wasn't a good idea to look any of the Da Hui in the eye on the water, so I had come to learn early on— also through my local friend Brock—to do the opposite while negotiating with them on land. Thank you, Brock.

Rather than look away, I did exactly what Brock had recommended. I looked at Tattoo Guy with a confident yet respectful gaze that was neither downcast nor too direct. I held his eyes for a long, silent moment.

"There's no problem here," I said finally. "I've paid my taxes. We're cool."

I shifted back onto my seat and pedaled away. To my amazement, they didn't try to stop me. I rode off toward the sunset. As soon as I did, my heart started pounding. What exactly had just happened?

Thinking about it now, I realize that I was able to defuse and stabilize the situation just by the way I used my eyes. In a single look, I was able to navigate a complicated power dynamic. On one hand, I was letting my antagonist know that I was not weak and that he could not scare me into submission. On the other, I was recognizing his strength and acknowledging a messy history in which I was linked to a long string of outsiders who had disrespected the Hawaiian people and their culture in all kinds of ways.

I may make my living as a producer, but what I really am is a storyteller. And stories are always about the communication of feelings. People have a tendency to see life as binary—right versus wrong, success versus failure—but feelings are more nuanced than that. They are both infinite in their variation and inarguable. You can't tell someone how they feel or how they experience the world. Feelings, like stories, are subjective, and what people need perhaps more than anything these days is to have their stories acknowledged and heard. Don't we all want that? To be seen in a way that recognizes our own sense of who we are? I believe what happened that day with the two Da Hui was exactly that. I didn't attempt to challenge their story of themselves. Instead, I looked at them in a way that allowed me to maintain my personal agency, while acknowledging their strength, their authority, and their experience of the world.

22

Honeymoon in the Holy Land

When God loves you, what can be better than that?

—*Aretha Franklin*

I was raised both Jewish and Catholic: Jewish on my mother's side and Catholic on my father's. Until I was about ten, I basically lived the life of a Catholic. I was baptized as a baby (oddly, my Jewish mother had insisted that I be, probably to respect my father's beliefs), and I went to catechism every Sunday as a boy. I even remember visiting Santa Barbara during the Cuban Missile Crisis and running across the railroad tracks to pray for safety at a nearby mission.

Despite all this, the fear-based aspects of Catholicism—my childhood terror of being in sin, the fear of dying and going to hell— were a bit much for me. I was always more at home with the traditions of my Jewish heritage, which felt warmer and more alive to me. My grandma Sonia and I would go to temple a couple of times a year, and she would tell me stories about the Jewish faith. She had me over for seders, and we celebrated the Jewish holidays together.

As I got older, my belief in God never waned, but I didn't particularly identify with either of the faith traditions in which I'd been raised.

Unlike me, Veronica was raised by a devout Catholic Filipina mother and a Catholic American father. She attended St. Columba

Catholic School and graduated from Georgetown, the oldest Catholic and Jesuit university in the country. She's deeply devoted to God and introduced me to her community at St. Monica Catholic Church. In fact, St. Monica is where we were married.

I often go to church with Veronica and have grown close with our pastor, Monsignor Lloyd Torgerson, a progressive, gifted, and beloved spiritual leader in the community and the city of Los Angeles. When he and I first met, what struck me immediately was the way he looked at me. I've met many priests in my life and have grown accustomed to seeing a hint of approval—or disapproval—in their eyes. Monsignor Torgerson's eyes, in contrast, hold nothing but deep love and humanity.

I had been brought up in a brand of Catholicism that emphasized guilt and judgment. The Catholicism that Monsignor preaches is completely different. He is a charismatic and gifted orator, and his weekly sermons are consistently powerful. No matter the theme, his message is always hopeful, relevant, and rooted in love. It hits you in the heart, not just the mind. Monsignor also has a special talent for using story and even his own personal limits and relatable struggles to help us make sense of our lives. I always walk away with something meaningful to reflect on, something that makes me think about the bigger picture of why we are here and what really matters in life. Monsignor and I have since become close friends, and he has had a profound impact on my spiritual journey.

When Veronica informed me one day that a group from our church would be traveling to Israel, I was interested but wary. I've never been one for group travel to begin with, and although I was feeling much more comfortable within Catholicism than I ever had before, I can't say I was 100 percent at ease with the idea of visiting Israel for the first time with a church group. That being said, I was definitely curious, and I knew the trip would mean a lot to Veronica. So I said yes, and just like that the plan for our honeymoon was hatched.

Off we went on a nonstop flight from LA to Tel Aviv. We spent one night in Tel Aviv to get settled and then set off again to join the group from St. Monica. Finally, we reached Tabgha, by the Sea of Galilee, where we would visit the Church of the Multiplication.

The Church of the Multiplication is the holiest of holy ground, where Christ performed the miracle of the loaves and fishes. The group was gathered around for Mass, and admittedly, I felt just a little out of place. As I often do, I found myself thinking of Grandma Sonia. But this time I wondered what she'd have made of my visit to the Holy Land with a Catholic church group. I could feel a spiritual crisis setting in: Was I betraying her? Was I betraying God and, by extension, my own beliefs? What *did* I believe?

The idea of a spiritual crisis might sound a bit grand, but when you travel to a place like Israel, and when you feel connected to people you've loved both in the past (Grandma Sonia) and in the present (Veronica), you can't help but ponder the big questions.

We were about to take Communion when I noticed Eli standing in the background. Eli was our tour guide. Early on in our trip, I had struck up a personal conversation with him. I shared that I was Jewish by birth, raised as a confused Catholic, and that my wife was a practicing Catholic. Eli told me about what it was like to be an Israeli Jew living alongside Christians and Muslims in a land that each claims as its own. (Remarkably, at the center of Jerusalem, in an area about twice the size of the Mall in Washington, sit three major holy sites: the Al-Aqsa Mosque, the third holiest site in the world for Muslims; the Western Wall, part of the holiest site in the world for Jews; and the Church of the Holy Sepulchre, which marks the place where Christians believe Jesus was crucified, entombed, and resurrected.) Over the course of the trip, that one conversation between Eli and me turned into hours of discussion about our respective journeys into faith.

On this particular day, as Eli watched me with his gentle, inquisitive eyes, I could almost read his thoughts: *You have a Jewish mother and a Catholic father. Hmm . . . What's going through your mind, Brian?*

As I glanced back at him, the image of my grandmother came to me. Right then, I knew that I was not betraying her. I was not betraying God or myself. Rather, I was discovering who I was and what I believed. Despite the long and continuing history of religious conflicts there, I had a feeling of oneness with the people I saw. I felt deep love as I walked the city. I felt safe even though people don't think it's safe. Maybe I felt this because I was in a place of deep significance for all three religions. Maybe it was because of events from the Bible taking place in the very place I was walking. I'm not exactly sure what it was, but I felt it.

Two days later, our church group was planning to walk the Via Dolorosa, or the "Way of Suffering." This street in the Old City of Jerusalem is believed to be the very one that Jesus walked on the way to his crucifixion. Marked with the Stations of the Cross and terminating at the Church of the Holy Sepulchre, the Via Dolorosa is an important processional route for Christian pilgrims. As they travel the winding path, the pilgrims sing and take turns carrying the cross in imitation of Christ.

Not surprisingly, Veronica wanted to share this experience together. So we set our alarm for four in the morning and made our way in the pitch black from the King David Hotel to the meeting point inside the walls of the Old City. We began. Our group of about forty people would take turns rotating who would carry the cross and who would follow and sing. At each of the fourteen stations, we recited a reading and prayer, then continued on to the next.

Monsignor tapped my shoulder. It was my turn. As I helped carry what must have been a ten- or twelve-foot heavy wooden cross along the narrow, ancient walkway, the sun started to rise. We sang and made our way to the final stations within Golgotha, or Calvary, inside the church. As we walked in, I caught Eli's eye. This time, however, it was different. His gaze was not one of curiosity, but one of connection. We looked at each other for a long moment—two human beings sharing a spiritual quest.

23

What It Means to Be Alive

I think that what we're seeking is an experience of being
alive, so that our life experiences on the purely physical plane
will have resonances with our own innermost being and reality, so that we actually feel the rapture of being alive.

—*Joseph Campbell*

Many years ago I was living in Malibu Colony, a residential community near Pepperdine University. It was a temporary situation while I
was having construction done on my place in the city. My house in
Malibu was at the very end of the colony, where the private access
meets a public beach. Ordinarily, that beach was extremely crowded,
so I liked to get up early and have my coffee out on the deck, where I
could enjoy the view before it filled up. There were usually a few
walkers or surfers, but it was generally very calm. One morning, I
was out—it was around 7:30 or so—and I found myself utterly alone.
The beach looked empty. I couldn't see a single person from where I
sat. As I sipped my coffee and stared down the beach, however, I
suddenly realized that there *was* someone. Way, way down the beach
and out closer to the water, where the tide pools were, was a person
lying on her side. The sight was so strange. It took me a moment to
realize I was looking at a human being. It took me another moment

to realize that the person was in some sort of trouble. I couldn't detect any movement in her body.

I took off running, sprinting down the beach in her direction. It took me a good minute or two to get there. As I drew near, I saw two young girls standing over her. Their faces looked frightened. And right then, I realized that the person I'd raced out to help wasn't an adult but a teenager. Her body was pulsing and her arms were flailing. From the looks of it, she was having some sort of seizure.

I dropped down next to her. The tide was lapping right where she lay, and her face was in the water while her arms flapped at her sides. I rolled her onto her back and managed to drag her to dry sand. I don't have any formal medical training—I'm not an EMT or anything—but I remembered in high school there'd been a boy in my class who'd had an epileptic seizure in the cafeteria, so I knew to clear her mouth of obstruction. I pulled out a piece of gum.

She was barely conscious and was clammy and still. Her eyes, which, to that point, had been half-shut, suddenly flashed open, revealing a blank stare without any trace of life or vitality. For a split second, my eyes fastened on hers, and I felt certain she was going to die. Then, just as abruptly as they had popped open, her eyes closed again.

I desperately scanned the beach for another human being, someone who might summon help, and I felt an overwhelming sadness course through me. I felt powerless. I couldn't connect with her. I felt her slipping away. Whether or not you've ever seen someone dying, as I had only once before, the moment has a metaphysical quality, an overwhelming spiritual power.

The other time was when I was just nine years old. I'd had a paper route out in Northridge, California, where we lived, and while I was making my rounds one day I saw an elderly man lying in the middle of the street near an upside-down car. It was early in the morning and the accident had clearly taken place just moments before. A camper had smashed into his Chevy, causing it to flip over and fling him from the car. I could hear the ambulance siren, and people were starting to gather. Though I was only a young kid, I felt an incredible, palpable sadness then too. This man was lifeless, gone. As I watched him lie there bleeding, I was stunned by what I now recognize as the pull of our shared humanity in that moment.

This moment on the beach was different. I was an adult and, by extension perhaps, a little closer to my own mortality, but this girl was just a kid.

"Georgia!" a woman's voice yelled.

It all took place within a span of seconds. It felt much longer, but it was almost instantaneous. I looked over my shoulder and—thank God!—there was a woman sprinting toward us.

"Georgia!"

I realized as she approached that I knew her: the woman was Melissa Mathison, the late screenwriter of *E.T.*, who was at that time married to Harrison Ford. She was the girl's mother. I think—it's hard to recall—I yelled to *her* to get help and dial 911.

Fortunately, there's a station right outside the colony gate, and the paramedics arrived almost immediately. But until they did, I stayed right where I was, kneeling down beside the girl and searching her semiconscious face. I was deep inside that fragile moment; I had no control over what would happen next. And that fundamental *uncertainty* seemed to me to exemplify the crux of the human experience. Would she live? Who knew? The part of the experience that remains indelible is the connection I felt, not just to her as a person, but to her fate.

She was airlifted to UCLA Medical Center via helicopter. Thankfully, she fully recovered.

About five years after the incident, I was walking through the lobby of the Mercer Hotel where I always stay when I'm in New York. I noticed Harrison Ford sitting on one of the couches. At the time of the incident, I had only known him as an actor. I'd been trying to make a movie about the Worcester Cold Storage and Warehouse Co. fire, a brutal and terrifying blaze that killed six firefighters in Massachusetts in 1999, and Harrison had agreed to star in it, but the film never got off the ground. He's a very strong guy, slightly brusque but powerful, as you'd probably expect from the roles he plays. He has tremendous integrity. Right after he found out what had happened, he called to thank me. For a long time I never told anyone what had happened, aside from my family. It seemed like another reality.

As I was crossing the Mercer lobby, Harrison called out to me. He waved me over to where he was sitting with a young woman in her early twenties.

"Come have a drink with us."

I joined them. The bar was crowded, as it happened to be Fashion Week, and so the three of us found ourselves huddled together in this densely packed room.

"Do you recognize this girl?" he said. "This is my daughter, Georgia."

Of course I recognized her, and she recognized me too. I was relieved to see her alert and full of life. We sat together and had a glass of wine. It felt like we were bound together by an indescribable connection—the ineffable experience of our shared humanity and fleeting mortality.

We are all human beings. We all have emotions. We all have something to share. We are made for connection. It is the source of growth, discovery, joy, and meaning in our short, sweet time here on Earth. We need only be willing to open our minds and hearts and choose to *see* the people standing with us face to face. Whether the connection lasts a moment or a lifetime, whether it's easy or challenging, we are always better for it.

Brian Grazer's Curiosity Conversations: A Sampler

As part of the work to write *A Curious Mind*, I did something I had never done before: assembled in one place as comprehensive a list as possible of the people I've had curiosity conversations with over the last thirty years. (Actually, some of the staff at Imagine did most of the work to create the list—for which I'm incredibly thankful.)

Looking through the list of people I've had the chance to talk to is, for me, like turning the pages of a photo album. Just like a single snapshot sometimes does, a name can trigger a wave of memories: where I was when I met that person, what we talked about, what they were wearing, even someone's posture, attitude, or facial expression.

Reading through the list over and over as we worked on the book, I was struck by two things. First, an incredible sense of gratitude that so many people agreed to sit and talk to me, to give me a sense of their world, when there wasn't anything tangible to be gained. All these years later, I wish I could call each of these people up and say thank you, again, for what they added to my life. Each person was an adventure—even if we were just sitting on the couches in my office—a journey well beyond the confines and routines of my own life. The breadth of experience and personality and accomplishment on the list is inspiring.

And second, although *A Curious Mind* is populated with stories from the conversations, we had so many more we didn't include that it seemed like it would be fun to offer a wider selection. What follows is a sampler—bonus material, we might call it here in Hollywood—from some of the curiosity conversations that have stayed with me.

Lunch with Fidel

The Hotel Nacional in Havana sits on the seaside boulevard, the Malecón, and it has two dozen rooms that are named after famous people who have stayed in them—Fred Astaire (room 228), Stan Musial (245), Jean-Paul Sartre (539), and Walt Disney (445) are examples.

When I visited Havana in February 2001, I was put in the Lucky Luciano suite, a pair of rooms named for the famous mafioso that are really too large for one person.

I had come with a group of guy friends—we'd decided we wanted to do one guys' trip a year, and we started with Cuba. The Cuba trip was organized by Tom Freston, who was the CEO of MTV at the time, and the group included Brad Grey, the TV and movie producer; Jim Wiatt, then the head of the talent agency William Morris; Bill Roedy, former head of MTV International; Graydon Carter, then editor of *Vanity Fair*; and Leslie Moonves, then the CEO of CBS, including the CBS News division.

This was long before the thaw in relations between the United States and Cuba, of course, and a visit to Cuba in those days was a challenge—you never knew quite where you would get to go or whom you would get to meet.

Before we went to Cuba, I invested a lot of effort trying quietly to set up a curiosity conversation with Fidel Castro, without making any headway.

We flew into a Cuban military base—and it turned out that several of us had separately tried to set up meetings with Fidel. We made it clear to the folks taking care of us that we would welcome a meeting with him.

Cubans, we learned during our visit, tried to avoid referring to Fidel by name. They had a gesture they used in place of saying his name—you used your thumb and forefinger to pull on your chin like you were stroking a beard.

We had a few false alarms. Once, we were leaving a Havana club at 2:30 in the morning, and an aide came and told us Fidel would see us at 4 a.m. We were exhausted. We all looked at each other and said, "Okay! Let's do it!"

Almost as soon as we said yes, word came back that the meeting wasn't going to happen after all.

The day before we left, we were told that Fidel would host us as a group for lunch the next day, starting at noon. We had been scheduled to leave then, so we had to push our departure back.

The next morning, we were ready to go. We were given a destination. We piled into the cars and headed off at high speed. Then, suddenly, the cars swerved to the side, did a U-turn, and accelerated in exactly the opposite direction, to a different destination.

Was that mystery? Theatrics? Was it designed to provide Fidel with some real security? Who knows?

As soon as we arrived at the new location, we were introduced to Fidel, who was dressed in his classic army fatigues. We were all given rum drinks, and we stood around talking.

I was with Les Moonves, talking to Fidel. Les was arguably the most powerful person in our group, and after William Paley himself (founder of CBS), he was arguably the most successful broadcaster of all time. Fidel clearly knew who Les was and treated him as if he were the "leader" of our group, directing a lot of his attention to Moonves. Fidel talked with such energy that he actually had two translators, who took turns.

Fidel, too, held a drink, but in an hour of standing around, I never saw the glass touch his lips. I also never saw him tire, either of the standing or of holding the drink. After more than an hour, I whispered to Les, "Do you think we're ever going to go inside for lunch?"

Les said loudly, and partly to Fidel, "Maybe we ought to go inside and have lunch!"

As if he'd completely forgotten about the meal, Fidel agreed immediately and ushered us into lunch. The meal consisted of two parts: many long courses of Cuban food; and Fidel, talking about the wonders of Cuba. He didn't talk with us—he talked at us.

He knew the details of everything. The weather for every part of Cuba. The kilowatts required to run a light bulb in a Cuban home. He could granularize anything about the country, its people, its economy.

At one point, Fidel turned quite pointedly to Les and said, "When you get back to your country and your president, Bush, I wish you would tell him my thoughts"—and he proceeded to unfurl a long dissertation he wanted Moonves to pass on to the United States president. As if Les would naturally, and immediately, report in with President Bush.

For literally hours, Fidel didn't ask a single question of us, or engage us in conversation. He talked, and we ate and listened.

Eventually, lunch stretched to 5:30. The jets were waiting to fly us back to the United States. Again, I nodded to Les that maybe it was time to go. And again, Les elegantly moved us along, telling Fidel it was really time for us to go.

Fidel presented each of us with a box of cigars as a parting gift. I was wearing a beautiful Cuban guayabera I had bought, and as we left, Fidel autographed the shirt, while I was wearing it, right in the middle of the back.

The Hero, the Prediction, and the Dangerous Baseball Cap

One day in 2005, the second stop of the afternoon was a magnificent office in the United States Capitol. It was generously appointed, with rich wood paneling and solid, elegant furniture. The space conveyed not so much a sense of power as something much deeper: a sense of authority. It was the office of Senator John McCain, and I had an appointment to have a curiosity conversation with one of the most interesting and influential men in the United States Senate.

It was shaping up to be quite an afternoon, that Wednesday, June 8. I had spent the previous hour in one of the least regal Senate offices before arriving at McCain's office, with one of the least influential members of the United States Senate at the time: Barack Obama.

And after my conversation with Senator McCain, I had to hustle a few blocks up Pennsylvania Avenue to the White House to have dinner and a movie with the most powerful person in the world—President George W. Bush.

Obama. McCain. Bush. One-on-one, within the same four hours. That's about as amazing a lineup as one guy from outside Washington can have in a single afternoon inside the Beltway.

John McCain was a real American hero. He was a pilot in Vietnam and was shot down, captured, and tortured; he survived and went on to become an important political figure. Even in the North Vietnam prison camps where he was held, McCain's fellow American prisoners regarded him as a leader. In the Senate and across the country in 2005, McCain had a reputation for smarts, independence, and determination.

The psychology and the character of heroes fascinate me—almost every movie we've made is about what it means to be a hero in some way or another.

But my meeting with McCain was oddly anticlimactic. We ended up talking not about substance but about oddly generic things—we talked about baseball, which I know very little about. We talked about the elderly.

McCain's presence was as impressive as his office. He was clearly in charge. He was polite to me, but I got the sense in the end that he wasn't quite sure what I was doing there. I was just a relatively well-known person on his schedule for an hour. One thing was clear: John McCain didn't have to worry about time, because everybody around him was paying attention to the schedule.

At one point in our conversation, his chief assistant came in and she said, "One minute, sir!" And I'm not kidding, sixty seconds later, that woman came back in and said, "You're up!"

Senator McCain rose. His jacket was already on, of course. He buttoned it as he stood, he shook my hand, and he was gone. A moment later, one of the aides pointed to the television in McCain's office—and there he was, striding onto the Senate floor.

In contrast to my previous conversation, meeting with Barack Obama couldn't have been more complete. Senator McCain had been in the Senate eighteen years, and just the last November he had been re-elected to his fourth term representing Arizona, with a stunning 77 percent of the vote. He was at the top of his influence, and rising.

Barack Obama had been in the United States Senate for five months. Just a year earlier, Obama was still an Illinois state senator.

But it was at the Democratic National Convention the previous summer—at the convention that nominated Senator John Kerry as the Democrat to challenge George W. Bush—that Barack Obama first came to the nation's attention, and mine as well. That's where Obama gave the galvanizing keynote address, with optimistic lines like "There's not a liberal America and a conservative America. There's the United States of America."

The day I met him for the first time, he was the only Black United States senator. When I arrived at his office, I was struck first by the number of people coming and going. It was in a basement; the light wasn't great. It was like some cross between a Saturday swap meet and the DMV. Obama's office was totally open—people were just coming and going, taking advantage of the chance to visit their senator.

There were a lot of fascinating people in the Senate I could have seen that afternoon, a lot of important people in Washington. I had asked for an appointment to see Obama, who was not even a significant senator, let alone a force on the national stage, because when I'd seen him speak on television, like everybody who watched, I was captivated and intrigued. To me, his communication skills were in another category. His communication skills were like Muhammad Ali's boxing skills. It seemed as if he were performing magic, rhetorical magic.

I'm in the communication business. My job is to make words into images and have those images ignite emotions in the audience, emotions that are more forceful than the original words.

Obama, when I saw him speak, in the same way one might have seen Ali punch, was doing something beyond any other speaker I'd seen. He was igniting emotions with words—the same way an image could.

Obama's office was very humble, but he was very welcoming—and he was totally present. None of the distraction you often find with busy, important people who are with you yet constantly checking the clock or their email, their minds in four other places at once. He's tall and wiry, and we sat on couches that were catty-corner—he greeted me, then he folded himself onto the couch with acrobatic fluidity, like an athlete would. He seemed completely relaxed and totally comfortable with himself.

We talked about our families; we talked about work—it was more of a personal conversation than a policy conversation. While we talked, energetic young people—his staff—were constantly coming and going from the office, but he was undistracted.

Obama conveyed a real sense of confidence. He was in office number ninety-nine, but he was completely self-assured. Obama was just a year out of the Illinois state senate and five months into the U.S. Senate, and not even four years later he would be president of the United States.

As I was leaving Senate office number ninety-nine, I bumped into Jon Favreau, the talented writer who was working for Obama as a speechwriter. They had met at the Democratic National Convention, where Obama gave the keynote.

"If you ever decide to get out of politics," I said to Favreau half-jokingly, "and you want to work in Hollywood, give me a call. You're awesome."

"Thanks so much," said Favreau, smiling. "But I think he's going to want me."

I hadn't told Senator McCain and Senator Obama that I was going to see the other one. But I had told them both I was going to the White House that evening to screen *Cinderella Man* for President George W. Bush.

As the pre-movie food was being served, President Bush got a tray for himself, put his food on it, and then sat down at a table all alone. He didn't seem to need his folks around him. That table filled up, of course. But I thought that was pretty impressive. President Bush stayed for the whole movie.

The only disappointing part of the evening had to do with a small gift I had for President Bush. I brought him a ball cap from the TV show *Friday Night Lights*. President Bush grew up in Odessa, Texas, of course, and I thought he would get a kick out of it.

I was standing in line to go through security at the White House gate, and I was so excited about the hat, I showed it to the security officers. "The president is from Odessa, Texas, and I brought him this hat from *Friday Night Lights* as a gift," I said. "I'm going to give it to him."

I thought that would make everyone smile.

Boy was I wrong. They looked at me. They looked at the hat. They took the hat from me. They put it through a couple of different machines. A couple more people examined it, inside and out.

Then someone nodded and said to me, "You won't be handing the hat to the president. We'll give the hat to the president for you."

I would have been better off not saying anything and just wearing the hat into the White House on my own head.

I never saw the hat again. I did tell President Bush about it—and I hope at some point someone handed it to him.

The Gloved One

In the early 1990s, I routinely tried to sit down with Michael Jackson. We would call his office a couple of times a year and ask for a meeting, invite him over. He wasn't interested.

Then, all of a sudden, he said yes. It wasn't clear why, although this was the period we were doing movies like *Parenthood* and *Kindergarten Cop* and *My Girl*, which were family friendly, and I had heard that Jackson was interested in doing movies like that himself.

When the day arrived, his advance people came up to the office first. There was a lot of excitement—as you might imagine—and then Jackson appeared.

Jackson was already known at that point for those shy, slightly unusual gestures of his. But there was none of that. He seemed like a totally normal person, although he was wearing the gloves—the white gloves.

I was a Michael Jackson fan, of course—you couldn't follow music in America in the 1970s and 1980s and not be a fan of Michael Jackson. But I wasn't a crazed fan—so I wasn't particularly nervous. I respected Jackson; I thought he was an amazing talent.

He was about five feet nine inches tall—he was thin, but you could tell he was strong. He stepped into my office and sat down.

"What a pleasure to meet you," I said. "This is great."

He was acting normally, so I decided to treat him normally. I had the thought, *I'm going to ask him to take off his gloves. Anyone normal coming in from outside would take off their gloves, right?*

It could have been the end of the conversation right there.

But I didn't hesitate. I said, "Would you mind taking off your gloves?"

And he did. Simple as that. I thought, *He took off the gloves—we're going to be okay.*

Michael Jackson was clearly not much of a small-talk person. And to be honest, I didn't know exactly what to talk to him about. I certainly didn't want to bore him.

I asked, "How do you create music?"

And he immediately started to talk about how he creates music— how he composes it, how he performs it, all in a way that was almost scientific.

In fact, his whole manner transformed. When we first started talking, he had that high, slightly childish voice people know. But as soon as he started to talk about making music, even his voice changed, and he became another person—it was like a master class, like a professor from Juilliard was talking. Melody, lyrics, what the mixing engineer does. It blew my mind.

We did talk a little bit about movies—Jackson had already done amazing videos, including the video for "Thriller," which was directed by John Landis. It was a curiosity conversation with a touch of business about it.

Although I never met him again, there was nothing odd or uncomfortable about the hour we spent together. I came away with a very different impression of Michael Jackson. It made me feel like he wasn't so much a weird guy, or a collection of weird affectations—he was just someone who struggled with fame. The behavior was somehow environmental. I was so struck by the fact that I could talk to him like an adult, and he talked back like an adult.

I could ask him to take off the gloves, and he'd take off the gloves.

The Missed Opportunity

In some interesting ways, Andy Warhol had a lot in common with Michael Jackson. They both had a distinctive physical presence, one that each had consciously crafted for himself. They both did such impressive, influential work that simply saying either name conjures a whole style, a whole era. And they were both considered mysterious, enigmatic, almost impenetrable.

I went to meet Andy Warhol in the early 1980s, when I was visiting New York City, during a period when I had gotten the chance to meet a lot of artists, including David Hockney, Ed Ruscha, Salvador Dalí, and Roy Lichtenstein. By then, Andy Warhol had become an institution—he did the famous Campbell's soup can silk screens in 1962. I met him at his studio, The Factory. He was wearing his classic black turtleneck.

Two things were interesting to me about Warhol. The first is that he wasn't a brilliant technical artist—he didn't have the skills of, say, Roy Lichtenstein, and he wasn't trying to gain them. For him, the message of the art, the statement, was the most important thing.

And the second thing that was so striking when I met him in person was his absolute refusal to intellectualize his work. He almost didn't want to talk about it. He wasn't just understated. Every question brought the absolute simplest answer.

"Why did you do the portraits of Marilyn Monroe?" I asked.

"I like her," Warhol said.

We were strolling through The Factory, and there were silk screens everywhere, both finished and in progress.

"Why would you do your art on silk screens?" I asked.

"So we can make many of them," he said. Just like that—never an elaborate explanation.

Warhol had a reputation for being detached. During that visit to his studio, he was totally with me. He was a little trippy, in that sixties way. "Hey, man, let's go over here," he would say.

And he was a little hard to talk to. But he was easy to hang out with.

I was back in New York City just a few weeks later, and I returned for a second visit.

He told me, "I'm going to go out to Los Angeles and do a *Love*

Boat episode." I thought to myself, *What's he talking about? Andy Warhol on* The Love Boat—*with Captain Stubing and Julie McCoy?* I couldn't picture it. I thought he was kidding.

"I'm going to act in an episode of *The Love Boat*," Warhol said. I didn't realize he'd done those kinds of pop culture appearances before. He liked to surprise people. And he did it: he was on a *Love Boat* episode broadcast October 12, 1985, along with Milton Berle and Andy Griffith.

At that second meeting, Warhol said to me, "I didn't realize your partner is Ron Howard. He's Richie Cunningham!"

Warhol had an idea.

"I would love to take a picture of Ron Howard and do two paintings—a before and an after. I want to take a picture of Ron Howard now, with his handlebar mustache, then I want to shave off the mustache, and I'll do another picture.

"Two of them. One with the mustache. One with no mustache. Before and after."

I thought immediately of Warhol's dual portraits of Elvis. But I didn't mention that. I told Warhol I would talk to Ron about it.

I got back to LA and I said to Ron, "Andy Warhol wants to do this thing with you. He wants to do portraits of Ron Howard, before and after. He wants to shave off your mustache." I was pretty excited.

Ron wasn't excited; he was more baffled than anything. "You know, Brian, I don't really want to shave off my mustache," he said. "It's part of my identity now. I'm trying to get out of that 'American boy' identity."

Okay. I could understand that. Kind of. Not everybody has Andy Warhol asking to do portraits of them, of course. But I also knew how important Ron Howard's grown-up identity was to him—how important it's been to all of us, in fact.

So that was the end of *Ron Howard, Before and After*. Or so I thought.

Many years later, our movie *Cry-Baby* opened. As had become our habit, Ron Howard and I went to the Westwood Avco theater in Los Angeles on opening night to gauge the popularity of *Cry-Baby* firsthand. The Avco was the theater where there had been lines around the block for *Splash*. That Friday, to see *Cry-Baby*, there were seven people in a theater for five hundred.

Ron and I went home, had a couple of bottles of red wine, and watched *Drugstore Cowboy* to soften the disappointment. Ron had to catch a red-eye flight from LAX back east, so around 10 p.m., he headed to the airport.

Before he flew out, he called me. He was a little buzzy. He said, "Brian, I want you to know I just went in the men's room here at the airport and shaved off my mustache."

And without thinking about it, I said, "Oh my God, you could have done that for Andy Warhol! Then we could have had two portraits of Ron Howard each worth fifty million."

These days, of course, Ron's mustache—in fact, his full beard—is back. Ron is an icon without a Warhol silk screen.

Curiosity as Art

You probably know Jeff Koons's art. It's fun; it's outsized. He's done huge stainless steel sculptures in the shape of the balloon dogs that clowns make. He rendered an inflatable toy rabbit in the same vivid stainless steel, and it became so well-known that it was reproduced as a float in the Macy's Thanksgiving Day Parade.

To me, Koons's work is both exuberant and playful. It seems simple too. But underneath is his rich understanding of history, of art theory.

I first met Jeff Koons in the early 1990s. As with Warhol, I went to Koons's studio in New York. When you walk into his studio, knowing about the rabbit and the balloon dog, you think, *I could do this*. When you walk out after having spent a couple of hours with Koons, you think, *No one could duplicate what he's doing*.

Although he worked on Wall Street as a commodities broker as a young man, Koons always wanted to be an artist. But he's not the kind of artist who bangs around his studio in blue jeans. He's more apt to dress like one of the great directors of the forties or fifties, like George Cukor or Cecil B. DeMille—in slacks and a nice shirt, fashionable and elegant.

He's a study in contrasts. Vocally, he's not loud. But his art and his actions are loud. For instance, in 1991, he got married for the first time—to the famous Italian porn actress La Cicciolina. Then they did art together—including pictures in which they both appear naked, or mostly naked.

Koons is an unpretentious man, but he's willing to do risky, even shocking things on behalf of his art. And unlike Warhol, Koons is happy to talk to you about the sources of his art as well as its intellectual principles and historical perspective translated into visual form.

His studio, where he was producing all this dramatic art, felt almost like an expensive, elaborate science laboratory. It was almost antiseptic. He was like the calculating genius, the scientist, thinking and creating.

I went to his studio a second time much more recently—it was in a different place, and it was like the first studio, the science lab, had been taken to a whole new level.

Later, when we started talking about art for the cover of *A Curious Mind*, I suddenly thought of Jeff Koons. What would his approach to curiosity be? What would his approach to a book cover be?

I didn't ask him directly—I passed word through a mutual friend that I would love for him to do a drawing for the book. Word came back that he would definitely do it.

A month later, in the summer of 2014, we met at the Aspen Ideas Festival and I said to him, "I'm so excited you're doing a piece of art for the book!"

He said, "Tell me about the book."

I described the years of curiosity conversations, the people, the sense I have that I wouldn't have had anything like the kind of life I've had without curiosity. I told him that the point of the book is to inspire other people to see the simple power of curiosity to make their own lives better.

Koons's face lit up. "I understand," he said. "I love that."

And the drawing he did for the cover captures what we were talking about—a seemingly simple line drawing of a face that conveys exactly the joy, openheartedness, and excitement that being curious brings.

Writer Puts Producer in a Headlock

Perhaps the greatest boxing writer in modern America was Norman Mailer. He was a great writer about many things—Mailer won the National Book Award and two Pulitzers—and also a huge force in America's cultural landscape starting in the 1950s, when he co-founded *The Village Voice*.

When we started working on *Cinderella Man*, the boxing movie that we ultimately got to show to President Bush at the White House, I decided it would be fun and valuable to talk to Mailer about the boxer Jim Braddock and the role of boxing in Depression-era America.

I met Mailer in New York City in 2004. I let him pick the place—he chose the Royalton hotel, one of those famous old Midtown hotels that had once been elegant but was then a little past its prime.

It was the kind of lobby that had those old lumpy couches covered with velvet. Slightly uncomfortable. We sat catty-corner to each other. Mailer sat very close to me.

When we met, he was eighty-one years old, but there was nothing old about him. We talked about boxing, we complained to each other about our relationships.

Even at eighty-one, Mailer was a tough guy. He was short and thick and very strong. He had a big, tough face. And he had a very interesting voice. He enunciated every word. Every word had drama to it. You leaned into his voice.

It was about three in the afternoon, but Mailer ordered a drink. I remember thinking it was a little early to start drinking—but probably not in the world Norman Mailer lived and wrote in. He was a bridge to the era of Hemingway. He had something you'd expect from a guy like Mailer—something old-fashioned, like a sidecar. A whiskey drink.

Mailer liked the idea of a movie about Jim Braddock. He was crabby—he was crabby about most things that afternoon. But he liked the idea of the movie.

He was kind of funny. We took some pictures—he was willing to take some with me, but he wasn't warm and fuzzy about it. "Okay, take it. You've got a second to do it," he said.

When he was talking about boxing, he talked about individual fights—he could remember the sequence of punches in specific rounds in specific fights—and he showed me the punches; he literally did the punches. He talked about the physiognomy of the boxers, how they study each other's bodies and faces, looking for the places where the punches will really hurt.

He was demonstrating an exchange of punches in a particular fight, and he said, "And then he threw him out of the ring."

I was surprised. I asked, "How'd that go? How did he throw him out of the ring?"

He just reached over, said, "It went like this," and then all of a sudden Norman Mailer had me in a headlock. Right in the lobby of the Royalton hotel. The famous writer put the Hollywood producer in a headlock.

I wasn't quite sure what to do.

With his arms wrapped around my head, it was clear how strong he was. It was slightly embarrassing. I didn't want to struggle. But I also wasn't quite sure what would happen next. How long would Mailer keep me in the headlock?

It lasted long enough to leave a strong impression.

Sharing a Bowl of Ice Cream with a Princess

For pure excitement, nothing quite tops a real prince and princess. In September 1995, we were invited to do a royal premiere of the movie *Apollo 13* in London for Prince Charles and Princess Diana and the royal family.

The way a royal premiere works is a little different than, for instance, the White House showings we do. You meet the royals at a movie theater in London, and then, in the case of *Apollo 13*, everyone is invited to dinner afterward at a different location.

Prince Charles and Princess Di had already formally separated, so we weren't quite sure who would come to the event. But as soon as we knew it was going to happen, I violated protocol by reaching out to the office of Princess Diana. I explained that I looked forward to the premiere and to meeting Her Royal Highness, and that I did these curiosity meetings and would welcome the chance to sit down one-on-one with the princess either before or after the evening's events.

Perhaps not surprisingly, I didn't hear anything back.

The premiere went off on September 7 at a theater in London's West End, and we all lined up to formally greet Princess Diana (Prince Charles did not attend). After the movie, several dozen of us adjourned to dinner at a big restaurant with long rectangular tables. We all took our seats, as instructed.

Now, when you do a royal premiere, before you even get on the plane to cross the Atlantic Ocean, the folks from Universal Studios come and brief you on the protocol for being in the presence of members of the royal family: how to greet them ("Your Royal Highness"), that you don't touch them, the moments when you should stand and when you should sit and when you should bow. You get a second briefing after you arrive in London.

So we took our seats for dinner, and the last person to walk in was Princess Diana. As she entered, everyone stood up. She sat, and we took our seats—and sitting directly across from me was Princess Diana.

Without being told, it seemed like I was going to get my curiosity conversation after all.

Diana was extremely beautiful—in fact, that night, Princess Diana was wearing a short black Versace dress that got a lot of notice in the London press as being perhaps the shortest dress she'd ever worn in public.

As soon as she sat down, I made a decision in my mind: I was not going to let our conversation conform to the stilted style that protocol would dictate.

I decided to be funny, to be jokey. She connected immediately— she joked right back. You could tell people around her were a little surprised at my behavior and at her playful participation.

She did love *Apollo 13*. She didn't get animated like I would have. With that wonderful British lilt, she said, "It was a tremendous film. Really, triumphant. An important movie."

Over dinner, we talked about movies. We talked about pop culture in America. Tom Hanks was sitting on one side of the princess, and he was in very funny form himself that evening. Ron Howard was on the other side of the princess. I'd say between Tom and me trying to make the princess laugh, I'm not sure Ron got the chance to talk very much.

Diana reminded me of Audrey Hepburn in the movie *Roman Holiday*—although in Diana's case, she was the ordinary person who became a princess, instead of the other way around. Diana's charisma came from her beauty, her poise, her attentiveness.

I was most surprised by her sense of humor. I didn't expect her to laugh at our jokes. I thought she would smile—but she laughed. It seemed liberating. She was the most famous person in the world but also a little trapped. The laughter was a touch of freedom.

At dinner, there was no ordering—the menu had been set in advance. As we were finishing the main course, I said to the princess, "You know, I really like ice cream. Do you think I could get some ice cream?"

Princess Diana smiled. "If you want some ice cream," she said, "why don't you order some from one of the waiters?"

I called a waiter over and said, "I was wondering if the princess and I could share a bowl of ice cream."

Princess Diana looked at me with an expression that seemed to say, *That was cute. That was ballsy. And I'm a little aghast.*

The waiters scrambled to get ice cream. I'd say I've never seen waiters scramble around quite like they did trying to find that ice cream, in fact.

Shortly, a bowl of ice cream was presented to me—a scoop of chocolate and a scoop of vanilla. Naturally, I offered the bowl to Princess Diana first, and she took a spoonful or two. Then I had some.

Then before it was all gone, I offered the bowl back to Princess Diana. And although I'd been eating from it, she took several more bites. She ate after me. That sort of stunned me. She was smiling.

Then, all of a sudden, the princess had to leave.

I said, "Why do you have to leave? We're having such a good time!"

She said, "It's protocol. I have to leave before midnight." Just like in a fairy tale.

Then the princess stood, and we all stood, and she was gone.

Appendix: How to Have a Curiosity Conversation

We've talked throughout the book about how to use questions, how to use curiosity, to make your daily life better. But maybe you want to try what I did: maybe you want to have some curiosity conversations, to sit down with a few really interesting people and try to understand how they see the world differently than you do.

Curiosity conversations can help give you a bigger life. They can do for you what they have done for me—they can help you step out of your own world, they can widen your perspective, they can give you a taste of experiences you won't have on your own.

Starter Conversations

Everyone has their own style, but I'd recommend starting close to home. That's what I did, in fact. Think about your immediate circle of relatives, friends, acquaintances, work-related colleagues. Maybe there are a few people with intriguing jobs or very different experiences—of education, upbringing, culture—or people who work in your business but in a different arena.

That's a great place to start, a good place to get a feel for how a curiosity conversation works. Pick someone and ask if they'll make a date to talk to you for twenty minutes or so—and specify what you want to talk about.

"I've always been curious about your work, I'm trying to broaden my sense of that world, and I was wondering if you'd be willing to spend twenty minutes talking to me about what you do, what the challenges and the satisfactions are."

Or . . .

"I've always been curious about how you ended up as [whatever their profession is], and I was wondering if you'd be willing to spend twenty minutes talking to me about what it took to get where you are—what the key turning points in your career have been."

Here are a few tips for when someone agrees to talk to you— whether they are a family member, an acquaintance, or a friend of a friend:

✦ Be clear that you want to hear their story. You're not looking for a job; you're not looking for advice about your own situation or any challenges you're facing. You're curious about them.

✦ Even if the person you're talking to is someone you know well, be respectful—treat the occasion with just a tinge of formality, because you want to talk about things you don't normally; dress well; be on time; be appreciative of their time even as you sit down to begin.

✦ Think in advance about what you'd most hope to get out of the conversation, and think of a handful of open-ended questions that will get the person talking about what you're most interested in: "What was your first professional success?" "Why did you decide to do [whatever their job is]?" "Tell me about a couple of big challenges you had to overcome." "What has been your biggest surprise?" "How did you end up living in [their city]?" "What's the part of what you do that outsiders don't appreciate?"

✦ Don't be a slave to your prepared questions. Be just the opposite: listen closely, and be a good conversationalist. Pick up on what the person you're talking to is saying, and ask questions that expand on the stories they tell or the points they make.

✦ Don't share your own story or your own observations. Listen. Ask questions. The goal is for you to learn as much about the person you're talking to as you can in the time you have. If you're talking, you're not learning about the other person.

✦ Be respectful of the person's time, without unnecessarily cutting off a great conversation. If they agree to give you twenty minutes, keep track of the time. Even if things are going well, when the allotted time has passed, it's okay to say something like, "I don't want to take too much of your time, and it's been twenty minutes" or "It's been twenty minutes; perhaps I should let you go." People will often say, "I'm enjoying this. I can give you a few more minutes."

✦ Be grateful. Don't just say thank you; give the best compliment for a conversation like this: "That was so interesting." And send a very brief follow-up email thank-you, perhaps highlighting one story or point they made that you particularly enjoyed or that was particularly eye-opening for you. That thank-you email shouldn't ask for anything more—it should be written so the person who gave you his or her time doesn't even need to reply.

Curiosity Conversations Farther Afield

Conversations with people outside your own circle or with strangers are harder to arrange, but they can be fascinating, even thrilling.

Who should you approach? Think about your own interests—whether it's college football or astrophysics or cooking, your community almost surely has local experts. When you read the news or scroll through social media, pay attention to people who make an impression on you. Search out experts at your local university.

Setting up curiosity conversations with people outside your own circle requires a little more planning and discretion:

✦ First, once you've identified someone you'd like to sit with and talk to for twenty minutes, consider whether you might know someone who knows that person. Get in touch with the person you know, explain who you want to talk to, and ask if you can use your acquaintance's name. An email that begins "I'm writing at the suggestion of [name of mutual acquaintance]" establishes immediate credibility.

✦ If you are trying to meet someone who is totally outside of your circle, use your own credentials and strong interest up front. "I'm a vice president at the local hospital, and I have a lifelong interest in astronomy. I was wondering if you'd be willing to spend twenty minutes talking to me about your own work and the current state of the field. I appreciate that you don't know me, but I'm writing out of genuine curiosity—I don't want anything more than a twenty-minute conversation, at your convenience."

✦ You may hear back from an assistant asking for a little more information—and some people may find the request a little unusual. Explain what you're hoping for. Be clear that you're not seeking a job, or advice, or a career change—you are simply trying to understand a little about someone with real achievements in a field you care about.

✦ If you get an appointment, make sure to do as much reading as possible about the person you're going to see, as well as their field. That can help you ask good questions about their career track or their avocations. But it's a fine line: be respectful of people's privacy.

✦ Pay attention not just to what the person you're talking to says, but how they say it. Often there is as much information in people's tone, in the way they tell a story or respond to a question, as in the answer itself.

✦ The tips about starter conversations apply—along with your own experience of having those starter conversations. Have questions in advance, but let the conversation flow based on what you learn; make your side of the conversation questions, not your own thoughts; be respectful of the clock; be grateful in person and in a very brief follow-up email. If an assistant helps set up a curiosity conversation, be sure to include that person in your thank-you note.

Curiosity Takeaways

What you'll discover is that people love talking about themselves—about their work, about their challenges, about the story of how they arrived where they are.

The hardest part is the very beginning.

In a formal curiosity conversation, I would recommend not taking notes—the goal is a good conversation. Taking notes might just make someone uncomfortable.

But when you've left a person's office, it's valuable to spend just a few minutes thinking about what the most surprising thing you learned was; what the person's tone and personality were like compared to what you might have imagined; what choices they've made that were different than you might have made in the same circumstances.

And you don't need to have curiosity conversations in formal settings that you set up. You meet people all the time. The person next to you on an airplane or at a wedding quite likely has a fascinating story and comes from a world different from yours—and all you have to do in that setting is turn, smile, and introduce yourself to start a conversation. "Hi, I'm Brian. I work in the movie business—what do you do?"

Remember that if you're trying to learn something, you should be asking questions and listening to the answers rather than talking about yourself.

Curiosity Conversation 2.0: The Curiosity Dinner Party

You can take the aforementioned principles and extend them into a group atmosphere by hosting a gathering. Think of two or three interesting friends or acquaintances—they can be people who know one another or do not—preferably from different lines of work and different backgrounds.

Invite those people and ask each of them to invite two or three of their most interesting friends or acquaintances. The result will be a group of selected people who are interconnected but (hopefully) very different from one another.

The dinner party can be as formal or informal as you like, but it should be in a place that is conducive to mingling. Use the suggestions mentioned previously to kick off the dinner conversation and encourage each person to follow their own curiosity, ask questions, listen, and learn about one another.

Acknowledgments

From *A Curious Mind*

Brian Grazer

The journalist Charlie Rose was the first person to seriously suggest a book about curiosity. He'd had me on his PBS interview show to talk about curiosity, and afterward he said, "You should do a book about this."

That was ten years ago. Charlie Rose planted the seed. Ron Howard—who knew about the incredible range of the curiosity conversations—would also occasionally nudge me to write a book. He feels like there is so much fun and insight packed into those decades of talking to people.

But I was always a little uncomfortable with the idea—a book about my curiosity seemed like it would be egotistical and not that interesting to anyone else.

One afternoon in 2012 I was talking about the curiosity conversations with Bryan Lourd, one of my show business agents, and he said, "Why don't you write a book about that? Why don't you write a book about curiosity?" Richard Lovett, Bryan's colleague at CAA, had suggested the same thing. I said that it didn't seem like a very interesting book. Bryan said, "No, not a book about *your* curiosity, a book about the journey curiosity has taken you on. A book about *curiosity*—not as some kind of accomplishment, but as something you use to explore the world."

That reframing of the idea—a book not about my curiosity, but about what curiosity has enabled me to do, about what curiosity can enable anyone to do—snapped the idea into focus for me.

I didn't want to write a book about all the people I'd had conversations with—I wanted to write about the impulse to have those conversations. I wanted to use the conversations to tell a story: the story of my steady discovery of the power of curiosity in my own life.

In the book, I tell the story of my grandmother, Sonia Schwartz, inspiring and nurturing my curiosity as a boy. There have been some similarly critical people who have supported my curious style as an adult.

The first among those is, in fact, Ron Howard, my closest professional colleague going back forty years, my business partner at Imagine Entertainment, and my best friend. Ron is my sounding board, my supporter, my conscience, and he never stops encouraging my curiosity.

Michael Rosenberg has been helping Ron and me make movies in a businesslike fashion for thirty-five years. We often have fifteen or twenty projects going at once, and I am sure Michael wasn't thinking I needed to add a book—requiring hours a week of time— to all our other demands. But he has been an enthusiastic supporter of the book from the start, and he has figured out how to gracefully add *A Curious Mind* to everything else we're doing. We would be lost without Michael's loyalty, determination, and quiet leadership.

Karen Kehela Sherwood was the first person to help me set up the "curiosity conversations," taking on a task I had done for years by myself. She brought the same determination to getting people to come and talk as I did, but she dramatically widened our range. She brought professionalism to the curiosity conversations, and she made my priorities her priorities—both things for which I am eternally grateful.

After Karen, many executives and assistants helped me continue the conversations over many years.

In 2006, Brad Grossman formalized the curiosity conversation process. He gave the curiosity conversations depth and structure, and he brought such honest interest in new people and new subjects that, with his help, I met people I never would have met on my own.

At Imagine, the help and guidance of many people have been indispensable, including Erica Huggins, Kim Roth, Robin Ruse-Rinehart Barris, Anna Culp, and Sage Shah. Hillary Messenger and Lee Dreyfuss get me through the day every day.

I want to thank my siblings, Nora and Gavin. They've been listening to my questions longer than anyone else. They keep me cheerfully connected to the real world, and the world in which we all grew up.

My kids are the joy of my life. Riley, Sage, Thomas, and Patrick are the best curiosity guides I've ever had—they each pull me into universes I would never get to visit without them.

My now-wife, Veronica, has been at my side throughout the creation of *A Curious Mind*, and she has been indispensable. Veronica sees the best in people, and she knows instinctively how to get the best out of me. Her generosity, her cheerfulness, and her sense of adventure are contagious.

In terms of getting curiosity from the idea for a book to the printed page, I am indebted to Simon Green at CAA for his work in getting the book published.

Jonathan Karp, the president and publisher of Simon & Schuster, understood the kind of book I wanted this to be from the beginning—and from the spark of the idea through the writing process, he has given us support and brilliant editing, and he has held on to a clear vision of the book and its possibilities, which have kept me focused.

Also at Simon & Schuster, Sydney Tanigawa gave *A Curious Mind* a careful and thoughtful word edit; the book is much better for her attention. We've had great support throughout Simon & Schuster: Megan Hogan, in Jonathan Karp's office; Cary Goldstein and Kellyn Patterson in publicity; Richard Rhorer and Dana Trocker in marketing; Irene Kheradi, Gina DiMascia, and Ffej Caplan in managing editorial; Jackie Seow, Christopher Lin, and Joy O'Meara in art and design; and Lisa Erwin and Carla Benton in production and copyediting, as well as Judith Hancock for creating the book's index.

Finally, I want to thank my coauthor and collaborator, Charles Fishman, a nationally renowned journalist. He asks questions for a living, and he asked questions about curiosity that had never occurred to me. I know how much work goes into a movie or a TV show, but I had no idea how much work goes into a book. Charles has done a remarkable job shaping our own curiosity conversations into a completely original narrative. I often start our calls with the greeting "The Mighty Fish!" He has been exactly that.

Charles Fishman

I first heard about Brian Grazer's book project when my agent, Raphael Sagalyn, called and said, "I'm going to say a single word to you. Let's see if this one word is a book idea you might be interested in. The word is 'curiosity.'"

He had me immediately. There aren't many single-word topics as engaging and important as curiosity. And then Rafe told me the author was the Academy Award–winning producer Brian Grazer.

I want to thank Brian for the chance to step into his world and to think about curiosity in ways I had never considered. Brian is a master storyteller, and it has been fascinating, fun, and illuminating to work with him day after day bringing curiosity to life. His core belief in the power of curiosity to make everyone's life better is an inspiration.

I also want to thank Jonathan Karp for thinking this might be a project I'd be interested in. His support from the earliest conversations about how to shape the book until the final editing has been indispensable. Sydney Tanigawa, our editor at Simon & Schuster, has been patient and insightful.

The book would not have been written without the team at Imagine Entertainment. No one there ever hesitated to help or refused a single request. Thanks to Ron Howard, Michael Rosenberg, Erica Huggins, Kim Roth, Robin Ruse-Rinehart Barris, Anna Culp, and Sage Shah. Hillary Messenger and Lee Dreyfuss made sure I stayed connected to Brian. Their good humor never failed.

No book gets finished without the counsel of Rafe, the guidance of Geoff, or the patience and support of Trish, Nicolas, and Maya. My best curiosity conversations start and end with them.

From *Face to Face*

Sage, Riley, Patrick, and Thomas: I hope you'll take in these stories and lessons from my life as you develop your own ways of creating meaningful connections and finding fulfillment within yourselves and out in the world. May our birthday speeches always live on.

This book has evolved thanks to the wise and creative input from friends and colleagues, among them Malcolm Gladwell, Bryan Lourd, Adam Grant, Michael Rosenberg, Risa Gertner, Julie Oh, Tara Polacek, Simon Sinek, Will Rosenfeld, Stephanie Frerich, and everybody else who offered guidance along the way. I want to especially thank our friends Jenna Abdou and Samantha Vinograd for the heartfelt heavy lifting, especially when the countdown was on. You understood the vision and made it better. Thank you, Jenn Hallam: you are every bit the superstar that Simon described at Toscana.

Almost every weekend, I see a close friend of mine, face to face, for coffee. Thank you, Bob Iger, for the immeasurable friendship.

Jon Karp, the president and publisher of Simon & Schuster, loved the idea of eye contact and personal connection from the very start. Thank you for your patience and encouragement.

I am deeply grateful to my friend, the celebrated artist Mark

Bradford, who generously created the "FACE TO FACE" artwork for this book. I have always been deeply moved by his story. Surviving by working in his mother's beauty shop in Crenshaw, he didn't have the money or opportunity to become an artist until his forties. It's super difficult and rare to reach his level of achievement as an artist when starting at that age. He is, and always will be, an original voice in our world.

Thank you to novelist and screenwriter Matthew Specktor, who helped form the book when it was just a whisper of an idea. We met over many breakfasts of huevos rancheros on the back porch while he took in my stories.

In my business as a movie and television producer, I make qualitative decisions every day. Whenever I make one of those decisions and tell myself it's "good enough," it nearly always means it's sh*tty. With this book, there was a point when the manuscript had been delivered, the book was listed on Amazon, and I thought we were ready to go. The day of the deadline, my brilliantly candid wife, Veronica, pulled me aside and said the book was only "good enough." I understood immediately. She was the catalyst—as well as my thought partner—who spurred me to dive back in and take the extra time to make this book better. She was relentless in pushing me hard, and I am forever grateful.

Every day, Veronica teaches me and our children about genuine human connection, not through words but in the way she takes the time to see people, listen to them, and make them feel like they matter. She is my blessing and my true collaborator on this book and in life. I'm grateful to God for you.

Notes

Introduction to the New Edition: Curiosity to the Rescue

1. Eleanor Roosevelt, "In Defense of Curiosity," *Saturday Evening Post*, August 24, 1935, pp. 8–9.
2. Robert Waldinger and Marc Schulz, "What the Longest Study on Human Happiness Found Is the Key to a Good Life," *The Atlantic*, January 19, 2023, https://www.theatlantic.com/ideas/archive/2023/01/harvard-happiness-study-relationships/672753/; Harvard Study of Adult Development: https://www.adultdevelopmentstudy.org.

Chapter 1: There Is No Cure for Curiosity

1. This quote—perhaps the most razor-sharp take on curiosity's power—is widely attributed to the writer and poet Dorothy Parker, but no scholarly or online source has a citation for when Parker might have written or said it. The quote is also occasionally attributed to someone named Ellen Parr, but also without attribution or any identifying information about Parr. The pair of sentences does have the particular interlocking snap that is characteristic of Parker's turn of phrase.
2. People who are younger than thirty years old might not know of a service that phone companies used to offer: If you needed a phone number, you simply dialed 411 on your telephone and an operator would look it up for you. The address too.
3. Fifty years later, that is still the main phone number at Warner Bros., although now you also have to dial the area code: (818) 954-6000.
4. What kind of character was Sue Mengers? Pretty big, pretty fearsome. The 2013 Broadway play about Mengers's life was called *I'll Eat You Last*.
5. Google reports that the average number of searches per day in 2022 was 9,072,000,000. That's 6,300,000 each minute (Jason Wise, "How Many Google

Searches Per Hour Are Made in 2023?," EarthWeb, Dec. 18, 2022, https://earth
web.com/how-many-google-searches-per-hour/).

6. In the CBS TV series *Dallas*, the question "Who shot J.R.?" became one of the
   most effective cliffhangers in modern storytelling—a masterful campaign in creating curiosity. The actor Larry Hagman, who played J.R. Ewing in the TV show,
   was shot in the concluding episode of the 1979–80 season, which aired March 21,
   1980. The character who shot him was not revealed until an episode broadcast
   eight months later, on November 21, 1980.

   Marketing—and curiosity—around the cliffhanger was so widespread that
   bookies laid odds and took bets on who the shooter would turn out to be, and
   "Who shot J.R.?" jokes even crept into the 1980 presidential campaign between
   Jimmy Carter and Ronald Reagan. The Republican campaign produced buttons
   reading, "The Democrats shot J.R."; President Carter joked that he would have no
   trouble with fundraising if he could find out who had shot J.R.

   CBS filmed five scenes, each with a different character shooting J.R. On the
   November 21 episode, the shooter was revealed to be Kristin Shepard, J.R.'s mis-
   tress (content.time.com/time/magazine/article/0,9171,924376,00.html#paid-wall,
   accessed October 10, 2014).

7. Adults tend not to know the answer to "Why is the sky blue?" because although
   it's a simple question, and a simple experience, the answer itself is complicated.
   The sky is blue because of how light itself is made up.

   Blue wavelengths of light are more easily scattered by the particles in the air
   than other colors, and so as sunlight streams from the sun to the ground, the blue
   light passing through the atmosphere gets scattered around, and we see that scat-
   tering as the sky being blue.

   The blue color fades as you get higher up in the atmosphere. In a passenger jet,
   flying at six miles up (thirty-two thousand feet), the blue is already a little watery and
   thin. If you look up as you fly higher, the sky starts to look black—the black of space.

   And the sky doesn't look blue when there is no light shining through it, of
   course. The blue goes away when the sun sets.

8. Genesis 2:16–17. The citation is from the New International Version of the Bible,
   www.biblegateway.com, accessed October 18, 2014.

9. Genesis 3:4–5 (NIV).

10. Genesis 3:6 (NIV).

11. Genesis 3:7 (NIV).

12. It's an astonishing output by a studio, in terms of lasting cultural impact and qual-
    ity in a short time. The movies by year:

A Clockwork Orange, 1971 (four Academy Award nominations)

Dirty Harry, 1971

Deliverance, 1972 (three Academy Award nominations)

The Exorcist, 1973 (two Academy Awards, ten nominations)

Blazing Saddles, 1974 (three Academy Award nominations)

The Towering Inferno, 1974 (three Academy Awards, eight nominations)

Dog Day Afternoon, 1975 (one Academy Award, six nominations)

All the President's Men, 1976 (four Academy Awards, eight nominations)

13. Geraldine Fabrikant, "A Strong Debut Helps, as a New Chief Tackles Sony's Movie Problems," *New York Times*, May 26, 1997.

14. When John Calley died in 2011, the *Los Angeles Times* used a picture of him sitting on a couch, one foot propped up on a coffee table (www.latimes.com/enter tainment/news/movies/la-me-2011notables-calley,0,403960.photo#axzz2qUME KSCu, accessed October 10, 2014).

15. My office at Imagine Entertainment does have a desk, but I don't sit there very often. I have two couches, and that's where I work, notes spread out on the couch cushions or the coffee table, a console phone sitting on the cushion next to me.

16. Stop and think about yourself for a minute. Regardless of what work you do—whether you work in movies or software, insurance or health care or advertising—imagine if you decided today that for the next six months you would meet a new person *every single day* in your industry. Not to have an hour-long conversation, just to meet them and talk for five minutes. Six months from now, you'd know one hundred fifty people in your own line of work you don't know right now. If even 10 percent of those people had something to offer—insight, connections, support for a project—that's fifteen new allies.

17. The piece ran in the *New Yorker*'s Talk of the Town section: "Want Ad: Beautiful Minds," by Lizzie Widdicombe, March 20, 2008.

18. According to the *Forbes* magazine list of the richest people in the world, Carlos Slim was number one when I met him; as of spring 2023, he was at number ten.

Chapter 2: The Police Chief, the Movie Mogul, and the
Father of the H-Bomb: Thinking Like Other People

1. The full line from Vladimir Nabokov is "Curiosity in its turn is insubordination in its purest form." It comes from the 1947 novel *Bend Sinister* (New York: Vintage Classic Paperback, 2012), 46.

2. President Bush used the speech to denounce the rioting, which he said was "not

about civil rights" and "not a message of protest" but "the brutality of a mob, pure and simple." But he also said of the beating of Rodney King, "What you saw and what I saw on the TV video was revolting. I felt anger. I felt pain. How can I explain this to my grandchildren?" The text of Bush's May 1, 1992, speech is here: https://www.presidency.ucsb.edu/documents/address-the-nation-the-civil -disturbances-los-angeles-california, accessed March 22, 2023.

3. In the wake of the Rodney King beating—before the officers were tried—there was an investigative commission into the practices of the Los Angeles Police Department, and into Gates's leadership, and Gates announced in the summer of 1991 that he would resign. He then postponed his retirement several times—and even threatened to postpone leaving after his successor, Willie Williams, the chief in Philadelphia, was hired.

Here are several accounts of Gates's reluctant departure:

Robert Reinhold, "Head of Police in Philadelphia Chosen for Chief in Los Angeles," *New York Times*, April 16, 1992, www.nytimes.com/1992/04/16 /us/head-of-police-in-philadelphia-chosen-for-chief-in-los-angeles.html, accessed October 10, 2014.

Richard A. Serrano and James Rainey, "Gates Says He Bluffed Staying, Lashes Critics," *Los Angeles Times*, June 9, 1992, articles.latimes.com/1992-06-09/news /mn-188_1_police-department, accessed October 10, 2014.

Richard A. Serrano, "Williams Takes Oath as New Police Chief," *Los Angeles Times*, June 27, 1992, articles.latimes.com/1992-06-27/news/mn-828_1_police -commission, accessed October 10, 2014.

4. Daryl Gates was a protégé of William H. Parker, the man for whom the old LAPD headquarters, Parker Center, was named. Early in his career, as a young patrol officer, Gates was assigned to be Chief Parker's driver, a job in which Gates got to see up close the everyday acquisition and use of authority. Later, Gates was Parker's executive officer. Parker was the longest-serving LAPD chief, at sixteen years (1950 to 1966); Gates was the second-longest-serving chief, at fourteen years (1978 to 1992).

5. Novelists and painters can rework the same topics, characters, and themes over and over again—many popular book series involve the same characters in very similar plots. Actors, directors, and others in Hollywood are supposed to avoid doing that, for fear of being typecast, or "falling into a rut."

6. I talked to Michael Scheuer just after he left the CIA in 2004, when his book *Imperial Hubris*, about being a front-line operative, came out. For an account of Scheuer's increasingly extreme views since then, read David Frum in the *Daily Beast*, January

3, 2014: "Michael Scheuer's Meltdown," www.thedailybeast.com/articles/2014/01
/03/michael-scheuer-s-meltdown.html, accessed October 10, 2014.

7. This list comes from the *New York Times* obituary of Lew Wasserman, who died
June 3, 2002: Jonathan Kandell, "Lew Wasserman, 89, Is Dead; Last of Hollywood's Moguls," *New York Times*, June 4, 2002, http://www.nytimes.com/2002/06
/04/business/lew-wasserman-89-is-dead-last-of-hollywood-s-moguls
.html, accessed October 10, 2014.

8. People have been trying to eat and drink in cars since roads were smoothed out,
but the search for a way of securing drinks inside cars really took off during the
1950s, with the invention of the drive-in hamburger stand. For a brief, charming
history of the cup holder, see Sam Dean, "The History of the Car Cup Holder,"
Bon Appétit, February 18, 2013, www.bonappetit.com/trends/article/the-history
-of-the-car-cup-holder, accessed October 10, 2014.

9. "Turning an Icon on Its Head," *Chief Executive*, July 2003, chiefexecutive.net
/turning-an-icon-on-its-head, accessed October 10, 2014. The story of Paul
Brown imagining himself as liquid silicone is found in this second account of the
invention of the upside-down bottle—the valve was first used in shampoo bottles:
Frank Greve, "Ketchup Squeezes Competition with Upside-Down, Bigger Bottle," McClatchy Newspapers, June 25, 2007, www.mcclatchydc.com/2007/06/28
/17335/ketchup-is-better-with-upside.html, accessed October 10, 2014.

10. Bruce Brown and Scott D. Anthony, "How P&G Tripled Its Innovation Success
Rate," *Harvard Business Review*, June 2011, www.hbsclubwdc.net/images.html?
file_id=xtypsHwtheU%3D, accessed October 10, 2014.

11. Sam Walton tells the story of creating Walmart, and refining his business practices
and his curiosity, in his autobiography, *Made in America* (New York: Bantam
Books, 1993, with John Huey). Walton's curiosity was legendary. One fellow retail
executive recalls meeting Walton and said, "He proceed[ed] to extract every piece
of information in your possession" (p. 105).

The word "curiosity" appears twice in Walton's 346-page book, most notably in
a quote from Sam Walton's wife, Helen, describing her distaste at having become
a public figure: "What I hate is being the object of curiosity. People are so curious
about everything, and so we are just public conversation. The whole thing just
makes me mad when I think about it. I mean, I hate it" (p. 98). The other use of
"curiosity" is Walton's surprise at being welcomed in the headquarters of his retail
competitors early on, while he was trying to learn how other people ran their
stores. "As often as not, they'd let me in, maybe out of curiosity" (p. 104). Walton,
too, didn't use the word to credit his own curiosity.

12. The frequency of the words "creativity," "innovation," and "curiosity" in the U.S. media comes from Nexis database searches of the category "US Newspapers and Wires" starting January 1, 1980. As the words appeared more and more frequently, the Nexis searches were done week by week for January and June of each year to get representative counts.

Chapter 3: The Curiosity Inside the Story

1. Jonathan Gottschall, *The Storytelling Animal* (New York: Houghton Mifflin, 2012), p. 3.

2. The up-to-date list is here: www.the-numbers.com/movies/franchises/, accessed March 22, 2023. Nash's *The Numbers* website also says that the movies I have produced in the last forty-five years have gross sales of $6,720,099,170. Details here: www.the-numbers.com/person/208890401-Brian-Grazer#tab=summary, accessed March 22, 2023.

3. What parts of the movie *Apollo 13* take liberties with what actually happened? If you're curious, here are a handful of websites that answer the question, including a long interview with T. K. Mattingly, the astronaut who was bumped from the flight at the last minute because he was exposed to German measles:

    Ken Mattingly on the movie *Apollo 13*: www.universetoday.com/101531/ken -mattingly-explains-how-the-apollo-13-movie-differed-from-real-life/, accessed October 18, 2014. From the official NASA oral history website: www.jsc.nasa.gov /history/oral_histories/MattinglyTK/MattinglyTK_11-6-01.htm, accessed October 18, 2014.

    From Space.com: "Apollo 13: Facts about NASA's Near Disaster," www.space .com/17250-apollo-13-facts.html, accessed October 18, 2014.

4. Miriam Krule, "How Biblically Accurate Is *Noah*?," *Slate*, March 28, 2014, www .slate.com/blogs/browbeat/2014/03/28/noah_movie_biblical_accuracy_how_the _darren_aronofsky_movie_departs_from.html, accessed October 18, 2014.

5. How did NPR discover its listeners were having "driveway moments"? A former senior news executive for NPR told me the network receives letters (and now emails) from listeners saying they did not go into the house when they got home—they sat in their cars until the story to which they were listening was over.

6. If you're not a regular listener to National Public Radio and don't know what it feels like to be so bewitched by a radio story that you can't leave your car, here's a collection of dozens of NPR stories that are considered "driveway moments." Lis-

ten to one or two. You'll see: www.npr.org/series/700000/driveway-moments, accessed October 18, 2014.

Chapter 4: Curiosity as a Superhero Power

1. James Stephens (1880–1950) was a popular Irish poet and novelist in the early twentieth century. This line is from *The Crock of Gold* (London: Macmillan, 1912), p. 9 (viewable via books.google.com).

   The full sentence, discussed later in the chapter, is "Curiosity will conquer fear even more than bravery will; indeed, it has led many people into dangers which mere physical courage would shudder away from, for hunger and love and curiosity are the great impelling forces of life."

   Stephens's death merited a seven-paragraph obituary in the *New York Times*: query.nytimes.com/mem/archive-free/pdf?res=9905E3DC103EEF3BBC4F51D FB467838B649EDE, accessed October 18, 2014.

2. Isaac Asimov's productivity as an author was so impressive that the *New York Times* obituary of him details the number of books he wrote decade by decade— in the obituary's fourth paragraph. Mervyn Rothstein, "Isaac Asimov, Whose Thoughts and Books Traveled the Universe, Is Dead at 72," *New York Times*, April 7, 1992, www.nytimes.com/books/97/03/23/lifetimes/asi-v-obit.html, accessed October 18, 2014.

   There is a catalog of every book Asimov wrote online, compiled by Ed Seiler, with the apparent assistance of Asimov: www.asimovonline.com/oldsite/asimov _catalogue.html, accessed October 18, 2014.

3. In 2014, while reconstructing this meeting, we exchanged emails with Janet Jeppson Asimov about my brief visit from twenty-eight years previously. She has no memory of it, and she apologized for any rudeness. She also said that, although it wasn't publicly known at the time, Isaac Asimov was already infected with the HIV virus that would kill him six years later, and he was already often ill. Janet Asimov said her impatience may well have been a result of—entirely understandable—protectiveness of her husband.

4. The *New York Times* story of the prostitution ring run out of New York's morgue is just as fun as I remember it—and is practically the outline for a movie script. It ran on August 28, 1976, opposite the obituaries in the Metro section. The opening sentence reports that the men running the call-girl ring often "chauffeur[ed] prostitutes to clients in the Medical Examiner's official car." The *Times* never did report what became of the charges against those men—nor did any other media

outlet. Here is the original story (PDF): query.nytimes.com/mem/archive/pdf?res
=F20617FC3B5E16738DDDA10A94D0405B868BF1D3, accessed October 18,
2014.

5. The movie executive and journalist Beverly Gray gives a detailed account of the
creation of *Night Shift* and *Splash* in her biography of Ron Howard, *Ron Howard:
From Mayberry to the Moon . . . and Beyond* (Nashville, TN: Rutledge Hill Press,
2003).

6. *Newsweek* did a story on the selling of the rights to *How the Grinch Stole Christmas!*: "The Grinch's Gatekeeper," November 12, 2000, www.newsweek.com/
grinchs-gatekeeper-156985, accessed October 18, 2014.

   Audrey's "GRINCH" license plate was noted in an Associated Press profile
from 2004, the year that Theodor Geisel would have turned one hundred:
Michelle Morgante, "A Seussian Pair of Shoulders," Associated Press,
February 28, 2004, published in the *Los Angeles Times*, articles.latimes.com/2004
/feb/28/entertainment/et-morgante28, accessed October 18, 2014.

   That Dr. Seuss had used the "GRINCH" license plate is noted in Charles Co-
hen's biography of him: *The Seuss, the Whole Seuss, and Nothing but the Seuss: A Visual Biography of Theodor Seuss Geisel* (New York: Random House, 2004), p. 330.

7. *Dr. Seuss' How the Grinch Stole Christmas* was a huge hit in the Christmas movie
season in 2000. It spent four weeks as the number one movie in the country, and
although it only debuted on November 17, it was the highest-grossing movie of
2000 (ultimately making about $510 million) and is the highest-grossing movie of
the Christmas season ever, having passed *Home Alone. Grinch* was nominated for
three Academy Awards—for costume design, makeup, and art direction/set
direction—and won for makeup.

8. James Reginato, "The Mogul: Brian Grazer, Whose Movies Have Grossed
$10.5 Billion, Is Arguably the Most Successful Producer in Town—and Surely the
Most Recognizable. Is it the Hair?," *W* magazine, February 1, 2004.

9. The *New York Post* did a brief story on the Cuba trip: "Castro Butters Up Media
Moguls," February 15, 2001, p. 10.

Chapter 5: Every Conversation Is a Curiosity Conversation

1. Brené Brown is a wildly popular author, speaker, podcaster—and research professor
at the University of Houston Graduate College of Social Work. Her research focuses on shame and vulnerability, and she is the author of several bestselling books.
She calls herself "a researcher and a storyteller" and often says, "Maybe stories are

just data with a soul." Her talk at TEDxHouston in June 2010—"The Power of Vulnerability"—is the fourth-most-watched TED Talk ever, at sixty-one million views as of mid-2023: www.ted.com/talks/brene_brown_on_vulnerability, accessed March 22, 2023.

2. Bianca Bosker, "Google Design: Why Google.com Homepage Looks So Simple," *Huffington Post*, March 27, 2012, www.huffingtonpost.com/2012/03/27/google -design-sergey-brin_n_1384074.html, accessed October 18, 2014.

3. From the website poliotoday.org. The history section is here, with cultural impact and statistics: poliotoday.org/?page_id=13, accessed October 18, 2014.

   Poliotoday.org was created and is maintained by Jonas Salk's research organization, the Salk Institute for Biological Studies.

4. This list of polio survivors comes from the compilation on Wikipedia, which contains source citations for each person listed: en.wikipedia.org/wiki/List_of _poliomyelitis_survivors, accessed October 18, 2014.

5. One account of the often-controversial development of the polio vaccine is here: www.chemheritage.org/discover/online-resources/chemistry-in-history/themes /pharmaceuticals/preventing-and-treating-infectious-diseases/salk-and-sabin .aspx, accessed October 18, 2014.

6. Harold M. Schmeck Jr., "Dr. Jonas Salk, Whose Vaccine Turned Tide on Polio, Dies at 80," *New York Times*, June 24, 1995, www.nytimes.com/1995/06/24 /obituaries/dr-jonas-salk-whose-vaccine-turned-tide-on-polio-dies-at-80.html, accessed October 18, 2014.

Chapter 6: Good Taste and the Power of Anti-Curiosity

1. Carl Sagan said this in a TV interview with Charlie Rose, May 27, 1996, *Charlie Rose*, PBS. The full interview is available on YouTube: www.youtube.com /watch?v=U8HEwO-2L4w, accessed October 18, 2014.

   At the time of the interview, astronomer and author Sagan was ill with bone marrow cancer. He died seven months later, on December 20, 1996.

2. Denzel Washington said he would only do *American Gangster* if, in the end, the character he was playing, heroin dealer Frank Lucas, got punished.

3. The ticker trading symbol for Imagine on the NASDAQ was IFEI—Imagine Films Entertainment Inc.

Chapter 7: The Golden Age of Curiosity

1. From Arthur C. Clarke's 1951 book predicting the future of space travel: *The Exploration of Space* (New York: Harper and Brothers, 1951, since reissued), ch. 18, p. 187.

2. Bees are surprisingly fast: they cruise along at about fifteen miles per hour and can go twenty miles per hour when they need to. So they are as fast as a slow-moving car—but up close, given their small size, they seem to be going quite fast.

   More on the speed of flying bees at this site from the University of California: ucanr.edu/blogs/blogcore/postdetail.cfm?postnum=10898, accessed October 18, 2014.

3. An excellent scientific biography of Robert Hooke: Michael W. Davidson, "Robert Hooke: Physics, Architecture, Astronomy, Paleontology, Biology," *LabMedicine* 41, pp. 180–82. Available online: https://academic.oup.com/labmed/article/41/3/180/2504959, accessed March 22, 2023.

4. Curiosity as "an outlaw impulse," from Barbara M. Benedict, *Curiosity: A Cultural History of Early Modern Inquiry* (Chicago: University of Chicago Press, 2001), p. 25.

5. "White Paper: China's Internet Population Reaches 1.05 Billion," November 7, 2022, China State Council Information Office, http://english.scio.gov.cn/m/press room/2022-11/07/content_78506468.htm.

6. The Karl Marx quote is often miscited as "Religion is the opiate of the masses." The full context of the quote is revealing, because Marx was making an observation on the oppression and misery of the working class, which he thought religion tried to both paper over and justify. The full quote, which comes from Marx's *Critique of the Hegelian Philosophy of Right* (Cambridge University Press, 1977, p. 131), is "The wretchedness of religion is at once an expression of and a protest against real wretchedness. Religion is the sigh of the oppressed creature, the heart of a heartless world and the soul of soulless conditions. It is the opium of the people.

   "The abolition of religion as the illusory happiness of the people is a demand for their true happiness. The call to abandon illusions about their condition is the call to abandon a condition which requires illusions. Thus, the critique of religion is the critique in embryo of the vale of tears of which religion is the halo."

Introduction to Part Two

1. "Can Relationships Boost Longevity and Well-Being?" Harvard Health Publishing, Harvard Medical School, June 2017, https://www.health.harvard.edu/mental-health/can-relationships-boost-longevity-and-well-being/.

2. "An Epidemic of Loneliness," *The Week*, January 6, 2019, https://theweek.com/articles/815518/epidemic-loneliness/.

3. Ceylan Yeginsu, "U.K. Appoints a Minister for Loneliness," *New York Times*, January 17, 2018, https://www.nytimes.com/2018/01/17/world/europe/uk-britain-loneliness.html.

4. Maria Russo, "The Eyes Have It," *New York Times*, March 25, 2015, https://www.nytimes.com/interactive/2015/03/25/books/review/25childrens.html.

Chapter 8: Do You See Me?

1. Flora Carr, "Rapping for Freedom," *Time*, May 17, 2018, https://time.com/collection-post/5277970/sonita-alizadeh-next-generation-leaders.

2. Steven Kotler, "Social Flow: 9 Social Triggers for Entering Flow," Medium, February 21, 2014, https://medium.com/@kotlersteven/social-flow-b04436fac167.

3. "Steven Kotler on Lyme Disease and the Flow State," *Joe Rogan Experience* podcast #873, YouTube, November 21, 2016, https://www.youtube.com/watch?v=X_yq-4remO0.

4. Jill Suttie, "Why Curious People Have Better Relationships," *Greater Good*, May 31, 2017, https://greatergood.berkeley.edu/article/item/why_curious_people_have_better_relationships/.

Chapter 9: Take a Chance on Connection

1. "Winfrey's Commencement Address," *The Harvard Gazette*, May 31, 2013, https://news.harvard.edu/gazette/story/2013/05/winfreys-commencement-address/.

2. Sue Shellenbarger, "Just Look Me in the Eye Already," *The Wall Street Journal*, May 28, 2013, https://www.wsj.com/articles/SB10001424127887324809804578511290822228174/.

Chapter 11: Together We Rise

1. Jill O'Rourke, "For Riz Ahmed, There's a Difference between 'Diversity' and 'Representation' in Media," *A Plus*, October 10, 2018, https://articles.aplus.com/film -forward/riz-ahmed-trevor-noah-diversity-representation/.

Chapter 12: Trust in the Vision

1. Simon Sinek, "How Great Leaders Inspire Action," TEDxPugetSound, September 2009, https://www.ted.com/talks/simon_sinek_how_great_leaders_inspire _action.
2. "The City: U.S. Jury Convicts Heroin Informant," *New York Times*, August 25, 1984.
3. Mark Jacobson, "The Return of Superfly," *New York*, August 14, 2000, http://ny mag.com/nymetro/news/people/features/3649/.

Chapter 13: What Do Your Eyes Say?

1. Ayanna Prescod, "9 Fashion Staples You Need Inspired by Cookie Lyon from *Empire*," *Vibe*, January 14, 2015, https://www.vibe.com/2015/01/9-fashion-staples -you-need-inspired-by-cookie-lyon-from-empire/.

Chapter 14: It's Universal

1. Adam Gopnik, "Can Science Explain Why We Tell Stories?," *The New Yorker*, May 18, 2012, https://www.newyorker.com/books/page-turner/can-science-explain -why-we-tell-stories/.

Chapter 16: Listen Up!

1. Mike Fleming Jr., "Netflix Wins 'Tunga,' Animated Musical from Zimbabwe-Born Newcomer Godwin Jabangwe; First Deal out of Talent Hatchery Imagine Impact 1," *Deadline*, February 14, 2019, https://deadline.com/2019/02/tunga-netflix -animated-musical-zimbabwe-newcomer-godwin-jabangwe-imagine-impact-1 -1202557570/.
2. Stephen Covey, *7 Habits of Highly Effective People* (New York: Simon & Schuster, 1989), p. 251.

Chapter 17: Adapt or Die

1. Celeste Heiter, "Film Review: The Man Who Would Be King," *ThingsAsian*, September 29, 2006, http://thingsasian.com/story/film-review-man-who-would-be-king/.

2. Martin Stezano, "One Man Exposed the Secrets of the Freemasons. His Disappearance Led to Their Downfall," January 24, 2019, https://www.history.com/news/freemason-secrets-revealed/.

3. Mo Rocca, "Inside the Secret World of the Freemasons," *CBS News*, December 8, 2013, https://www.cbsnews.com/news/inside-the-secret-world-of-the-freemasons/.

4. Stezano, "One Man Exposed the Secrets of the Freemasons. His Disappearance Led to Their Downfall."

5. "List of Presidents of the United States Who Were Freemasons," Wikipedia, accessed April 14, 2019, https://en.wikipedia.org/wiki/List_of_Presidents_of_the_United_States_who_were_Freemasons.

6. Rocca, "Inside the Secret World of the Freemasons."

7. "Freemasonry under the Nazi Regime," *Holocaust Encyclopedia*, United States Holocaust Memorial Museum, accessed April 14, 2019, https://www.ushmm.org/wlc/en/article.php?ModuleId=10007187/.

8. "Suppression of Freemasonry," Wikipedia, accessed April 14, 2019, https://en.wikipedia.org/wiki/Suppression_of_Freemasonry.

9. "A Standard of Masonic Conduct," *Short Talk Bulletin* 7, no. 12 (December 1929), http://www.masonicworld.com/education/files/artfeb02/standard%20of%20masonic%20conduct.htm.

Chapter 19: Where Life Begins

1. Adrian Ward, Kristen Duke, Ayelet Gneezy, and Maarten Bos, "Brain Drain: The Mere Presence of One's Own Smartphone Reduces Available Cognitive Capacity," *Journal of the Association for Consumer Research* 2, no. 2 (April 2017), https://www.journals.uchicago.edu/doi/10.1086/691462.

2. Olivia Yasukawa, "Senegal's 'Dead Sea': Salt Harvesting in the Strawberry-Pink Lake," CNN, June 27, 2014, https://www.cnn.com/2014/06/27/world/africa/senegals-dead-sea-lake-retba/index.html.

3. Kevin E. G. Perry, "Where the Magic Happens: Baaba Maal Interviewed," *The Quietus*, January 19, 2016, https://thequietus.com/articles/19559-baaba-maal-interview/.

Chapter 20: Venturing into New Worlds

1. Rahima Nasa, "Timeline: How the Crisis in Venezuela Unfolded," *Frontline*, PBS, February 22, 2019, https://www.pbs.org/wgbh/frontline/article/timeline-how-the -crisis-in-venezuela-unfolded/.

Chapter 21: In the Blink of an Eye

1. Geri-Ann Galanti, *Caring for Patients from Different Cultures* (Philadelphia: University of Pennsylvania Press, 2004), p. 34, https://books.google.com/books?id= nVgeOxUL3cYC&pg=PA34#v=onepage&q&f=false/.
2. Robert T. Moran, Philip R. Harris, Sarah V. Moran, *Managing Cultural Differences: Global Leadership Strategies for the 21st Century* (Butterworth-Heinemann, 2007), p. 64.
3. Alicia Raeburn, "10 Places Where Eye-Contact Is Not Recommended (10 Places Where the Locals Are Friendly)," *The Travel*, September 12, 2018, https://www .thetravel.com/10-places-where-eye-contact-is-not-recommended-10-places -where-the-locals-are-friendly/.
4. Ailsa Chang, "What Eye Contact—and Dogs—Can Teach Us about Civility in Politics," NPR, May 8, 2015, https://www.npr.org/sections/itsallpolitics/2015/05 /08/404991505/what-eye-contact-and-dogs-can-teach-us-about-civility-in -politics/.

Index

About the Author

Academy Award–, Emmy-, Golden Globe–, and Grammy Award–winning producer **Brian Grazer** has been making movies and television programs for forty years. His work has been nominated for forty-seven Oscars and 228 Emmys, winning over a hundred significant awards, including the best picture Oscar for *A Beautiful Mind*.

In addition to *A Beautiful Mind*, Grazer's films include *tick, tick . . . BOOM!*, *Apollo 13*, *Friday Night Lights*, *American Gangster*, *8 Mile*, *Frost/Nixon*, *Liar Liar*, and *Splash*. Grazer's long-running television series include the award-winning *Genius* anthology series, *24*, *Arrested Development*, *Parenthood*, *Empire*, and *Friday Night Lights*.

Grazer has also produced numerous documentaries, including Emmy-winning *Lucy and Desi*, directed by Amy Poehler; *We Feed People*, profiling renowned chef José Andrés and his World Central Kitchen; the Grammy Award–winning best music film *The Beatles: Eight Days a Week*; and the docuseries *Light & Magic*, about George Lucas's pioneering visual effects house Industrial Light & Magic.

Grazer cofounded Impact, a content accelerator whose mission is to discover, cultivate, nurture, and connect creative storytellers around the world. To date, Impact has built a community of over seventy-five thousand writers across 140-plus countries.

Profiled by *Time* magazine as one of the 100 most influential people in the world, Grazer believes that curiosity is the superpower that has helped him create his best life, and he is passionate about turning that curiosity toward doing good in the world. He has been honored for his global humanitarian work by organizations including the Simon Wiesenthal Center, the Alfred Mann Foundation, the Alzheimer's Association, World of Children, and the Atlantic Council. He serves on the board of the University of Southern California's School of Cinematic Arts, where he also teaches a course entitled Starting from Zero.

Grazer grew up in the San Fernando Valley and is a graduate of USC's School of Cinematic Arts. He began his career as a producer developing television projects. It was while producing TV pilots for Paramount Pictures in the early 1980s that Grazer first met his longtime friend and business partner, Ron Howard. Their collaboration began in 1982 with the hit comedies *Night Shift* and *Splash*, and soon after, the two cofounded Imagine Entertainment, embarking on what is now one of the longest-running partnerships in Hollywood. They continue to run the company together as executive chairmen.

Grazer lives in the Brentwood neighborhood of Los Angeles and has four children.

Charles Fishman is an award-winning reporter and *New York Times* bestselling author. His journalistic curiosity has taken him from the nation's only bomb factory to its busiest maternity ward, to the surface of the moon. He is the author of the *New York Times* bestseller *One Giant Leap*, the acclaimed account of the race to the moon in the 1960s. He is also the author of *The Wal-Mart Effect*, the first book to crack Wal-Mart's wall of silence and explain how the world's largest company really works, and *The Big Thirst*, the standard for understanding how to manage water in the era of climate change.

Fishman grew up in Miami, went to Harvard, and started his journalism career as a reporter for the *Washington Post*. He went on to work at the *Orlando Sentinel*, the *News & Observer* in Raleigh, and *Fast Company* magazine. He lives in Washington, DC, with his wife, who is also a journalist; they are the parents of two adult children.